FIRST AMERICANS

FIRST AMERICANS

U.S. Patriotism in Indian Country
After World War I

THOMAS GRILLOT

Yale

UNIVERSITY PRESS

New Haven and London

Published with assistance from the Mary Cady Tew Memorial Fund.
First published in English by Yale University Press in 2018.

Originally published as *Après la grande guerre: Comment les
Amérindiens des États-Unis sont devenus patriotes (1917–1947)*.
Copyright © éditions de l'EHESS, 2014.

Yale University Press books may be purchased in quantity for
educational, business, or promotional use. For information,
please e-mail sales.press@yale.edu (U.S. office) or sales@yaleup.co.uk
(U.K. office).

Set in Janson type by Integrated Publishing Solutions,
Grand Rapids, Michigan.
Printed in the United States of America.

ISBN 978-0-300-22433-7 (hardcover : alk. paper)
Library of Congress Control Number: 2017953543
A catalogue record for this book is available from the British Library.

This paper meets the requirements of ANSI/NISO Z39.48-1992
(Permanence of Paper).

10 9 8 7 6 5 4 3 2 1

Contents

Acknowledgments

THIS WORK OWES MUCH to many individuals and institutions. Its subject matter is gift giving, and gifts have been given to me more than once throughout the course of its conception. It would have been impossible, in particular, without the help of the people I met in North Dakota and South Dakota. At the Standing Rock Reservation, I have been welcomed, entertained, and educated in many interactions, short or long, during the visits I've made there since 2008. Many elders have been especially generous with their time and willing to share memories. Some of them have since passed away. I permit myself to single out especially the generosity and kindness of Everett Chasing Hawk and Adele Little Dog in Little Eagle; Etta Taken Alive in Bear Soldier; Germaine Eagle, Cecilia Brownotter, and Olley Little Eagle in Bullhead; Wilbur Flying By in McLaughlin; Alfred Blue Earth in Cannonball; Maxine White Bull, Elaine Saint John, Alma Little Bear, and Isabel Crow Feather in Kenel; and Melvin Shoots the Enemy in Fort Yates. At the tribal offices of the Standing Rock Sioux Tribes, the staff at the tribal historic preservation office, including Ladonna Brave Bull Allard, Byron Olson, and Wasté Win Young, have been helpful beyond measure. At Sitting Bull College, I'm particularly grateful for the support given me by Mark Ohlman and Mike Moore. Not too far from the reservation, Jim Davis at the State Historical Society of North Dakota in Bismarck and Ken Stewart at the South Dakota State Historical Society in Pierre have assisted me in countless requests for material. Farther away, at the National Archives, I want to extend special acknowledgment to William Davis (Washington, D.C.) as well as Tim Rives and Stephen Spence (Kansas City), who never hesitated to go out of their way to help me locate documents and even send some "across the pond."

At a crucial time in the development of the project, a grant from the Georges Lurcy Charitable and Educational Trust facilitated a year of research and study at the University of Virginia. In Charlottesville, Olivier Zunz and Christian McMillen provided me with friendly and expert guidance and remained wonderful supporters years after I left the master's program. The History Department and the Maison française extended me exquisite hospitality. The first requirement to complete research studying in another country is to find a home there: Jennifer Bing, Florence and Robert Brodkey, and Rachel Kerwin and Victor Nemchenok have taken turns hosting me during my stays in the U.S. capital. I'm still awed by their extraordinary willingness to open their door and help me make it through the ups and downs of archival research. Researchers in American Indian studies, history, and anthropology throughout the country have contributed suggestions, comments, and documents. I'm especially grateful to Russel L. Barsh and Raymond DeMallie. Their scholarship has been an inspiration and shaped this project in more than one way.

In France, the project developed at the Centre d'études nord-américaines (CENA) of the École des hautes études en sciences sociales (EHESS). François Weil directed the dissertation and introduced me to a research center where help is always offered gracefully. Several grants received from the CENA and the EHESS have been crucial to the traveling back and forth between France and the United States. The comments and suggestions of Nicolas Barreyre, Sara Le Menestrel, Pauline Peretz, Yann Philippe, Cécile Vidal, Jean-Christian Vinel, and many other graduate students, researchers, and visitors at the CENA have been critical throughout the different stages of a project that started in 2005. Annick Grandemange-Gurgel and Flavie Holzinger have helped me with maps, Elizabeth Rowley-Jolivet brought a precise and delicate touch to help me with the translation of a book that was originally published in French by the Éditions de l'École des hautes études en sciences sociales in Paris.

To all, thanks are in order. But to Peggy Lefebvre, I have a special debt of gratitude. She has been an inspiration in more ways than she would care to admit.

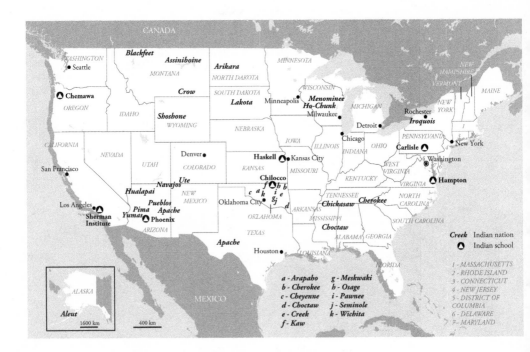

Indian nations and schools mentioned in the book

FIRST AMERICANS

Introduction
The Problem of Indian Patriotism

The Indians are getting out. In every department of life he
is found. He is side by side with the Whites. In business, in
politics, in law, in medicine, in the arts, in the ministry, in
agriculture, he has no mean representatives. There are more
of them in the Army, in proportion of their numbers, than
of any other class of our citizens. He is in the offices, on the
farms, in Congress, in the shops, and "somewhere in France."

— C. L. HALL, 1918

THE PATRIOTISM OF MINORITY GROUPS is a complex phenomenon,
especially when these groups, like Native Americans in the United
States, claim a distinct political existence as nations. But patriotism
is almost by definition a contested notion for all groups, whether or
not they belong to the majority. In the United States, patriotism has
revolutionary origins and a more conservative history. "Patriots," in
1775, were the members of the population of settlers originating
mostly in the British Isles who decided to rebel against English "tyranny." Based on an act of defiance and what self-identified "loyal-
ists" regarded as treason, the revolt of North American colonists par-
adoxically launched the career of a word, *patriotism*, that eventually

I

came to be identified, at the beginning of the twentieth century, precisely with loyalty and compliance. The transatlantic ties of immigrant groups, rivalries with the British Empire, and conflicts with Mexico tested the boundaries of this loyalty more than once over the course of the nineteenth century. Uncertain citizenship, insufficient knowledge of English and American political and social institutions, socialist leanings, or racial identification by U.S.-born Americans made immigrants of various origins the targets of campaigns that questioned their willingness or ability to assimilate and their determination to stand on the right side of international conflicts involving the United States.

Despite their ambiguous position both outside and inside the U.S. nation, the loyalty of individual Native American groups was also tested in that era. The Civil War in particular forced tribes in the Northeast, the Old Northwest, and Indian Territory to demonstrate their adherence to treaties of alliance signed with the federal government—although not all remained on the side of the Union. Yet for the most part Natives both inside and outside U.S. territory stood in a position that made patriotism and loyalty problematic for them. "Friendly" or "hostile," they were allies or enemies. A handful of them were citizens. Some began to be regarded as wards under the exclusive purview of the federal government. And for a century, the idea of fostering U.S. patriotism among them was not part of national Indian policy. Only by the last decade of the nineteenth century, when Native American children started being sent to U.S. schools, did a new, positive doctrine coalesce that mandated something more than not taking up arms against the United States. Only then did Native Americans begin to be asked to know and love the whole country, not just the birthplaces of their people; to defend the U.S. Constitution and U.S. values of individualism and enterprise; to remember U.S. history and U.S. heroes; and above all to be aware of and act according to their rights, privileges, and duties as citizens. Only then did Indians' patriotic integration in an empire-nation competing with other world powers become paramount.

In 1917, for the first time after the end of the continental expansion of the United States, a major international conflagration tested the new type of loyalty, one that went beyond mere alliance and diplomatic friendship. For Native Americans, World War I was new on more than one level. It involved universal registration and a draft; overseas combat; service alongside other recruits in majority-white units; compulsory participation until official demobilization, as opposed to seasonal raiding or six-month contracts as scouts; and finally, engagement with an enemy they had never met in an industrial conflict the likes of which the world had never seen. None of these novelties deterred Native participation in any major way. Among the some three hundred thousand self-identified Natives in the 1910 census, there was no real rebellion against the draft, not even of the unorganized, passive type; no attempt at sabotage, or espionage; no pro-German propaganda in the reservations to which, almost since the beginning of the U.S. republic, Native Americans had been relegated, one group after the other, one war or treaty at a time. Much heralded, Native American compliance was promptly naturalized and then half forgotten. Loyalty was an Indian's second nature, or so most non-Natives liked to think—and not a few Natives as well.

For people involved in Indian lives, especially the federal agency known as the Indian Office, the Indian Bureau, or the Bureau of Indian Affairs (BIA), Native service in World War I was the vindication of a century-old project that many detractors denounced as a costly utopia: civilizing the Indians. Native compliance to military recruitment was also a very paradoxical victory—for the BIA had done all it could to erase Indian institutions of war.

The civilization project was a multifaceted, indeed all-encompassing enterprise of social transformation addressing Native American difference and seeking to erase it for the benefit of all. Every group, whatever the length of its contact with whites, whatever its social and political organization, was involved. At the root of the program lay the Jeffersonian ideal of the white Christian yeoman, owner of his plot of land, able through his property and his work to assert his economic independence and political ability to participate in community affairs. By turning Indians into such yeomen, self-proclaimed "Friends of the Indians" declared, the United States would be able to do more than just push aside the aborigines of the continent on its expansionist course. It would save them from utter destruction by making them white—the only strategy that could possibly work in a white-dominated world. The ownership of land, therefore, was simultaneously the bane of Indian life, for it mandated the cession of huge swaths of "unproductive" Indian territory to non-native settlers and resulted in often tense or debilitating contact with whites, and their proposed salvation. After the Dawes Act of 1887, agents of the BIA surveyed and allotted tribal land for Indian families on the model of white homesteads. This policy went hand in hand with an all-out attack on Indian institutions. None were more maligned than those that sustained Indians' ability to wage war.

Indeed, throughout the nineteenth century civilization decidedly finished second to pacification for U.S. Indian policy makers. Western reservations started out as mere expedients to control the movements of Indian groups, variously known as bands, tribes, or nations, in an effort to minimize the risk of conflict with white settlers and the necessity of a costly display of federal military might. BIA agents tried to ply native groups with rations and annuities and helped the military disarm them. Policing reservation boundaries, confiscating weapons and horses, forbidding raids and calling in the Army, imprisoning or killing rebels—none of it seemed enough to suppress what many agents, using the old colonial idiom of savagery, regarded as a native propensity to violence. To counter this tendency, whether innate or acquired, Christian education was in order. But a major stumbling block stood in the way of civilization propagandists: dances.

Ceremonies involving dancing compounded most of what "Friends of the Indians," basing their opinion on old literary examples set in the East or on the new, ongoing traditions of the Plains and the West, regarded as unredeemable institutions of backwardness. Dances called forth images of scalping, torture, and self-mutilation, of the raising of war parties and calls to murder whites. As agents and missionaries became more familiar with Indians, they also noted that dances encouraged what in their eyes constituted an intolerable assault against civilization: gift giving on a massive scale, which could in a matter of hours undo months of indoctrination regarding the value of property. While American military personnel had often been of two minds regarding the martial virtues of Indians, sometimes praising their stealth, endurance, and sheer bravery, sometimes degrading them to mere treachery and bloodthirstiness, Indian agents could not have been more clearly opposed to fostering native military traditions and ceremonies, for them the root of all that was bad in Indians. The Ghost Dance movement that swept across the Plains in 1889–1890, raising fear of Indian rebellion, only confirmed this conviction, albeit in a self-fulfilling way. Indian dancing brought military intervention and the "last Indian war."

Few, then, regarded Indians' warlike qualities as in any way likely to be useful to the United States. After a short-lived integration of Indian scouts in Western regiments at the beginning of the 1890s, all attempts to harness Native military skills fell by the wayside. In 1898, isolated voices recommending the raising of Indian regiments in the war against Spain went unheard. Civilization, its proponents claimed, could only be compatible with individual military service. Tribalism needed to make room for true patriotism. Native warriors needed to be reconstructed as Indian American citizen soldiers. But even if, by 1916, two-thirds of American Indians were U.S. citizens, whites as a whole were still uncertain what their behavior would be in the event of war; many harbored grave doubts as to the advisability of arming them at all. The war in Europe changed everything.

On April 6, 1917, the United States joined Britain, France, and their allies in the fight against Germany, Austria-Hungary, and the Ottoman Empire, the so-called Central Powers of Europe. The question of arming Indians and asking them to demonstrate their patriotism became a burning one—and it severely tested BIA officials' determination to have their Indian wards enlist just like any other American citizens. By the summer, with the draft getting into its stride, images of the Indian warrior and his value in the fight against the barbarous "Huns" entered the public sphere. For Army officials as for journalists on the lookout for morale-boosting news items, the propaganda value of pitting one (Indian) savagery against another (German) one was simply too high to resist. And the return of the repressed was not confined to official declarations. On reservations, in the name of patriotism and of raising money for the war effort, ceremonies were given a stamp of approval that for decades BIA agents and missionaries had tried to deny them. Nor did praise for warriors stop at the door of the training camp. While Indians were assigned to white units (partly out of the fear that all of the civilization work would be undone if they were exposed to the influence of African Americans), military and civilians alike praised their racially distinct value as natural-born fighters. All the barriers to arming Indians had evaporated.[1]

The unanimous reappraisal of Native American military heritage supported a distinctly American and racialized mixture of political inclusion and distinction for Native Americans. On the Western front, native troops hailing from European colonial territories had since the beginning of the war served under white officers in segregated regiments. Famed military theoreticians in France or Britain had long classified colonized native peoples from Africa and Asia according to their supposed ability to wage war in a European-style army. Part of an imperial policy of divide and rule, this identification of "martial races" remained throughout World War I at the center of policies of recruitment and, perhaps more importantly, at the foundation of the tactical insertion of indigenous troops in battle plans. The specific integration of Indians in the military armed forces of the United States was never as explicitly theorized. With around twelve thousand recruits, Native Americans were but a fraction of the more than four million American soldiers who served in World War I. Indian contingents were integrated in white units, and they never came close to representing a "Red Force" that mustered the same impact as the *Force Noire* ("Black Force") of the French colonial territories in West Africa. At the same time, Indian soldiers' experience on the front remained heavily framed by racial expectations.

The position of Native American soldiers was indeed paradoxical. On one hand, fellow soldiers rarely forgot that their Indian brothers in arms were descended from warriors, some of them quite famous, and they often held them up to impossibly heroic ideals. On the other hand, military service was an unparalleled experience of Americanization and cultural assimilation that tested native soldiers' ability to live according to social norms they had often been able to keep at bay on their respective reservations. Legitimized against a despicable German enemy, native violence no longer drew a bloody line between savagery and civilization. It symbolized the ambiguous Americanness of those who were at one and the same time the first patriots of the Western hemisphere and the former enemies of their new country, the last warriors and the new soldiers of its Republic.

After the conflict ended, the ambivalent framing of Native experience in the war continued to shape memories, public discourse, and commemorations. Indian patriotism—the mix of gestures, ceremonies, and utterances demonstrating love of the country and military loyalty—remained a paradox that orators both Indian and white alternately naturalized and problematized. While Indians' military compliance had reassured non-Indians, it had also underlined the unclear political position of the nation's indigenous populations. Once the dust settled on the front lines, Indian patriotism developed, rather than subsided, as an attempt to both prolong and make sense of the massive, if puzzling, demonstration of loyalty that the war had occasioned. In the process, patriotism was repurposed for new goals. Should Natives' compliance during the war speed up their political integration into the U.S. body politic? Would their rights as patriotic citizens be compatible with the rights they derived from treaties? Would their patriotism allow them to claim emancipation from the omnipresent control of the Bureau of Indian Affairs? Would veterans of the conflict be reintegrated in their home communities in the same way as their warrior ancestors? Which dispositions should be taken to ensure that the memory of their loyalty and their sacrifice would not promptly vanish from memory?

This very short summary of Native American soldiers' position both during and after the war cannot do justice to the myriad of individual and collective experiences that shaped a greater "Native American experience of World War I." But it will have served its purpose if it has staked out the premise of this book: Indian patriotism, mandated by whites or claimed by Natives themselves, was neither inevitable nor in any way obvious. Patriotism, for Indians as for non-Indians, was the product of historical contingencies and a mixture of contradictory projects and motivations that each individual had to make sense of on his own. And on *her* own too, for patriotism was not limited to soldiers, at the time an exclusively male grouping. Patriotism tested, shaped, and was shaped by families, reservation communities, and urban Indian organizations in inter- and intra-generational dialogues. And because it was heavily constrained and influenced by non-Natives as well, it was also the product of interracial interactions and conversations.

For all of these reasons, it seems justified to look at World War I as a beginning rather than as the mere reenactment of century-old patterns. No matter how long Native peoples had engaged with war, World War I brought forth entirely new questions regarding the rightful place of Native Americans in the body politic. It forced a reinterpretation of the compatibility of Indians' identity and pride in their history with their newfound attachment for a country that had subjugated their ancestors. Indeed, it is precisely by looking at what happens after, rather than during or before the war, that one can most clearly understand how a specific type of patriotism developed that was inextricably Indian (under that word or various ethnonyms) and American. It is also my contention that, although not an *absolute* beginning, the Native American patriotism born of World War I constituted a major and often overlooked inflection in the discourse and the practice of expressing Indians' national belonging, whether American or tribal.

Native American participation in the U.S. war effort has received scholarly attention since the 1990s, but it is mostly the war experience itself that has been studied, not patriotism per se.[2] While an enormous amount of scholarship has looked at the impact of wars and at the various and shifting meanings of patriotism in the United States at large, Indian "loyalty" has had few students and has in general remained a side interest in research dealing more broadly with citizenship, land claims, the history of Indian dancing and the powwow, or individual tribal histories.[3]

More than thirty years ago, the New Western History and the New Indian History revolutionized our understanding of Indians' formidable determination to shape their encounters with whites and Euro-American colonialism. The New Historians, however, have mostly ignored the impact of twentieth-century wars on native communities. After decades of pro-assimilation discourse, their welcome emphasis on Indian agency and on Indians' ability to preserve their values has equally precluded the serious investigation of Indian patriotism, a complex social phenomenon that cannot be reduced to a pretext for resurrecting Native traditions.[4]

Political barriers have also limited our understanding of Indian patriotism. Tribal governments and American Indian studies scholars have insisted on the importance of not equating Indians with other minority ethnic groups—a valid political point perhaps, but one that has also contributed to obscuring the manifest similarities of Native Americans' and African Americans' takes on U.S. patriotism as a resource for gaining rights and asserting identities.[5]

Even when directly addressed by historians, Indian patriotism has remained heavily framed by moral and political issues. Outside of academia, the activism of Vietnam War–era veterans and their determination to see their grievances addressed by the state have resulted in emphasizing above all other aspects the traumatic sides of the war experience. Veterans' activism easily merged, in the case of Native Americans, in a broader denunciation of colonization's impact on Indian lives and of the less than satisfying state of Indian health on Indian reservations.[6] More generally, historical investigation has remained strongly associated with the celebration of Indian bravery and Native contributions to national history, a take much too close to historical actors' strategies to be satisfying for most historians. The vibrant literature on Navajo code talkers in World War II stands as the most obvious witness of that trend. Even a century after World War I, therefore, Indian patriotism remains the contested property of various stakeholders and a heavily fragmented historical object. The only point of agreement seems to be the rather unquestioned belief that, for an explanation of Native engagement with war, one need only look to Indians' "military traditions" and "warrior ethos."[7]

Indian patriotism obviously poses serious challenges to the historian. Military service has touched virtually every Indian group in the United States and has been the object of centralized policies in a way that makes it legitimate to talk of "Native Americans" in general. But an appropriate understanding of each patriotic gesture or utterance also requires painstaking contextualization within local histories and individual trajectories. It often taxes our ability to generalize about the role patriotism as a historical phenomenon played in each Indian community. While this is a common dilemma in the writing of history in general, especially when looking at social phenomena whose reach is as enormous as their definition is vague, it is especially evident in the case of Native Americans. Their self-understanding as "Indians" and members of a coherent racial or ethnic, cultural, and political group had been acquired under duress and remained problematic at the turn of the twentieth century. The risk of ignoring distinct groups' understandings (or ignorance) of patriotism and merging them artificially under the rubric of "Indian patriotism" is ever present. It is all the more problematic as it could be interpreted as an attempt by the historian to further the goal of the assimilationists and erase Indian difference(s).[8]

The imposed nature of patriotism poses another, equally formidable problem. Is tracking down, on and off reservations, the use of national symbols, flag ceremonies, Memorial Day speeches, or even the word *patriotism*—building, in historical parlance, a corpus and a research topic, as I have done—legitimate? When so much of what Native Americans thought about the United States can be expected to have gone unsaid and repressed, for obvious reasons, are those the proper sources to look at Indians' relationship to the United States? Will a history of Indian patriotism be a history of defeat and submission? A history of resistance? Of hidden opinions and double entendre whose real meaning we cannot approach?

More traditional perhaps, but no less difficult, is the question of the starting and end points to give to this research. Even if one admits my premise that World War I can be regarded as a beginning, it is clear that what happened on Indian reservations and in Indian communities in the years preceding the conflict is of exceeding importance to a proper understanding of what followed. At the other end of the problem, if it is the impact of World War I on Native patriotism that I follow, should I stop before World War II? After the Vietnam War? Or only after the last person to have lived through the war has passed away?

To address these three series of methodological problems in a way that fully accounts for the massive role played by patriotism in recent Indian history, I have followed a two-pronged approach. It consists in studying patriotism as a phenomenon both generational and profoundly local. My strategy throughout the book has been to replace patriotic gestures and utterances within a social history of Indian veterans of World War I. It is only through veterans, on and off reservations, that we can hope to get at the core of the patriotic experience of Native Americans. Because they were themselves the embodiment of Natives' (and non-Natives') conflicting relationship with patriotism, they are our best chance of escaping both unwarranted generalization and excessive fragmentation. By focusing my research on the years between 1917 and the end of the 1940s, I have made sure to look only at the years when World War I veterans were most active, indeed often politically dominant in their respective communities. In this way, I feel I have been able to connect patriotism to specific events and specific people, to produce, in short, a situated history. As will become clear in the course of the book, patriotism is both a political ideology linking (in various ways) rights and military participation and a series of teachings, symbols, and ceremonies centered on collective belonging. Although ideology and practices can be and indeed are implemented as part of a coherent program by state officials or patriotic organizations, the links connecting symbols, ideology, and feelings are experienced by individuals and groups in ways that are not necessarily prescribed by the program.

The generational approach has also proved to be an efficient way to place the history of Indian patriotism in a larger framework so as to answer another series of questions that have yet to be addressed. What has the Indian appropriation of patriotism in the years following World War I changed in native lives? What effect has it had on Indian affairs at the local and national level? How has it affected the interactions between Indians and non-Indians? The years between 1918 and the end of the 1940s were crucial ones in recent Indian history. Beginning in the 1920s, reservation groups were allowed to claim reparation for broken treaties from the American government in the U.S. Court of Claims. A few years later, they were encouraged to write constitutions for their tribal governments. The New Deal saw the first major attempt to reverse the most undesirable effects of the assimilation policy the federal government had followed since the last decades of the nineteenth century. World War II occasioned the massive reenlistment of yet another generation of Indian soldiers. Finally, at the end of the 1940s, the major assault on the existence of reservations as separate territories known as "termination" began.

Throughout these decisive decades, patriotic ceremonies imposed in the war and public invocation of Indian patriotism during the war were put to an extraordinarily diverse number of uses. When they played the patriotic game, Indians did more than simply fend off attacks for disloyalty. Because World War I saw a major redefinition of what the United States as a nation was expected to give back to its veterans, patriotic manifestations became not just a way to demonstrate love for one's country or to avoid being chided for not loving it enough but also a discourse to remind one's fellow citizens, and the state, of one's sacrifice. After the Great War, patriotism was more and more regarded as a two-way street, an exchange, not a blank check given the country by veterans and their families. Patriotic ceremonies and utterances were carefully scripted shows imposing a norm on whoever participated in them. But they were never totalitarian events. Control was real but not omnipresent. Participation, in a word, required consent. In this context, patriotism developed as a moral position from which to look at one's own and one's community's relationship to the nation. More often than previously, the idea that the nation owed a debt to its veterans emphasized this relationship as one of mutual obligation. Because they had been colonized, and because they emphasized gift giving as a central aspect of social life, Indians, as this book will show, were well positioned to embrace this change in the social and political uses of patriotism in the interwar period.[9]

As a historian, I would not have been able to follow this change if I did not pay attention to how the relationship between Indians and the U.S. nation was shaped at the local level. This required two further methodological choices: first, a regional focus, and second, oral history. Although I have looked at Indian groups throughout the continental United States, I have paid special attention to what happened on the Plains. This is not because I believe that Indians on the Plains are "more Indian" than those in other places or because they were central to all parts of the story I tell. Iroquois, Eastern Cherokees, Ojibwas, Pueblos, and many other Native groups produced forceful articulations of patriotism and figure prominently in this book. But because the Plains Indians' relations with the United States were both recent and marked by war, I found that a focus on this region would provide the richest case study. Arguably, Indians were more visible on the Plains than anywhere else in the country. That their visibility was reinforced by debates and practices surrounding patriotism is of course part of the story. The stereotype of the mounted warrior and the expectations regarding Indians' patriotism were closely connected to non-Indians' understanding of native life on the Plains. Numbers mattered in my choice as well. With a focus on the Sioux or on the largest Oklahoman groups, I could expect to see more, and more in one place, than if I concerned myself equally with all Indian communities.

I also decided to pay special attention to a place whose history runs through this whole book: the Standing Rock Sioux Reservation, famous for having seen the last years of Sitting Bull. I would not have been able to identify the specific Indian take on patriotism had I not had the opportunity to spend time with veterans and descendants of veterans on Standing Rock. Although I never came close to the year-round sojourn recommended for anthropological field-workers, these stays helped me gain insight into aspects of Indian patriotism that archives, at first glance, seemed to have little to say about. Written records, the majority of which were produced by the federal government, refer to Memorial Day and the Fourth of July; they mention veterans and monuments—sometimes. Doing oral history, going to powwows, identifying monuments marked by patriotism, observing the honors rendered to veterans' graves—these were not just unique personal experiences. They revealed the essential role played by families in local appropriations of patriotism. It is only when I realized how intensely personal and familial patriotism could be, by talking to living people, that the archives began to reveal traces of the same family-centered phenomena in the 1920s, 1930s, and 1940s. Going back and forth between the current manifestations of patriotism and what transpired of it in archival material allowed me to emulate, albeit in a very modest way, the strategy of *upstreaming* followed by ethnohistorians. By taking the present as an inspiration to investigate the past, the emotional aspects of patriotism, not as an ideology but as lived experience consisting of marching, singing, dancing, taking off one's hat, or picking up an eagle feather that fell during a dance, became research objects in their own right—and part of the social history of patriotism in Indian communities.

The book begins with an examination of ceremonies in the years immediately following the end of World War I. Chapters 1 and 2 look at the role played by the commemoration of Native Americans' participation in the conflict in modifying the traditional understanding of Indians as a "dying race" and as an enemy race. Contrary to what happened for the majority population of the United States, Indian participation did not result in a flurry of personal and official, fictional and nonfictional literature. Indeed, for multiple reasons that I address in chapter 1, the story of Indian participation proved unwieldy to all who could have been interested in recounting it. While documentation was produced and sometimes published, neither the federal government nor the Bureau of Indian Affairs, nor the states, nor even anthropologists displayed an interest in looking at the war experience or investigating its effects on Indian veterans and communities. With rare exceptions, these actors treated war as a parenthesis, albeit one that proved that the Indians were not dead and that they could contribute to national life. Indian activists, especially in the cities, turned out to be the only ones interested in capitalizing on the war to push for a national holiday that would pay tribute to the Native American contribution: Indian Day.

Conversely, chapter 2 emphasizes the significance of the war in rearranging relations between races at the local level. In a colonial spirit of "closing the frontier," settlers living on or near Indian reservations appropriated Indian military participation. When raising funds for monuments or creating local heroes, whites invoked a brotherhood-in-arms and celebrated the true end of the Indian wars. Indians took advantage of their neighbors' willingness to include them in their celebrations and reactivated memories and heroes of the pre-reservation era.

Chapter 3 looks at these interracial interactions from the point of view of Indians in an effort at writing a historical anthropology of Indian patriotism. At the core of Indians' military participation and commemoration of the Great War, the practice of giving, to non-Indians or to Indians, to outsiders or to insiders, to family members or to complete strangers, structured the expression of patriotism in Indian communities. Examining Memorial and Armistice Days, in particular, chapter 3 looks at the role these holidays played in allowing Indians to maintain boundaries with their white neighbors and develop a series of adaptations of patriotic symbols and ceremonies that acclimatized patriotism for reservation life on an unprecedented scale.

Chapter 4 switches perspective again and takes as its object the veterans themselves. When looked at through an ethnographical lens,

World War I veterans appear to have been ambiguous heroes on reservations. They were honored but at the same time elicited mistrust, jealousy, and attempts on the part of the Bureau of Indian Affairs, as well as on the part of their own communities, to control and direct their behavior. Their identity as a group developed as much from local cultural traditions as from this ambivalent position on reservations, alternately central and marginal.

Chapters 5 and 6 apply the insights of the previous chapters to the examination of the role of patriotism and veterans in shaping Indian policy from the 1920s to the end of the 1940s. For veterans and non-veterans alike, Native American participation in World War I was an opportunity to ask the state and the general public for moral and material recognition. Although they derived few tangible benefits from this mobilization, the ability of veterans to claim the attention of non-Indians allowed them to accumulate a level of political savvy and social capital rarely encountered in their communities.

As chapter 6 makes clear, contradictions and frustrations surrounding veterans came to a head with the onset of the "Indian New Deal" initiated by Franklin D. Roosevelt's Indian commissioner, John Collier. As Collier pushed his agenda of reform and return to communal landholding on Indian reservations, patriotism became the privileged weapon of an active minority of veterans spearheading resistance to the New Deal. World War II proved a very favorable moment to realize a rhetorical and organizational connection that linked patriotism, the conservative defense of Indians' civic rights, and the rising tide of termination. At the end of the 1940s, the World War I generation reached the peak of its influence in Indian country and demonstrated the complexity of Indian patriotism. A new generation of Indian soldiers was soon to take their place. They would turn ceremonies popularized with World War I into a new, modern Indian tradition.

I NDIAN PARTICIPATION in World War I has been looked at since the war through a set of fixed propositions, an unquestioned doxa of popular opinion, that holds that Indians joined the U.S. armed forces in 1917 even though they were not citizens; they joined in far greater proportion than their numbers in the total U.S. population warranted; they received U.S. citizenship as a reward for their loyalty but massively refused it; and, last but not least, their status as super-patriots, then as now, should ultimately be ascribed to tribal "traditions," indigeneity, and Indians' common identity as a warrior race. Despite inevitable variations and adaptation, this core set of beliefs has survived and has even been reinforced by Indians' subsequent participation in conflicts waged by the United States. Examining how Indian military service was narrated in the two decades following the end of the Great War is a good vantage point for understanding how, and by whom, these beliefs were first held to be true and propagated. Myth-making and history-making are obviously inseparable here. Yet this chapter does not set out to debunk these myths as much as it purports to investigate the historical conditions that made them possible, desirable, and, to a certain extent, self-fulfilling. By looking at various attempts to integrate Indian participation in World War I into a national narrative, it emphasizes the role of racial ideologies in shaping popular belief and in creating its central paradox: The war made the Indian race part of history again, yet very little history writing was devoted to Indian soldiers.

Chronicling the Return of the Indian Race

Historians have abundantly noted the racial and racist nature of American nationalism and the diverse ability of ethnically and racially identified groups to take advantage of it by claiming loyalty and patriotism and by reminding the "majority" of sacrifices made for the country. In 1917, the limits of a patriotic stance had been clear to African Americans since at least the Spanish-American War.

previous page: Raymond Desvarreux-Larpenteur, *Odus [Otis] W. Leader, 16th Infantry, 1917* (Copyright Musée de l'Armée, Paris, France © Adagp, Paris, 2016)

The end of World War I further signaled to African Americans how little they would be allowed to benefit from their own participation in a war waged in Europe in defense of liberty and "civilization." As white mobs murdered African Americans, including veterans, in several major cities throughout the country in 1919 and 1920, the point was made that participation in the war would not result in challenging the racial status quo. Fighting for liberty in Europe was not the same thing as advocating against segregation at home. Consequently, as had already been the case after the Civil War, the memory of black soldiers' service was not to become part of a national narrative of American self-assertion on the international scene through military efficiency, bravery, and decisiveness.[1]

The years immediately following World War I were marked by extreme racial and political conservatism. The Red Scare used accusations of "bolshevism" to disqualify workers' movements, attack foreigners, and suppress the African American struggle for civil rights. Immigrants and minorities were, as they had been throughout the war, asked to demonstrate "Americanism," understood as a set of national goals but also as a characterization of the United States' collective persona; better still if that Americanism could be "one hundred per cent." Nativism, a component of American nationalism and American political life since the first decades of the nineteenth century, influenced the passing of the most restrictive immigration laws ever to be enacted in the country. At the same time, the 1920s were also the years when cultural pluralism began to be defended in the United States as a specifically American value, in line with an already long history of immigration, progressive acculturation of newcomers, multilingualism, and de facto diversity. Even before the fight against Nazism made these ideas central in American identity, the New Deal was an opportunity for social workers, anthropologists, and activists to reaffirm them: America was diverse, and patriotism could be demonstrated by all kinds of people.

American Indians were better positioned than African Americans to make the most of these apparently contradictory trends. During the war, non-Indians had demonstrated that they embraced Indians' racialized difference as warriors and valued their tenacity, their "savagery" even. For Indians much more than African Americans military service in the war was presented by whites as an incontrovertible motive of "race pride." The legitimization of Indian racial qualities and the fact of integrated service with white soldiers made it possible for Indians to enter the national narrative not as tribes or individuals but as a race—a possibility that was usually denied to non-white groups. In the United States as in European democracies, the ideology of the citizen-soldier associated political participation and military service as two sides of the same coin. Military service was the duty of every adult male citizen, a duty justified by and justifying the exercise of political rights such as the right to vote. But because American society was heavily racialized and ethnicized, military service was also implicitly a collective duty. Men stood as representatives of the ethnic or racial group with which they were identified. Consequently, serving the nation entailed a form of collective compensation in the form of recognition, at the national level, of each group's distinct contribution to the defense of the country. After World War I, several non-Anglo groups tried to avail themselves of this promise of symbolic inclusion in the national narrative. Foremost among their claims was the integration of their group in history textbooks.[2]

The histories produced by these groups were rarely an academic affair. They were also never a national concern. Activists fought over local history textbooks, commemorative war histories sponsored by the states, cities, and counties, with the limited objective of seeing their group's loyalty and patriotic excellence acknowledged and commended. History books should, for these entrepreneurs of memory, vindicate members of their ethnic groups against accusations of treachery and lukewarm patriotism. African Americans tried and failed to get the same kind of recognition that came easily to Central European immigrants, even though some of the latter had been suspected of sympathy for the Central Empires during the war. Race proved more malleable for American Indians, because they had always stood in an ambiguous position vis-à-vis American nativism.

The incontrovertible fact of Indians' anteriority on the North American continent had never been in doubt. Ever since the beginning of the American Republic, politicians and writers had acknowledged Indians' status as "aborigines of the continent" and as "the original Americans"—while at the same time applying the term "native American" to Euro-American colonists born in the country.

Aborigineity entailed no special rights, however, and anteriority was closely related to decadence. To many, the Indian race was old, doomed, and vanishing. Racist thinkers saw Indians as threatened, like any other race, by bastardization and degeneration, with only a few conceding the potential benefits of white admixture. As deplored as it was anxiously anticipated, the disappearance of the Indian race was also actively promoted by the federal state. One of the most influential laws in Indian affairs, the Dawes Act of 1887 (and its companion, the Burke Act of 1906) conditioned Indian assimilation and survival in American society to an individual's amount of white blood and adoption of white ways of life. If all Indians were allotted a portion of their respective tribe's reservation lands, only those "white" enough could claim the right to fully own and sell their land, manage their bank accounts, and live free of the otherwise inescapable supervision of the Bureau of Indian Affairs.

Until the mid-1910s, the set of self-fulfilling prophecies linking Indians' disappearance as a race and their assimilation could be regarded as amply justified by the census. In 1900, the Indian population of the entire United States numbered no more than 250,000, a historical low point that may have said more about the appalling state of health services on reservations than about historically linear trajectories of decline. Yet by 1910, the trend was, modestly, reversed. The understanding of American Indians' racial contribution to the war was framed by this demographic context of transition and timid recovery. Because aborigeneity ceased to be demographically associated with extinction at the very same time that World War I broke out, American Indian soldiers' participation in the war effort was early on (and contradictorily) understood as both the last gasp of a dying race and a testimony to its renewed dynamism, but the latter interpretation rapidly triumphed. The war brought about a new way of imagining not just the Indian race itself but also its place within the American body politic, a place that for the first time several observers could imagine as lasting and oriented toward the future rather than the past.[3]

To be sure, as the following examples will show, the new understandings of the Indian race permitted by the war and the new demographic context did not result in any coherent body of work. And while they were expressed in various genres—journalistic and novelistic literature, memoirs, the cinema, and a historical tract—and by thinkers both Indian and non-Indian, the attempts at historicizing Indian participation in the Great War never concerned more than a fringe of American fictional and historical productions on the conflict. Their diverse relations to ideologies of assimilation or racial evolutionism testified, however, to the new ideological space opened by the war with regard to Indians' symbolic place in U.S. history and society.

In his unique cinematographic representation of a Native American World War I veteran, George B. Seitz, a screenwriter and director known mostly for his "action" movies, tackled the problem head on in 1925. Fittingly titled *The Vanishing American*, his feature-length motion picture was an adaptation of a newspaper serial by the famed "western" novelist Zane Grey. After a long preamble chronicling the story of the U.S. Southwest as a succession of races in the tradition of racial evolutionism, the film focused on a Navajo Indian named Nophaie. Played by the white actor Richard Dix, Nophaie is remarkable mostly for his love of a non-Indian schoolteacher, until he answers the patriotic call to arms in 1917. Having volunteered in the Army, he is sent to the French front, where he becomes a sergeant and saves his commanding officer in an act of outstanding bravery. "In all the annals of the Great War," an intertitle reminded the audience, "there were no more thrilling pages than those written by these first Americans." The greater part of the movie subsequently addressed in a romanticized manner the problems encountered by Nophaie after he comes home to the arbitrariness of BIA supervision and the outright thievery of the local agent of the federal administration. While his fellow Indian veterans, duly decorated, sadly injured, and even amputated, plan a vengeful uprising against white settlers, Nophaie intervenes. He is killed during his attempt to defuse the situation.

Undeniably, all the then dominant stereotypes of Indian fiction are present in *The Vanishing American*—albeit in noticeably altered ways. Interracial love is doomed—but here, it concerns an Indian man and a white woman, not, as usually, an Indian "princess" and a white frontier hero. The contemporary setting and direct criticism of the BIA are equally rare and notable in a genre characterized by a historical bent and a predilection for frontier situations. The hero

himself is the typical "Friend of the Whites," but he is also an educated Indian with a war record who wears (approximately) traditional garb.[4] The movie cannot be taken as representative of a sea
change in the cinematographic representation of the Indians, comparable to the one that took place in the 1960s when Indian wars
were used by "western" directors to portray and criticize the war
in Vietnam. As an example of the "exceptional normal," however, it
testifies to what the war made possible, if not commonplace: a public restructuring of century-old emotional frames of reference to address the "Indian problem." After the war, even the most hackneyed
stereotypes had to be redefined in the face of recent events.

Few went as far as Seitz in problematizing in a work of fiction
the failed links connecting military service, citizenship, and justice
for American Indians. After the war, Indian soldiers became hard to
market. The only recorded project to document their participation
in the world conflict never got past the drafting stage. In 1923, one
editor at Houghton Mifflin tried to explain to the author Joseph K.
Dixon why this was so but could only point to the whims of readers:
"There has been for the last two or three years, a curious phenomenon of an acute repugnance on the part of the reading public, toward any book dealing with the war, in any way." Dixon, although an
amateur, was no beginner. In fact, when he received this disappoint-
ing letter turning down his tentatively titled *From Tepees to Trenches,*
he had more than ten years' experience in exploiting the myth of the
Vanishing American—the title of his bestselling book, published in
1913. Trying to emulate Edward S. Curtis, Dixon had, the same year,
toured Indian reservations with his camera, taking pictures of reservation leaders pledging allegiance to the American flag. He even envisioned the building of an Indian memorial on Staten Island. The
monument, the first stone of which was actually laid, would have
featured a massive sixty-foot bronze statue of an Indian warrior,
an impressive sight for immigrants that would have paralleled the
Statue of Liberty. Dixon's involvement with Indians did not stop
with this failure. From 1917 to 1920, he actively lobbied for the
creation of all-Indian regiments in the U.S. armed forces, emphasizing the unique racial abilities of Native Americans for military duty.
Undeterred by another disappointment, he decided to use the material he had accumulated during his campaign as the first step in

an effort at documenting the Indian participation in the war effort. Dixon was not alone in this undertaking. In 1919, Lieutenant John R. Eddy at the U.S. Army Historical Section sent out questionnaires to selected commanding officers in an attempt to assess their Indian subordinates' efficiency at night work, orientation, or intelligence gathering—a fact-finding endeavor that could support the promotion of all-Indian regiments in the peacetime Army. Dixon availed himself of the material and added to it by collecting interviews with wounded Indian veterans in Army hospitals and sending out his own questionnaire, transmitted to Indian veterans dispersed on reservations thanks to the help of the BIA. By 1921 he had accumulated enough information for a book-size publication.[5]

Dixon's questions to Indian veterans were closely aligned with his political and commercial project of glorifying the Indian race. Had a soldier been drafted or had he volunteered? Had he been wounded, killed, decorated? Where had he served and with whom? A section of the questionnaire devoted to "Remarks" was intended to elicit a short summary of each veteran's whole military career, from enlistment to demobilization. Another section addressed the specific contributions of the soldier's tribe to the raising of war bonds and in-kind contributions to the war effort as well as any sort of loss incurred because of the conflict. The status of tribal land (allotted or not) was to be mentioned to give an idea of each group's degree of backwardness or advancement. Individual itineraries and the collective trajectory on the road to citizenship and civilization were thus to be closely enmeshed in the book, but military gore and glamour would take pride of place.

Indexing a racial group's progress toward civilization and whiteness on its most brilliant members was an old strategy of activists interested in promoting minority rights in general and citizenship in particular. Long before the war, promoters of assimilation among Indians as well as blacks were actively collecting information about graduates of elite minority schools, informing the public about their students' success in dedicated journals, and printing photographic portraits displaying the outward signs of sartorial assimilation to the white middle class. For Native Americans, the Hampton Institute in Virginia or the Carlisle Indian School in Pennsylvania had already familiarized their students with these procedures. Several respondents to the Dixon questionnaire, alumni of these schools, appeared to be willing to play along.

In his interviews, Dixon was on the lookout for glorious anecdotes and acts of bravery. If one is to believe the prospective table of contents he sent to Houghton Mifflin, two-thirds of the work would have consisted of transcripts of interviews documenting Indian service on the front in the various branches of the military. Chapters already drafted insisted on the central part played in the war by the "17,000" Indian recruits and went as far as contending that it could not have been won without them. Indians, said Dixon, were the first to volunteer despite their subjugated condition. On the front, using their natural instinct, they rescued American patrols lost in the no man's land. Before the Tennessee hero Alvin York was able to go into action, Indian Alvin Yorks had already collected German scalps. Aborigineity, for Dixon, meant excellence in patriotism and bravery but also, literally, anteriority. He explicitly articulated the fight against Germany with "Ethnic Values and a New Odyssey" for Native Americans—the title of one of his concluding chapters.[6]

Dixon hoped to capitalize on a new edition of *The Vanishing American* to launch *From Tepees to Trenches*. Like Seitz, his approach attempted to achieve previously contradictory objectives: reasserting Indian racial identity not as a heritage from the past but as a current contribution to the U.S. nation and a justification for, rather than an impediment to, citizenship.

Seitz and Dixon had, however, few imitators in the ranks of "Friends of the Indians," the influential group of Eastern philanthropists and civil servants who had monitored the Bureau of Indian Affairs since the end of the 1860s and were the most active promoters of Indian citizenship. Most of them had stood on the other side of the Indian regiment controversy in 1917, including General Hugh L. Scott of the Army, probably one of their most prestigious members. A lieutenant commanding a troop of mounted Indian Scouts from 1892 to 1897 and a high-ranking professional soldier until his retirement in 1919, Scott then joined the Board of Indian Commissioners, the first and most official group of "Friends of the Indians." He was still in office in 1928 when he published his memoirs. In it, Indian participation figured briefly as an aside in the chapter dealing with his own service during World War I. "As a race,"

Scott explained, the Indian "played a higher part in the war on the side of patriotism than the ordinary white man, notwithstanding the fact that it was but a short time since we were pointing guns at him. He put aside his long list of grievances against his white brother, without waiting to be drafted, and of about fifteen thousand men able to pass our military examination, ten thousand served in the Army and Navy, a greater proportion than was furnished by the white man [. . .]. We may indeed all be proud of our red race and its record in the World War."[7] In its brevity and patronizing tone, Scott's account offered as official a summary of Indian contribution as would ever reach the general audience. Scott's emphasis was on loyalty rather than bravery. Explicit comparison of Indians with colonial troops in previous chapters made it clear what "our red race" meant: In a global conflict that had involved representatives of all the major empires, Indians had demonstrated their own imperial patriotism. This, however, had to be read into a short and allusive paragraph. Because it was written by one who had explicitly refused to generalize his own experience with race-based troops, the text hints at a larger problem in commemorating Indian patriotism in print. Aside from any question of marketability, Scott worked under a double bind: The Indian race had to be promoted in its effort to assimilate, but assimilation meant precisely renouncing any separate existence for Native Americans. Brevity was not simply a mark of indifference; it was also a rhetorical strategy to avoid delving into the politically troubling question of Indians' place within an American republic that had also become an empire.

There was only one way of addressing this problem, and it was also one most of the "Friends of the Indians" could sympathize with: the jeremiad. Lamenting Indian suffering at the hand of the whites had a long history in American letters, and its most resounding example had been Helen Hunt Jackson's *A Century of Dishonor* in 1881, a biting criticism against the shortcomings of the Bureau of Indian Affairs' dealings with its wards. For Jennings C. Wise, World War I proved an opportunity to renew the tradition. Trained in law, Wise was a professor at the prestigious Virginia Military Institute, his alma mater, from 1912 to 1915 and served as a lieutenant colonel in the American Expeditionary Force during World War I. He converted to the Indian cause in 1920, when he took up the claim of the Yankton Sioux. A year before, he had come into contact with Lieutenant John R. Eddy and was familiar with his effort to promote all-Indian regiments. In 1931, Wise published *The Red Man in the New World Drama*. This sweeping account of Indian history starting with the first contact between whites and Indians on the North American continent devoted a full chapter to "the Indians and the First World War." Wise quoted Scott's opinion of Indians but disagreed with his assessment of the advisability of segregating Indians. Psychiatric tests performed in the Army, he contended, had highlighted Indians' greater ability to withstand strain, a crucial concern of all protagonists in the recent conflict. While "the so-called Nordic must [. . .] still be taken as the foremost 'killer' of the human race," Native Americans had in fact demonstrated than they were not inferior to white soldiers in that regard. If they had been allowed to serve in segregated regiments, they might even have proved superior to East Indians serving in the British Army. In specific comparisons with the Gurkhas, Wise was careful not to be too conclusive on Indians' supposedly racial abilities. Environment, he explained, could account for the much-vaunted Indian quality of stealth; it was "common to frontiersmen of whatever breed." Contrary to Scott, Wise further noted the use of Indian languages in radio transmission to fool "Professor Fritz" but again insisted that there was nothing racial in this militarily beneficial use of Indian difference. Emphasizing Indian suffering "in the ranks of democracy," he concluded: "May the nation profit by that record, of which the red man has every reason to be proud. Who today shall say what was the color of the Unknown Soldier of America?" His development on World War I was surrounded by two chapters on Indian citizenship. His was as scientific a look at Indian specificity as would ever find its way into print in the years following the conflict.[8]

Despite differences in length, style, and overall objectives, Seitz's, Dixon's, Scott's, and Wise's treatment of Indian participation in the war operated under the same principles. They were evaluations by non-Indians of the specific contribution of Native Americans and attempts to draw conclusions from the very limited number of facts available regarding Indian soldiers. Their work, in various ways, testified to the two major constraints that weighed on making an inventory of Indian patriotism: assimilationism and a paucity of official sources. The latter was not corrected by the personal memoirs and war stories that non-Indian soldiers, whites especially, produced in abundance. Here again, we have to make the most of the exceptional, namely, the work John Joseph Mathews. Mathews was by his own account a "mixed-blood." His claim to Indianness was an Osage great-grandfather on his father's side. When Mathews published *Sundown*, a novel dealing with the war experience of an Oklahoma mixed-blood, he had, however, had time to make sense of his own racial identity. Mathews joined the Army in 1918 and went to France as a pilot. Disappointed by the treatment reserved for veterans at the University of Oklahoma, he returned to Europe and studied at Oxford and Geneva on his own money, part of the exceptional wealth the Osages derived from oil in the 1910s. Aimless traveling through Europe and North Africa brought about a personal epiphany: Witnessing the mock charge of Kabyle warriors in Morocco, he was reminded of a similar scene among the Osages in his childhood. Determined to go back to the United States and to his roots, Mathews returned to Oklahoma in 1929 and embarked on a project to recover his and his people's Indian past. *Sundown* was a first, fictional step in a personal itinerary that ultimately led to the creation of an Osage museum.

In many ways a classic coming-of-age story, *Sundown* chronicled the personal travails of Chal, Mathews's alter ego. A mixed-blood like his creator, Chal is an apparently perfectly assimilated individual who graduates from high school and goes to university. Hearing of the war on campus, he joins a flying school after learning that the United States would not engage any cavalry on the front—his first intuition on the best way to reconnect with his Indian heritage. Having become proficient at flying, he begins thinking "of himself as separated by a great abyss from Sun-on-His-Wings and Running Elk," his Indian childhood friends, "and from the village with the people moving among the lodges." Chal personifies the mixed-blood plagued by a feeling of displacement and the temptation of resorting to alcohol to assuage his identity conflicts. His aimlessness is compounded by the fact that the war ends before he is able to put his flying skills to use in combat. Returning home, depressed and on the verge of alcoholism, he drives to an Indian dance and finds himself "suddenly flooded with emotion that felt like needles pricking him, and he thought that he could not stay any longer. The singers were singing the song of his own ancestors." This first reconnection with his roots proves overwhelming, but later on Chal goes back to a dance as a participant. Unable to achieve the release he is after, he nevertheless feels that "he was an Indian now"; "He wanted by some action or some expression, to express the whole meaning of life: to declare to the silent world about him that he was a glorious male; to express to the silent forms of the blackjacks that he was a brother to the wind, the lightning and the forces that came out of the earth." In a final twist, it is not by flying or singing that his "warrior's heart" finds peace but in projecting himself in the "glory" of becoming a Harvard-trained lawyer, "a great orator."[9]

The contrast between Mathews's and Chal's trajectories expresses the force of stereotypes—as well as novelistic condensation. While it took the author several years and long-distance travel to formulate his project of returning to the "red race," his alter ego's identity crisis occurs over a matter of months, if not days. War is but a context justifying the emergence of deep-seated contradictions within him—contradictions that contemporary readers could immediately ascribe to the stereotype of the individual of mixed ancestry caught "between two worlds," forever unable to adjust fully to either. Gone is the confrontation with other colonized people in a faraway empire, which had been crucial in Mathews's decision to come to terms with his Indian ancestry and eventually transformed him into a historian of the Osage people. In *Sundown*, the "return" to the Indian race is not an intellectual construct but a powerfully embodied urge. Suffering does not come from combat wounds but from soul wounds, inflicted not by whites but by oneself. Internalized and dehistoricized, the travails of the mixed-blood neither end nor begin with the world war. They have a quality of eternity that only a novelist can bring to light.

The Problem of Culture Change

Race was a powerful and tricky concept, impossible to ignore when writing the history of Indian participation in the Great War but particularly unwieldy. Indians had long been identified as a vanish-

ing race, but the war had signaled just the opposite: Indians were
not a vanishing race, they were there to stay. It comes therefore as
no surprise that, of all professional writers, cultural anthropologists
were the ones to seize upon the situation and lobby for the use of a
new concept that had become central in their profession: culture, a
concept that could be seen as crucial to the understanding of American Indian patriotism. Admittedly, the American anthropological
profession, powerfully shaped since the beginning of the twentieth
century by the efforts of Franz Boas and his disciples, had not repu-
diated the concept of race. But Boasian anthropologists had proposed
to place strict limits on its use. Placing culture at the heart of a theory
of cultural relativism, anthropologists first emphasized the systemic
nature of culture and the culturally destructive effects of contacts
between white industrial societies and indigenous peoples. By the
1930s, however, a new line of inquiry emerged: the study of culture
change. Margaret Mead's groundbreaking work *The Changing Culture of an Indian Tribe* (1932) proposed an entirely new and scientific
way to address change when contact between two different cultural
groups was involved. Rather than the inevitable decadence of "weaker"
Indian cultures giving way to a triumphant white civilization, she
underlined conflict within Indian societies themselves.[10] The agenda
she sketched was expanded on by Robert Redfield, Melville Hersko-
vits, and Ralph Linton, who replaced folk understandings of assimilation with the more complex notion of acculturation. By the 1940s,
the study of acculturation was a bona fide academic field that informed scientific research throughout the Americas and in other
areas of the world.

The focus on conflict and an interest in contemporary Indian
societies did not lead anthropologists to a specific anthropological
interest in Indian veterans of World War I. For anthropologists,
veterans could be informants; they were often interpreters; they
could appear in field notes; but they did not make it to print. To be
sure, this testifies first to how slow change can be, even in an academic world that strives on new programs and places special emphasis on innovation. In line with an old tradition documenting Indian
chiefs, their oratory and fateful trajectories, the dominant genre of
the 1930s in work addressing Indian life was the biography of out-

standing individuals. In 1930, Frank B. Linderman published *American: The Life Story of a Great Indian, Plenty-Coups, Chief of the Crow*. Two years later, he followed suit with *Red Mother*, the biography of another Crow tribal member, Pretty Shield. That same year, *Black Elk Speaks*, the (auto-)biography of an Oglala spiritual leader, written by John G. Neihardt, was published. In 1933, Thomas Marquis retraced the steps of Antelope Woman, a Cheyenne, in *She Watched Custer's Last Battle: The Story of Kate Bighead*. In 1936, Ruth Underhill released *The Autobiography of a Papago Woman: An Intimate Portrait of American Indian Culture*. Based on fieldwork and interviews, the genre of Indian biography participated in the contemporary presence of Indians. War figured prominently in all these biographies, but in the form of intertribal conflicts or wars with the United States. The dominant historical narrative of the frontier, first conceptualized by Frederick Jackson Turner, remained an undisputed frame of analysis. The closing of the frontier signaled the end of pure, unadulterated Indian cultures. Even writers who served in France in 1917 and 1918 did regard the conflict as bearing on the history of Indian cultures. In 1930, Walter Campbell, for example, writing under his pen name of Stanley Vestal, concluded a biography of Sitting Bull based on exhaustive fieldwork that had put him in contact with several World War I veterans of the Standing Rock Reservation, with an ecstatic paean to the frontier:

> We Americans owe a great debt to our old enemy. Because it is not the smooth path, but the rough trail, which makes us strong; it is not our friends, but our foes, who commonly have most to do with forging our characters. Consider what the history of these states would be had there been no native peoples on this continent—a dull chronicle of plodding clodhoppers, placidly moving each year a little farther into the vacant lands, carrying along their petty, outworn European ideas and institutions, their bastard European culture, unchanged and unchanging—so many rubber stamps! But as it was, thank God, we had a Frontier, and, as historians are forever reminding us, that Frontier shaped America, moulded a nation unlike any other. That Frontier formed these states, made us what we are—and the Indian made the Frontier.[11]

Because of the omnipresence of the frontier paradigm, the line between those interested in veterans and those who were not had little
to do with the line separating "popular" and "serious" writers. On
the Oglala reservation of Pine Ridge, H. Scudder Mekeel, an anthropologist trained at Yale by Clark Wissler, spent two summers in
1930 and 1931 researching culture change in "a modern American
Indian community." War was not part of the modernity under investigation. On Pine Ridge, 126 young men had been called to the
colors during World War I. Mekeel did not ignore their existence.
In fact, two of them were his informants. One, Tom White Cow
Killer, told him about travels as a soldier that had taken him to the
Far East and allowed him to confront non-American cultures, even
test the validity of the theory that Indians had come from Asia. The
other, William Fire Thunder, an employee of the BIA, was Mekeel's
own interpreter. He volunteered information about his service on
the Western front and related the ambivalent effects of the conflict
for him. Both veterans exhibited no desire to hide their experience
as somehow problematic or un-authentic. Yet despite his attention
to generational differences and his distinction of Indians according
to their relationship to "traditional" culture, Mekeel did not see in
his veteran-informants a potential research topic or even a coherent
group that could have served as a starting point to address the problem of culture change. Fire Thunder appeared in his unpublished
dissertation as "Paul Big Wound," but his military service was not
mentioned. Although, as the title announced, Mekeel analyzed a society "in light of its past," this past stopped somewhere around the
end of the nineteenth century.[12]

Mekeel was heavily involved in the BIA's attempt, during the
New Deal, to bring anthropology to bear on contemporary Indian
problems. His position was not that of the antiquarian, nor that of
a man merely deploring the changes wrought on Indian societies
by colonization. Understanding culture change was for him part of
a project to control and redirect it, so as to ease Indians' transition
into modernity. Anthropological research could help identify cultural values and practices likely to hinder or facilitate modernization,
whether agricultural or political. Modernity drew a line between,
essentially, mixed-bloods and full-bloods. But participation in the
war did not have the power to create such categories of analysis. As

the work of his colleague Gordon Macgregor made clear, Mekeel's myopia was not isolated. Trained at Harvard, Macgregor worked for the Bureau of Indian Affairs as an anthropologist in various positions from 1936 to 1949, under Mekeel. His main project during the World War II years involved working with the same communities that his superior had studied on Pine Ridge a decade earlier. Funded by the Committee on Indian Education Research, which the BIA and the University of Chicago jointly sponsored, Macgregor's research focused on the psychological and social problems of adjustment faced by Lakota men unable to fulfill their traditional role as warriors. Realizing that the relation between culture and personality was essential in shaping individual and collective problems on the reservation, Macgregor characterized Pine Ridge men by an expression that was barely a metaphor: They were "warriors without weapons." For him and his collaborators, Indian men had been deprived of the opportunity to prove themselves in war or in hunting, and the reservation community had not developed new expectations for them. Apparently oblivious to the fact that hundreds of them were fighting Nazi Germany and Imperial Japan at the time when he was writing, just like the previous generation had fought in the Great War, Mekeel offered one solution: livestock raising. Cattle appeared the only economically viable venture likely to fit traditional values and restore Lakota men's self-esteem.[13]

It was not, in fact, until 1949 that Indian veterans became a legitimate concern of the anthropologists John Adair and Evon Vogt, who were working in the Southwest. The return of veterans understood as acculturated to both Indian and white ways through their service in Europe or the Pacific brought a new understanding of their relevance as a group to analyze change and conflict in Indian communities. The World War I generation had simply been bypassed, and the first autobiographies of Indian veterans of the Great War would have to wait until the 1990s.[14]

One exception to this trend allows us to understand how participation in the war would likely have been interpreted before 1949, had it been recognized as a full-fledged research topic. Leo Srole received his Ph.D. at the University of Chicago in 1940 with a dissertation titled "Ethnic Groups and American Society." That same year, he conducted fieldwork among the Ho-Chunk (Winnebago) under anthropologists Fay-Cooper Cole and Fred Eggan. In a short paper read at the annual meeting of the American Anthropological Association in December 1940, "The Winnebago and Modern War," Srole offered a candid analysis of his difficulty in grappling with the problem. "Let me first confess," Srole began, "that I was not explicitly aware of the problem while I was in the field. In the course of interviewing among all elements of the tribal population I had here and there picked up stray bits of information, the full significance of which did not come to me until much later when I was in the stage of organizing and analyzing my material. This is a situation, I am sure, which all field workers experience repeatedly. I mention it, however, to explain in self-defense the gaps obvious in my treatment of the problem here."

Srole did not immediately realize that World War I had been a moment of important theoretical import, but when he did, he was struck by its role in Winnebago life. In 1917, "many of the old procedures associated with warfare reappeared from a state of dormancy," which thereby explained the "very high proportion of Winnebagos enlisting in the armed forces. [. . .] Upon the return of the warriors to Wisconsin, at the close of the war, the surviving culture literally took a new lease on life." This was especially apparent in dances and songs, but the war also reestablished the warriors as a status group on the Winnebago reservation, Srole continued: "And its members immediately assumed the customary prerogatives associated with that status." The "contemporary bastard or mongrel culture" could not hide the fact that "the trinity of spirit, warrior and warfare—which for convenience sake I shall refer to as the war complex," had survived. "For all of the devastation" brought about by recent culture change, Srole explained, "the Winnebago culture pattern has been left intact at its core, namely, in the war complex I have referred to. The facade is and has been in ruins, but the framework, to be sure shrunken and bent, is standing fast." He concluded: "I am not able at this point to offer an explanation which would account for the persistence of the Winnebago war complex. But I do have a hunch that its persistence may be rooted, at least partially, in the very powerful and only thinly disguised feelings of aggression which the Winnebago have long been harboring for the whites around them." This conclusion is not unrelated to the fact that Srole would go on to serve as a military psychologist in World War II. But Srole's "hunch" remained untested, as did its similarity with folk understandings of Indians' embrace of military service in the Great War.[15]

Clearly, cultural anthropologists' engagement with the Indian experience in World War I challenges any linear description of the profession's intellectual trajectory. Anthropologists were under no obligation to talk about the Great War. But that they ignored it while at the same time launching the study of culture changes is telling. War, for anthropologists interested in Native Americans, was mostly a phenomenon of the past; its current version had no relevance in Indian lives; it took three decades after the end of World War I for these principles to be questioned. No matter how interested in the present anthropologists were, it was a present without events. They were unable to use the concept of culture to write Indian participation in the war as other than "the return of the Indian."

Federal Silence

The tendencies to sum up Indian participation with a few handpicked figures and formulas, on the one hand, and to inscribe the world war in a series of events in which its specificity tended to get lost, on the other, was, to be sure, not specific to writers, anthropologists, or others. The dehistoricizing potential of race was to be felt in government circles as well. Indians, in fact, were simply absent from the official history of the World War produced by the Historical Section of the U.S. Army. Indians, like other groups regarded as minorities, were made invisible in a narrative that focused strictly on combat and whose actors were regiments and divisions, not the races and ethnicities that had helped fill them to capacity. But in the case of Indians, the phenomenon was compounded by the fact that the Bureau of Indian Affairs, the group of specialists most likely to produce aggregate data on Natives, proved unable, just like anthropologists but for very different reasons, to produce knowledge on the war experience of its wards.[16]

This was not for lack of objective motivation. The Bureau had a vested interest in disseminating figures on Native Americans, soldiers or not—but on soldiers especially. Understood as a test of loyalty and assimilation, Indians' willingness to join the fight and face death was also a test of the institution's own success at its work of "civilization." Aside from the sample survey of the Historical Section of the U.S. Army, the BIA was the only agency of the federal government that attempted to conduct a systematic appraisal of the war's impact on Indian communities. Its first efforts, however, were strictly, and narrowly, statistical. While all governments were confronted with great difficulty in assessing their respective countries' human losses, the BIA found it especially hard to keep track of the precise number of Indians who had joined. Throughout the conflict, its estimates oscillated between 5,000 and 9,000, sometimes going as far as 17,000 (actually the number of Indians who registered for the draft), and stabilized around 12,000 after the end of the war. High figures demonstrated the quality of the BIA's collaboration with the Selective Service and the armed forces; their variation showed that, once they had left reservations, Indian soldiers became very difficult to track for their federal guardians. Classified as whites, Indians who enlisted under non-Indian surnames became virtually indistinguishable among the millions of American recruits, unless they themselves chose to report to their reservation's BIA superintendents. Attempting to produce the most meaningful figure of them all—the number of Indian deaths—BIA officials drafted a list that numbered no more than 337 killed in action, even though half of the Indian recruits they identified were thought to have seen combat. While the difficulty of identifying corpses in trench war did not help, the peculiar colonial positions of Native Americans, fully integrated in white troops, made the task of turning them into statistical material incredibly frustrating. The invisibility of Native American servicemen as such is peculiarly exemplified by the portrait of the American soldier painted by the French painter Raymond Desvarreux-Larpenteur reproduced at the beginning of this chapter. No one could even guess at the Choctaw origins of its uniformed model, Otis Leader.[17]

The BIA's efforts at documenting the war service of its wards were ostensibly a response to requests for figures coming from both public and private correspondents. They promptly turned into a new attempt to assess the durable effects of contact with whites on individual Indians and their ability to "manage" in the white world. In

his circular no. 1535 of April 28, 1919, Cato Sells, the wartime commissioner of Indian affairs, requested from field employees that they
collect information on veterans to show the "value to [the Indian] of
his experience under discipline and contact with foreign life." The
effort was in line with a larger effort of the Bureau to produce a statistical picture of Indian advancement. Already present at the beginning of the decade, the turn to statistics became a prominent feature
of Bureau policy in the 1920s, when "industrial surveys" of Indian
reservations were conducted throughout the country. The same logic
combining the monitoring of individuals at the local level and the
aggregation of nation-wide figures in Washington, D.C., was apparent in surveys on veterans and non-veterans. Correspondence with
local superintendents revealed that Indian soldiers were not necessarily more easily identified after the war than they had been during
it. Information on tribal affiliation, current location, status as draftee
or enlisted, branch of service, and combat experience was painstak-
ingly compiled and found its way into a card file accompanied by
heavy volumes of wartime clippings and photos—which later disappeared. The Catholic Church, in an internal recommendation to its
members to steer Indian soldiers to the National Committee on Historical Records, seemed interested in participating in the effort.[18]

The collection allowed the BIA to furnish state history committees with lists of "their" Indian soldiers, which in turn allowed the
committees to notify the relevant state commissions of the need to
pay Indian soldiers their "bonus," the small monetary compensation
several states offered their returning soldiers. The states also distributed certificates of recognition to the families of soldiers killed
in action. On November 11, 1926, Armistice Day, the "Liberty
Memorial" to the World War was dedicated in Kansas City. It contained two panels listing the number of Indians who had registered,
had been drafted, killed, or wounded, and had served as officers or
been decorated, as well as the amount of money spent on Liberty
bonds by Indian tribes. The figures appear to have been furnished
by the BIA. The card file, then, did not lie idle. Yet the energy ex-
pended in compiling it appears to have been disproportionate with
its actual use. Mediocre returns (only four thousand soldiers were
identified) were not the only culprit. Although it was updated until
1930, the project must also have lost steam after the first years. De-

spite all the appearances of systematicity, it was never possible for BIA employees to progress beyond the exploitation of information that it had favored during the war: individual portraits and *exempla*, or exemplary cases.[19]

The Bureau of Indian Affairs was but one compiler among many. The sources of its agents were, more often than not, newspapers. Dixon's questionnaires provided some information as well. The information they put forward had little to do with assimilation and everything to do with the mishmash of curios journalists on the lookout for sensationalist examples of patriotism had favored during the war. War heroes, descendants of famous chiefs (preferably "hostile" like Sitting Bull), and, above all, heroics that had allowed Indians to rank first in the patriotic competition with other races were most prominent: first Indian to join, first officer to die in France, first American Indian soldier to receive a medal, first to be wounded in the battle of the Marne, to cross this or that French river under fire, first Indian of his state to die or be buried. The card file of the BIA reduced the war to a sporting event, and its fact-finding mission produced only a list of brilliant exceptions. Here and there, as if to testify to the original aim of pursuing the investigation past the end of the conflict, a few individual success stories of Indian soldiers turned farmers, actors, and doctors were identified. They were insufficient to hide the overall failure of the Bureau to accomplish its civilizing mission, a fact that became painfully clear in 1928, when the Meriam Report, an investigation of the "Indian Problem" funded by the Rockefeller Foundation, documented the appalling life statistics of the Indian population throughout the country.

Schools were the only institution within the Bureau of Indian Affairs that might have been able to make regular use of the data collected on Indian soldiers. This was especially the case because they had been the prime recruiting ground for the armed forces throughout World War I. Not all school directors had aggressively encouraged enlistment. But because they promoted military discipline, the use of uniforms, marches, and drills, and a patriotic vision of Indians' place in U.S. citizenry, BIA schools weighed heavily in the almost immediate naturalization of military service among Indian youth. School newspapers published honor rolls listing "their" enrollees, thereby fostering competition among the students—and among schools. After the war, school administrations often raised money to turn the rolls into more lasting monuments. At Haskell, a Kansas institute that attracted Indian students from the entire country, rich Quapaw donors even funded the construction of an archway to the school's football stadium dedicated to the memory of soldiers from the school who served in the war. Aside from these spectacular commemorative displays, there is precious little evidence that the war changed in any way how history, both U.S. and Indian, was taught in Indian schools. Official programs recommended that teachers tell about the causes of war, the organization of the Selective Service, the control of national resources, the War Risk Insurance offered soldiers, or combat and the Armistice. The contribution of Indian soldiers to the national cause was not specifically suggested as a valid point of entry into the history of the conflict—even though BIA teachers located on reservations showed some willingness to include former Indian participants in the Indian wars when addressing this part of the national narrative. Furthermore, there was no sign that courses of study were used to disseminate centrally produced statistics on Indian participation in the war.[20]

The limited amount of information produced through official channels and the lack of enthusiasm in exploiting the little that had been gathered are not easily explained. It might be that the propaganda value of Indian soldiers proved not to be on a par with the enormous challenge that the BIA faced during the 1920s. With the Bureau's very existence called into question by critics as acerbic and talented as John Collier, a social worker turned Indian rights activist, American Indian compliance with the Selective Service turned out not to yield the expected prestige. The very fact that Indian soldiers had eluded BIA control during the war meant that the entire war experience could be interpreted as proving the uselessness of the Indian Bureau. Early on in the 1920s, the BIA lost the initiative in documenting this experience.

It could have regained control with the New Deal. In the years following Franklin D. Roosevelt's nomination of John Collier as the new commissioner of Indian affairs, the Federal Works Progress Administration worked with the Bureau on several Indian-related projects. To be sure, the Indian-Pioneer History Project directed in Oklahoma by historian Grant Foreman bypassed the Bureau entirely. In the thousands of interviews collected, only three were conducted with Native American veterans of the Great War. The focus on "pioneer days" and the frontier was, here also, impossible to question.[21] In other cases, however, the relationship between the BIA and the WPA was more direct. Working closely with the BIA, the Indian Arts and Crafts Board promoted Indian arts and sponsored museums, such as the one built in 1938 for the Osage Nation by John Joseph Mathews or the Museum of the Plains Indians inaugurated in 1941 in Browning, Montana. As was also the case in the rest of the United States, several Indian reservations were scoured by interviewers looking to document the experience of ordinary Americans hit hard by the Depression. The Federal Writers' Project launched the Oneida Language and Folklore Project in New York state (1938–1941) and the Oneida Ethnological Study in Wisconsin (1940–1942). Here again, veterans could be interviewed—and when they were, they made sure to mention their experience in the war. On several local projects, the WPA lent a hand in erecting monuments to world war dead and veterans. WPA state guides contained an occasional allusion to the military service of Indians. The Arizona volume reminded its readers that "the first native Arizonan to die in France [. . .] was Mathew Rivers, a Pima Indian youth." In South Dakota, a tourist circuit passing through the Standing Rock Reservation included a listing for "a monument to Indian soldiers who died in the World War" at Little Eagle, which was followed by several pages devoted to Sitting Bull's death, the reservation's most compelling claim to fame.[22]

Among what appears in retrospect as a series of missed opportunities to assess the impact of the war on Native communities and perhaps to anticipate the effects of the coming conflict, the one project conducted by the WPA most directly connected to veterans was also the one most disconnected with their living memory: graves registration. Answering the call of the American Legion, the foremost organization for veterans of the world war, the WPA funded local posts' efforts at documenting former servicemen's graves. On reservations, Indian Legion members were mobilized to question their comrades and their families and assess the cause of death, place of service, and place of burial of deceased fellow veterans. The example of Ralph Eagle Feather, chosen to manage the project on the

Rosebud Reservation in South Dakota, shows how even this apparently straightforward focus on World War I could easily be derailed. Eagle Feather, who had enlisted in the U.S. cavalry in the 1890s, did not stop at the graves of the Great War. He went further and documented the burial places of those who, like him, had served in the U.S. military in the nineteenth century. Although in line with other trends that tended to marginalize the specificity of World War I, this one, at least, demonstrated the connections drawn by Indians themselves between the different conflicts in which they had been involved. It also testified to Indian communities' need for commemoration that was to play a much larger role in shaping the way the war would be remembered than the action of the Bureau of Indian Affairs or the Works Progress Administration.[23]

Indian Day Narratives

If so little work was attempted to integrate Indians into the national narrative beyond simply recognizing the continuing value of the "race," it was not because Indians were unwilling to set the record straight. On the contrary, the need was keenly felt, and many Indians were not ready to settle for just any form of recognition. Joseph K. Dixon experienced this firsthand. In 1920, contacting for his project George Buckland, an Indian veteran from Anadarko, Oklahoma, who taught in BIA schools, Dixon found an interlocutor aware of his track record and wary of letting the writer-photographer use his testimony in a work he had little control over. "I know too little of your motives to be interested," Buckland explained.

> If you are preparing some book to sell, I am not much in sympathy with your efforts, which is to say I am opposed to commercializing the public interest in the Indians. I recall some of your writing on the Vanishing Race etc. The Indians are increasing. I do not take to this "vanishing" stuff. However I may be, and trust I am, wrong in my estimate of you.

Others were less reluctant than Buckland but no less clear about their conviction that Indians had been remembered the wrong way and not enough. Writing from Pine Ridge, South Dakota, Mrs. Brown, the mother of four Sioux soldiers, took her correspondence with Dixon as an opportunity to explain her motivations and not simply pass along information:

> I think the Indian boys are entitled to a history cause there are good many of our boys done some brave deeds this county has 6 gold stars we have 109 service stars here. [. . .] I am taking a kind of interest in the great History you are trying to get because the other books don't give the Indian boys Brave deeds they done and I don't think thats fair.

On the neighboring reservation of Cheyenne River, Sam Charger put it more succinctly. The vice chairman of his tribe, Charger was to play a central role in mobilizing his fellow reservation denizens in favor of a monument to Indians who fought in the war. He wrote unambiguously: "I am greatly interested in your work." But, asserting in one sentence both his credentials and his determination to keep Dixon on the right track, he added: "I am a full blood Indian and I feel it my duty to help you so that you can accomplish your work *accurately*."[24]

While these were not isolated voices, they were loosely organized. In the interwar years, American Indians were generally ill equipped as a political group to prevent the memory of their participation in World War I from falling into limbo. African Americans could count on powerful media to prevent their own contribution to the war effort from being completely erased from the record. *The Crisis*, directed by W.E.B. Du Bois, and Marcus Garvey's Universal Negro Improvement Association were institutions of national reach that defended the cause of black veterans and demanded that their sacrifice be made part of the national narrative. Native Americans had no such mouthpiece. The Society of American Indians (SAI), founded in 1911, had attempted to replicate the model of the National Association for the Advancement of Colored People. Like the NAACP, the SAI was a national organization defending minority rights against white prejudice, pushing for race pride, assimilation, and citizenship. Its membership, like that of the NAACP, was made up of the best-educated members of their respective communities; all were graduates of BIA schools. Yet, limited by intertribal rivalry and the tiny pool of Indians from which to recruit, the SAI was always an elite club. The world war did not make things any easier. While it was an opportunity to promote their civil rights agenda, it also forced some members to reconsider their previous lack of interest for tribal rights at a time when the United States was promoting self-determination for "small peoples" in Europe. The resulting contradictions, both ideological and personal, proved too much for the organization. After the end of the conflict, its most prominent members started to lose interest and went their own ways.

One project of the SAI survived these divisions, as well as the organization itself, and it had a bearing on the memory of World War I: a campaign for the recognition of a national "American Indian Day." Promoting a day of recognition for a specific group was not an especially Indian enterprise. Since the nineteenth century, ethnic or racial groups in the United States had organized to promote specific holidays. African American Texans commemorated the abolition of slavery on Juneteenth. Columbus Day became a focus of celebration for Catholic immigrants. And BIA schools started celebrating Indian Citizenship Day in 1898. A decidedly assimilationist affair, Indian Citizenship Day was part of a larger pedagogy of assimilation that tried to impart Indian students with a sense of the duties of citizenship and ownership. Since 1887 and the Dawes Act, all Indians were supposed to be set on a road that led to full ownership of their individual allotments and participation in the social and political life of the country at large. Indian Citizenship Day took place alongside Washington's Birthday and the Fourth of July as a celebration that specifically connected students to the rest of the U.S. body politic while at the same time reminding them of the work remaining to be done if they were to deserve full equality with their fellow citizens.

Arthur C. Parker, an Iroquois (Seneca) archaeologist and a major figure in the Society of American Indians, decided to transform Indian Citizenship Day into a larger, more ambitious occasion. After first considering the Boy Scouts of America to be the best vehicle for his project, Parker turned to the SAI to promote his "Indian Day." The society itself was provocatively founded on Columbus Day in

1911. In 1915, Indian Day was discussed during its annual convention. The following year, in May 1916, the governor of New York, Parker's native state, declared Indian Day as a time to celebrate the Indian heritage of the United States. Having succeeded in moving the celebration beyond the context of BIA schools, Parker redefined it as "a nation-wide holiday (official or otherwise), devoted to the study or recital of Indian lore. Picnics, parades, Indian games, music, ceremonies, dramas, speeches, orations, recitals of history, exercises by schools, clubs, societies, and out-door lovers—see the scheme?" Intentionally playing on the multiple connotations of the color red, he suggested that "every red-blooded American, whether just born or just imported from cradle to dotage, would yell long and loud for American Indian Day." The project to force the insertion of Indians in the national narrative while at the same time rewriting it was best exemplified in his provocative suggestion that "Land of the pilgrims' pride," perhaps the most famous phrase of the patriotic song "My Country, 'Tis of Thee," be replaced by "Land of the red man's pride."[25]

Cato Sells, the then commissioner of Indian affairs, did not ignore Indian Day. He was careful to frame the celebration in a way that fit his overall project of putting Indians to work. Indian Day, he reminded his agents in May 1916, was not to be a holiday, not a "lazy man's lay-off day" but a "thinking man's consideration day," a day of "resolution and patriotism." This stance became even stronger when the war reached America. In May 1917, reservations superintendents and school principals were asked to use Indian Day to disseminate the contents of Sells's "Declaration of Policy Statement," a document that fit the commissioner's policy to speed up the granting of citizenship to Indians and announced the imminent end of federal guardianship over them. "If any precept is to be given prominence," Sells argued, "I think [Indian Day] should teach the pupils under your care that industry and self-reliance, coupled with a definite vocational aim, will be essential if the Indian boy or girl is to be prepared for the inevitable day when he must stand or fall according to his own resources, just as his white brother does."

The SAI could not ignore the war context either. For years, SAI members had denigrated the stereotype of the bloodthirsty savage and made it a point instead of recommending that Americans ac-

knowledge Indians' peaceful contributions to the nation even before
it was born (with a special focus on Thanksgiving). With the war,
the SAI had to resurrect the warrior past of its members to assure its
non-Indian readers that Indian soldiers would be loyal and efficient.
Attempting, on the one hand, to ward off projects that purported to
segregate Indians based on their racial distinctiveness, a SAI edito-
rialist writing in 1917 could not avoid evoking, on the other hand,
"the qualities of racial blood." In the process, some SAI members
were seduced by the idea of vaunting the supposedly race-based
combat performances of fellow Indians. After the war years, these
contradictions became a matter of public conflict between members
vying over the best way to hold the celebration.[26]

For the war helped the cause of Indian Day. In 1919, Washington state and Illinois joined New York in proclaiming their Indian
Day. The next year, the celebration moved from May to September.
In Chicago, a minimum of four thousand people (some accounts
tripled that figure) attended the local Indian Day, with forty Indian
soldiers from the nearby Naval Station Great Lakes attending. The
SAI, by then virtually extinct, had locally ceded its leadership role
to the Indian Fellowship League, a group made up of urban Indians
who showed less compunction about selling the image of the Indian
warrior to the general public. (White) crowd-pleasing war dances
were a prominent feature of the day. It was to little avail that society
members denounced Indian Day as a modern-day Indian Barnum
extravaganza and that William Madison, secretary of the SAI and
one of its last active members, "expressed his regrets that it is only
when he exhibits Indian war dances and ancient ceremonies that the
public evinces any interest in the Indian." The shift was massive and
did not escape the attention of the Bureau of Indian Affairs. Troubling reports coming from reservations hinted that the association
of Indian Day with supposedly bygone traditions started raising the
interest of the most unprogressive wards of the Bureau. From Pine
Ridge, Robert Gillispie, hesitating between demonstrating concern
and divulging interest, reported: "Some say it is to revive the old
Indian customs and for the old timers to teach the younger people
some of their old ways of living and dressing."[27]

Indian Day, with its association of patriotism and race-based pageantry, proved too powerful to stamp out. Isolated individuals and local organizations found it a readily usable tool to gain more visibility and attention. David Arapahoe, a.k.a. "Chief Buffalo Bear," a Lakota from Pine Ridge, toured the United States in the years following World War I to gain citizenship for all Indians and obtain the transformation of Indian Day into a national holiday. His argument centered on the "10,000" Indians who had fought during the war and, according to the journalists who reported on his efforts, the eight thousand that had not come back. In Los Angeles, other urbanized Indians coming from different tribes organized a "Wigwam Club" to do charitable work with the Native Americans who started congregating in the city in the 1910s. The organization's annual picnic in the municipal park of Sycamore Grove drew thousands of participants in the 1920s. Basically a fundraising function, the picnic was also designed to gather support for making a national holiday out of Indian Day. Regularly mobilizing Indian actors working in Hollywood studios for spectacular war dances, the Wigwam Club did not stop short of politicking. In 1928, the club's annual gathering was organized in American Legion quarters, and fundraising organized for needy Indian veterans relocated in the city. At the same time the club publicly supported Republican Herbert Hoover's presidential bid.[28]

In Chicago, another Indian organization, the Indian Council Fire, mixed the promotion of Indian Day with electoral politics even more forcefully. In 1927, taking their cue from more prominent ethnic groups of European origin who tried to get better recognition for the participation in the war, Indian leaders adopted Chicago Mayor "Big Bill" Thompson's chauvinistic slogan "America First" and turned it on its head. In the writings of the Council Fire's foremost activists, Francis Cayou and Scott Henry Peters, the nativist politics that had just brought Thompson to power and his call to observe "One hundred per cent Americanism," became opportunities to claim aborigineity and rewrite a more inclusive history of the United States. "You tell all white men 'America first.'" Cayou and Peters wrote the mayor. "We believe in that. We are the first Americans. We are the only ones, truly, that are 100 per cent. We, therefore, ask you while you are teaching school children about America first, teach them truth about the first Americans." Indian participation in the war figured for them as a long line of contributions unjustly forgotten and unmentioned in history books:

> Tell your children of the friendly acts of Indians to the white people who first settled here. Tell them of our leaders and heroes and their deeds. Tell them of the Indians such as Black Partridge, Shabbona, and others who many times saved the people of Chicago at great danger to themselves. Put in your history books the Indian's part in the World War. Tell how the Indian fought for a country of which he was not a citizen, for a flag to which he has no claim, and for people that have treated him unjustly.
>
> The Indian has long been hurt by these unfair books. We ask only that our story be told in fairness. We do not ask you to overlook what we did, but we do ask you to understand it. A true program of America First will give a generous place to the culture and history of the American Indian. We ask this, Chief, to keep sacred the memory of our people.[29]

Indian Day was a natural vehicle for such ideas. In the postwar context, aborigineity stopped being used merely to claim anteriority or land rights and began to be used to tell a different history of the United States. At the end of the 1920s, an increasingly radical Peters even used Indian Day to promote not simply recognition but also self-determination for Indians. His call to remember the "First Americans" echoed the efforts of other Americans to encapsulate Indians' special place in the history of the nation in a single phrase. In 1919, Franklin D. Lane, secretary of the interior and as such in charge of the Bureau of Indian Affairs, began to talk of "the Indian" as "the True American." The nationalistic bent of the phrase was to the point: Lane used it in an endorsement of representative Homer P. Snyder's bill to allow Indian ex-servicemen with an honorable discharge to claim U.S. citizenship. Surprisingly, it was part of an argument that emphasized the possibility for Indians of claiming both specific tribal rights and the rights of citizenship. The war, which had been fought for civilization, had obviously created a fault line between designations of Native Americans as "the red race," "Indians," "redskins," or "savages" and their newfound status as fighters of German savagery. For So Lat Dowanee, a Mohawk hailing from the St. Regis reservation of New York state, "It was never more notice-able that during the late war the absolute need of this Government to correct this mistake. While the 'Amerind' members of the AEF were in England the press and public in order to give expression to their admiration of the fighting qualities of the 'Amerinds,' were forced to use 'Red Indians' for want of a better or proper name to distinguish them from the Hindu, or East Indian, though they were in no way similar."[30]

Riding on the wave to better recognize Indian specificity within the United States, Indian Day continued its expansion in the 1930s. To be sure, its celebration was always fraught with ambivalence, es-pecially in the New England states that adopted it all the more will-ingly, as the Indian populations who requested it in their territories were small and politically uninfluential. In New York, where the movement had started, the 1936 celebration of Indian Day demon-strated how closely it remained linked to an understanding of Indi-ans as a vanishing race, even as the day was an opportunity to dem-onstrate Indian loyalty and patriotism by adopting leaders of the American Legion. Usually held on Manhattan, the celebration was moved that year to Prospect Park in Brooklyn. The exercises focused on the inauguration of a memorial to the first inhabitants of the place, designed by an honorary member of the Museum of the Amer-ican Indian. "Here," it claimed, "Rest the Last of the Matinecocs." Despite the involvement of a native community boosted by the in-flux of veterans after the end of World War I, Indian participants themselves were not certain that they had not been made to give their seal of approval to a mere "farce."[31]

The major merit of the movement was to maintain the memory of Indian soldiers until another conflict made the oblivion into which they had fallen more scandalous. On December 11, 1941, four days after Pearl Harbor, S. 1240, "an act designating the fourth Saturday in September of each year as American Indian Day," was introduced in the House of Representatives. Several new bills followed between 1941 and 1946 promoting Indian Day as "a memorial to the aborig-ines of this Nation and their contributions to the establishment and maintenance of this Nation." Under BIA patronage, the movement became international after receiving the sponsorship of the First Inter-American Indian Congress organized in 1940. In the process, the Indian Council Fire and Arthur C. Parker, still active in promoting the Indian contribution, received the support of several Indian and non-Indian organizations. While the effort failed at the national level, new states added Indian Day to their official holidays. Notably, they were western states. In 1946, for example, Montana governor Sam Ford proclaimed Indian Day and explained:

> American Indians have proved themselves loyal to the government in many ways. In World War I, there were 17,000 Indians who answered the call to arms voluntarily. In World War II, 22,000 Indians were in Army service and 2,000 in the Navy [...] there are only 500,000 Indians in the country. American Indian day is a tribute, just and fair, to honor the Aborigines of this nation, and their contributions to the establishment and maintenance of our form of government.[32]

World War II, therefore, helped replicate and consolidate a mythology created at the outset of World War I: Indians were few but overrepresented in the Selective Service, and this effort, out of proportion with what could be demanded from them, deserved symbolic recognition. The feeling that history was repeating itself was inescapable. World War I had not brought about the revolution in Indian representation that some had hoped for. Race was as crucial as ever to the recognition of American Indian participation in the war effort. Yet, as will be apparent time and again in this volume, it was not against but from within the constraints imposed by a racialized patriotism that American Indians were able to formulate claims and demands on non-Indians in general and the federal state in particular. Indian Day, in that sense, was representative of other, less symbolic struggles for recognition. Participants in the myth-making process that accompanied the writing of Indian participation were numerous. They included civil servants in the Bureau of Indian Affairs, influential "Friends of the Indians" interested in Native American welfare and assimilation, and also people identified as Indians themselves, whether they lived in reservations or in urban areas. All circled the wagons around a coherent idea of what made Indian patriotism specific and Indian participation in the war notable. Tensions abounded but did not endanger the four myths of Indians' war experience, which were as close to an official history as Indians' part in the Great War would receive for a long time. In the absence of reliable national statistics or consistent efforts in documenting the experiences of Indian soldiers, the myths that developed in the interwar years offered easy summations of Indian specificity within the nation. The glorification of Indians as super-patriots recycled wartime propaganda and served the interests of reservation and urban groups. Not even the war was sufficient, however, to nationalize the celebration of Indian Day, which would have helped accomplish the goal of integrating Indians in non-Indians' memories of the war. The idea of a vanishing race took a long time to vanish. But the few writings chronicling the Indian war effort did not remain without echo in the concrete experiences of Indians. As countless individuals of Indian ancestry showed in the interwar years, the desire to see Native Americans' contribution to the war effort recognized and commemorated was as intense as it was locally grounded.

©1921.

CHAPTER TWO

The Names of Local Heroes

OURNALISTS OR AGENCIES such as the Bureau of Indian Affairs propagated narratives touting Indian participation in World War I. Such narratives wouldn't have mattered much after the war if they hadn't been given relevance by local societies. For Indians and their white neighbors, official reports on Indians in the war were but scripts on which to base their own interpretations of the event. To have a lasting impact outside of the government or the national press, narratives celebrating *all* American Indians had to be adjusted to local memories, and World War heroes had to be connected to the figures of local chiefs or "good Indians." Stories of Indian heroism, loyalty, sacrifice, or patriotism had to be taken up by populations in or around reservations to become part of a common history—the very possibility of which would have sounded all but ludicrous to many before the war.

Making room for Indian heroism meant including the Indian war dead in communities divided by race. Commemorating the actual participation of Indians in the war effort was only one aspect of a more general rethinking of their place in local histories in the light of World War I. Some—mostly whites—tried to use monuments to shore up racial hierarchies while appearing to mitigate them. Claiming that the war had strengthened the bonds of interracial fraternity was one of their most common strategies. Others—mostly Indians—tried to open wider the door of memory that the war had left ajar, to reclaim forgotten Indian heroes.

Dead Indian heroes were commemorated in cemeteries and in the names of American Legion posts. The war monuments that memorialized them on several reservations often did little else but list their names and dates of service. But their very existence resulted from a complex struggle in which tribes, bands, chiefs and chiefs' descendants, town notables, and white and Indian elites tried to appropriate for themselves the national legitimacy that military sacrifice carried. In Indian country, monuments had none of the "contagious necessity, or unanimous obviousness" that the historian Antoine Prost identified in French monuments of the World War I era. They

previous page: Chief Plenty Coups and French Army (© L. Tom Perry Special Collections, Harold B. Lee Library, MSS P 16 Item 190, Brigham Young University, Provo, Utah)

were sites of contention and hotly debated affairs. Controlling their interpretation was a least as important as putting them up.

West of the Mississippi especially, their erection revived memories of Indian wars and colonization and, whether for whites or for Indians, pointed to a glorious past, which after the war appeared almost mythical. The end of the conflict coincided with the "golden years" of the generation that had colonized Indian lands. The dream of a rural, pastoral America solidly planted in agricultural landscapes and open to immigrants began to look more and more like a utopia from the past. American populations were urbanizing at a fast pace, and the country was closing its borders to foreigners. In this context, monuments and soldiers' graves were more than tokens of appreciation for the brave deeds of local heroes. They were milestones that allowed local communities to anchor their sense of identity in memorable events in a time of rapid change. Graves and monuments materialized and spatialized the past. They set in stone the link that bound local, regional, and tribal identities to national points of reference. They indexed local memories on the national map. And in communities located near or on reservations, the Indian soldiers, dead or alive, played a crucial role in these processes.[1]

Remembering the Dead and Becoming Brothers

Few state histories of the war made more than a passing mention of Indians—Oklahoma being perhaps the only exception to this rule. Authors of county books, however, almost always included a section paying tribute to the patriotism of "their" Indian soldiers. After the war, in the newspapers and at official functions on patriotic celebrations, the "Red Brethren" were duly thanked for their contribution, especially on Memorial Day and Armistice Day. Commemorating the war dead and claiming brotherhood among the living allowed celebrants to serve widely different purposes, from mildly questioning the existing order, to reinforcing it, to making revolutionary claims against the status quo.

Before World War I, claiming brotherhood between Indians and whites invoked a concept of friendship that had first and foremost a military, diplomatic meaning: Brothers were friends, friends were allies, allies were not enemies, allies helped each other. In history books around the United States, the category "Friends of the Whites" covered the very specific group of Indians who could be said to have positively helped Euro-American colonization. Pocahontas, Sakakawea, the Dakota warriors known as the "Fool Soldiers" who brought white captives back to "civilization," or the Indian policemen who killed Sitting Bull—those were the individual Indians who were worthy of admiration and celebration, and few others. After World War I and its twelve thousand Indian recruits, this category expanded to the point of breaking up. More important than numbers was the fact that the war had produced no "bad Indians," no "hostiles." Friendship made way for unadulterated brotherhood, a brotherhood in arms, sealed in bloody sacrifice, which appeared to close the era of interracial conflict. As soon as the first victory celebrations were started in Indian country, it became obvious that 1918 was not just the end of the war in Europe. It was the real end of the Indian wars. Every public event was an opportunity to remind whites and Indians of that fact.

This was experienced firsthand by Herbert McDuffee, a white veteran of the European conflict who visited White Earth, the largest Ojibwa reservation in Minnesota. On Sunday, June 13, 1920, the anniversary date of the creation of the reservation, McDuffee ventured on White Earth, looking for "full bloods" and genuine Indianness. He was not disappointed. The aged "Chief Waters" greeted him and offered him a peace pipe. Waters made a speech in which he specifically reminded his audience, white or Ojibwa, that they shared the same god. He added that American Indians were true Americans who had always fought for the flag and who would henceforth use this day to commemorate their dead—not just the creation of their reservation. Waters put special emphasis on the blood bond that had united Native Americans and whites since the war, and several orators reinforced that point after he did. In a symbolic gesture, another "chief" invited white and Indian veterans to come together in the center of the dance circle for a special ceremony. After this was over, the wife of an Ojibwa soldier killed in action gave gifts to McDuffee in memory of her son, his brother in arms. Awed by the generosity of his hosts, McDuffee concluded from the ceremonies that whites needed to do a better job of defending Indian rights. Moreover, he vowed to learn more about the conditions of existence of his Ojibwa neighbors. Embedded in Indian ceremonies, brotherhood in the fight implied justice at home—or so McDuffee interpreted it.[2]

The monument erected on July 4, 1923, by the "Ah-Dah-Wa-Gam" chapter of the Daughters of the American Revolution of Wisconsin Rapids, Wisconsin, testified to a much more traditional interpretation of friendship and brotherhood between the races. The monument, which was an engraved boulder located on the banks of the Wisconsin River, called for the "recognition of the Loyalty & Patriotism of the Winnebago Indians" whose seven names followed this inscription. All had been killed in action or died from their wounds. In 1923, the DAR was still thirteen years away from having a national subcommittee on Indian affairs, and this socially and racially very conservative organization obviously did not intend the monument as an exercise in historical revisionism. Celebrating Winnebago identity in Wisconsin Rapids made good business sense. The local powwow sponsored by the tribe was a major tourist draw that contributed to the town's prosperity. Moreover, the monument foregrounded the Decorahs, a model family. Father and son had volunteered and died in the war, and their ancestors had been prominently involved in the history of the state since the war of 1812, when they had sided with the United States against Great Britain. At Wisconsin Rapids, the link between soldiers of the Great War and "Friends of the Whites" was at its most obvious. For the DAR, celebrating brotherhood meant first and foremost stressing loyalty and the Indians' willingness to accept or even help in their own colonization.[3]

Brotherhood could inspire much more subversive interpretations. Its religious and moral connotations and connection to blood symbolism opened interpretive opportunities for Native Americans interested in celebrating the memory of their soldiers. The options went from asserting whites' big-brotherly paternalism, a brotherhood of both races in Jesus Christ, the values of civilization, to decidedly less Christian images of communing in the German blood spilled on the battlefield. Some Native Americans could even claim that interracial brotherhood had been honored only in the breach by certain segments of the U.S. population. In Western sections of the country with large immigrant populations, this meant asserting

brotherhood with Anglo-Americans only, at the expense of the sometimes recently arrived German settlers. This was the case in the Dakotas, where many counties had been only recently populated—and
created—when the war broke out. In many of them, German, Nor-
wegian, and Swedish communities were organized on an ethnic basis,
in enclaves whose inhabitants kept to themselves and spoke their
original languages. In Fort Yates, on the Standing Rock Reservation,
the Lakota proved interested in exploiting, alongside whites, this
aloofness in the nativist context of the postwar era. By the end of the
war, many there had become convinced of the malignity of Germans. In the Bullhead District of the reservation, the death of local
soldier Barney Brought on October 12, 1918, was widely attributed
not to disease, as U.S. authorities had it, but to poisoning at the
hands of Prussian soldiers operating in American hospitals, who, as
one Korean War veteran later remembered, were ultimately identified and shot by a firing squad. In February 1919, forty-six Lakotas
joined their non-Indian, Anglo neighbors in denouncing the lack of
patriotism of the Germans from Russia who had settled the northern side of the reservation. In a petition addressed to the state legislature, they claimed for themselves the status of "True Americans"
and accused "people of foreign birth" and more specifically "large
numbers of such people of German birth or German descent" of
having "either openly or secretly espoused the cause of Germany."
They impugned their "disposition to band together in colonies"
and "to preserve the institutions of the countries from which they
came," while receiving land and American citizenship. The remedy
the petitioners outlined ironically mimicked the policy that had been
imposed on the Lakota and other American Indians. Education in
English emphasizing American history and institutions should be
imposed on the supposedly undeserving German Russians. The government should stop selling them land. Brothers against the Germans abroad, Indians and whites could also be brothers against the
Germans at home.

Some whites, such as the Catholic bishop of nearby Bismarck,
violently objected to the proposition, to the point of doubting whether
the Lakota had been aware of what they were signing. There is good
reason, however, to believe that as early as 1919, Native Americans
in the area were ready to use patriotism and brotherhood against

some Americans. Using wartime anti-German propaganda against local settlers made sense. It combined nativism with an assimilationist stance to denounce the double standard in the granting of citizenship and land to immigrants and Indians. By World War I, two generations of American Indians had already gone through government-funded schools promoting "Americanization." It was not impossible for Indians to affix their signature to a petition demanding that this principle be applied to "foreigners" as well. Linking access to land with patriotism could also appear a rational way to forestall colonization or shore up the remaining Indian lands. As for the meaning of citizenship, it was a central preoccupation of "Friends of the Indians" in the 1920s, and of quite a few Indian veterans as well. On Standing Rock or on White Earth, claiming brotherhood with whites was clearly a way to claim more rights, if necessary at the expense of a third party: supposed slackers, traitors, or tepid patriots. While the campaign to assimilate the Indians was still in full swing, using the memory of their participation in the postwar years allowed Native Americans to claim a place for themselves in the debate, not as victims or protesters but as full-fledged participants. And on a less conscious level, anti-German propaganda had made a lasting impact on the Lakota.[4]

Whether radical or conservative, claims of brotherhood were played out in an environment modified by the arrival of a new actor in the field of commemoration: the American Legion, which made it its business to promote the continued "comradeship" of returned soldiers. Founded in Paris in 1919 and soon to become the dominant organization of World War I veterans in the United States, the American Legion organized local "posts" across the nation, and Indian country was no exception to the rule. There, as elsewhere, the Legion's success was in no small measure due to the lack of rival, ethnic-based, or race-based organizations. Specifically, Indians from the Carolinas, the Great Lakes area, and the Plains tried and failed to create a national group that would address the needs of Native war veterans. In 1920, five of them gathered in the Minneapolis–St. Paul area, and made plans for an organization they called "American Indians of the World War" (AIWW). In a move that gestured toward the mother of all national Indian organizations, the Society of American Indians, they planned to ask the legal advice of one of its founders, the Seneca anthropologist and activist Arthur C. Parker. The presumptive fathers of the AIWW were George Peake, an Ojibwa; Anderson Warren Cash and Henry J. Flood, Dakota and Lakota members of the Santee and Rosebud reservations; and James M. Levy and David Owl, Eastern Cherokees hailing from North Carolina. Besides their war service, they all shared a BIA boarding school experience. Perhaps inspired by the American Legion itself, which held a convention in Minneapolis in 1919, they were not, however, able to replicate its success. Indeed, the AIWW never got past the planning stages, and its would-be founders soon followed diverging paths. Peake became an important Indian activist in Minneapolis and New York, developing a career as an "Indian dancer." Cash was prominent in Minneapolis in locally important Indian organizations, the Council Fire and the Teepee Order. Flood went back to his home reservation of Rosebud. Levy left the big city to become a medical doctor on the Cheyenne River Reservation. Owl was ordained a pastor and became the chairman of the National Fellowship of Indian Workers of the National Council of Churches. He practiced his ministry on the Seneca Cattaraugus Reservation in the state of New York. After the failure of the AIWW, and in line with a trend visible in other sectors of public life, American Indian veterans, unable to rely on a national organization, had to join local structures. The American Legion filled that gap, ensuring a virtual monopoly in organizing veterans on most reservations and promoting the discourse of brotherhood.[5]

Dominated by whites, the Legion was far from racially neutral. In fact, all-white posts were created on and around reservations. But all-Indian posts were chartered as well. This ensured that the Native American constituency of the organization would not be entirely drowned by numerically more important white populations and, depending on locally variable patterns, allowed Indians some measure of control over the way the war dead, the most precious patriotic commodity, would be handled on their reservation.

That the dead would need to be shared was new: On reservations that had experienced major inroads from white settlers, cemeteries were race-based and often miles apart. Had the war been celebrated on a strict community basis and Legion posts founded along those lines, wartime brotherhood between the races could have ended with the return of the bodies of soldiers killed in action to their respective, segregated communities. Because the patriotism promoted by the Legion celebrated national unity, it did not end there. Specifically, the organization emphasized in the preamble to its constitution the need to "preserve the memories and incidents of our associations in the Great War" and "consecrate and sanctify our comradeship by our devotion to mutual helpfulness," alongside the defense of the U.S. constitution, state, nation, religion, justice, peace, democracy, and Americanism. For most Americans, these principles were hardly new: They were directly inherited from the Great Army of the Republic (GAR), the organization that had organized the Northern veterans of the Civil War. With regard to the war dead, the Legion also inherited the GAR's foremost funeral invention: national cemeteries. For most Indians, however, the principle of merging all war dead within national rites and in national graveyards was a novelty. Comradeship between fellow soldiers resulted in forced brotherhood between surviving veterans, parents, and communities of different races. Practically, this meant sharing the war dead.

Like other American families, Indian families demanded and often obtained the repatriation of their sons killed on the battlefield. But far from being private affairs, the repatriation and interment of their remains were highly public events that incorporated families as mostly silent participants. From the nearest railroad station, the casket was generally accompanied by an honor guard of Indian and non-Indian members of veterans' organizations. Evidently the nationalization of the dead performed in these local ceremonies was heavily skewed toward assimilation. Witness the funeral of Charles Solis, a Cherokee living among the Pimas whose casket, wrapped in the American flag, was triumphantly received by the local population in Tucson, Arizona, at the end of February 1918. Next to the family, the local press featured the local Army and Navy Union, the Tucson Rifle Club, University of Arizona cadets, and a marching band. Accompanied by clergy, the local Indian agent, prominent members of the Tucson community and Indian schoolchildren, the group escorted the body to the San Xavier mission, which marked the boundary of the Pima (Tohono O'odham) reservation of the same name, where they paid military tribute to Solis. The war hero also received his title as "First Indian warrior from Pima county to die for his country," a title, the mission priest added, that redeemed his personal shortcomings: "He had his faults but his virtues, his courage, his patriotism more than balanced them." For a member of the Army and Navy Union, the ceremony proved "the unity of us, regardless of the blood that courses through our veins."

Calls for monuments were closely tied to repatriation, continuing the theme of the unity between races. It seems to have been especially important in Arizona, a territory admitted to statehood only five years before the United States entered the European conflict. It was precisely on the anniversary date of statehood that Solis was reburied in 1918. That same year, on the Hualapai reservation, spirits were very publicly chased away during the funeral of war hero Sam Swaskegame. In the nearby town of Kingman, he was offered a poem in the local newspaper and became the namesake of the local Legion post. Three years later, the reburial of another Native American from the Southwest brought the issue of patriotic unity to the fore again. On November 30, 1918, Lee Rainbow's father was informed of his son's death by a telegram that reached him on his Yuma reservation, a territory straddling California and Arizona. Lee Rainbow's body was not to be repatriated until 1921. But in September 1919, the local agent of the Bureau of Indian Affairs lobbied his father for authorization to build a monument in his memory, arguing like his colleague at San Xavier that Lee was the first of "a noble race" to die for his country. Having apparently weighed the pros and cons of the offer, Lee's father granted the request to hasten his son's return: "All right, I am glad I had a son who went to fight for his country. It is a custom of the Yumas never to speak the name of one who has died, but I believe we should make an exception to this case, and I am willing that the Yumas should erect a monument to Lee Rainbow, as the superintendent has suggested. I want his body brought home, so that he may be cremated according to Indian custom."[6]

On reservations, uniting races in patriotic brotherhood first meant exchanging symbolic goods under pressure from the state. To recover his son's body and perform traditional ceremonies, Lee's father had to renounce a traditional taboo and let his son's name be spoken out loud and even celebrated by non-Indians. While the monument to his name was used to validate the state's project of assimilating the Yumas and set in stone its success at turning natives into exemplary members of the nation, the body was also unmistakably appropriated by the white residents of the area. On October 22, 1921, when it finally reached home, the event prompted the publication of a celebratory poem in the local newspaper. The American Legion had by then replaced the Army and Navy Union as the main military-type organization involved in the ceremony. Accompanied by a firing squad, the Legionnaires met the body at an undertaking parlor and escorted it to the Methodist mission on the reservation. There it received proper military honors. The wish of the dead soldier's father was honored and the body cremated. The juxtaposition of Indian and non-Indian rituals, often held up as a concrete example of the union between the races, was clearly predicated on relations of power.[7]

An opportunity for public gatherings in small, often isolated reservation communities, the funerals organized in the interwar period under the aegis of the American Legion made it possible for Native groups to affirm a collective identity or hold hitherto banned religious ceremonies. Locally, they were still vividly remembered for a long time, sometimes as late as the 1970s. This was predicated on the very specific position of Legion posts in Indian country.[8]

As they took over their funeral duties from wartime organizations, American Legion posts positioned themselves as central actors in the transactions associating the States, the federal government, local communities, and populations on Indian reservations in the fabric of the local World War I hero. Soon their duties extended from coordinating the return of the Indian war dead to burying all veterans, including those who had not been members of its organizations. This rejection of racial segregation in the case of Indians was all the more remarkable as it certainly did not extend to African Americans in other parts of the country. Most emblematic of the Legion's politics of racial inclusion was the naming of Legion posts on or near reservations after an Indian soldier, a custom which the Veterans of Foreign Wars had pioneered after the Spanish American War.[9]

It could of course be argued that Legion posts were simply perpetuating a long-held American tradition of appropriating native names, costumes, or rituals to distinguish themselves from rival or-

ganizations. The availability of the Indian war dead could be said
to have been based on the education that Indians had received in
BIA boarding schools, with their emphasis on military discipline
and physical fitness, coupled with a low level of academic expecta-
tion, which made most of their graduates ideal recruits for danger-
ous assignments to infantry regiments, the front lines, and, eventually, death. The relative rarity of Indian deceased soldiers within
the pool of American war dead made them an even more precious
commodity.

Yet the availability of the Indian war dead was not entirely predicated on the colonization of native communities. First, the Legion
made it a rule of principle to name a post after the first soldier of the
county that had died during the conflict. This gave local posts an
"objective" motivation to appropriate Indian soldiers' names in their
bid to harness the war dead for their own purposes. Thus did Richard Blue Earth, from the Cannonball district of the Standing Rock
Reservation, become the namesake for post 142 of the Legion in the
white-dominated town of Solen, in North Dakota. In Wisconsin,
Legionnaires in Odanah County chose Ojibwa soldier John A. Sky.
Other examples could be cited in the Dakotas as well as in Oklahoma, New York, Oregon, even Mississippi. Although small in numbers, these posts testified to the specific status of the Indian war dead
in the local communities where these posts were chartered, a status
that seemed at odds with the actual power granted there to Native
Americans.[10]

This rule was clearly amenable to local preferences, which made
appropriation more a political gesture than a knee-jerk cultural re-
flex. In 1930, the white rancher and Legion commander Orvil Ogle
suggested Sam White Bear as the namesake for a new post on the
Pine Ridge Reservation, but he had to contend with strong opposition. He managed to impose the Lakota soldier's name only after
considerable debate. The explanations given by the post historian,
with all their repetitive emphasis, warrant a lengthy quotation:

> There was no little discussion in choosing a name for this
> new Post. It was customary in other parts of the country to
> select the name of a veteran who served in the World War

and who had given his life as the last full measure of devotion to his country in the sacrifice of his life for the same ideals that the rest of us fought to uphold and defend. It was the opinion of most of the local ex-service-men that the name should be that of an Indian, since it is to be located in Pine Ridge, the seat of this Indian Reservation, also since it is the only Post to represent the Indian boys who served in the World War. Several boys were killed in action [. . .] but the first one to lose his life during the War period from this reservation was Sam White Bear. The records show that he died in Camp Cody, New Mexico on March 29, 1918. A dissension arose in the selection of this name since it was known on the Reservation that Sam White Bear was of a disreputable character, and had been incarcerated several times for various misbehaviors. The originators of the new Legion Post stood firm, however, in their selection of the new name, on the ground that regardless of the reputation of the individual whose name was to be used, he served his country as a soldier in the same cause as all others who served in the World War, both living and dead; had given his life as the last full measure of devotion to his country. He was the first man to die in line of service from this Reservation. He represented the great army of soldiers, sailors, and marines who stood between our homes, our country, and our flag and a common enemy of the nation.[11]

Taken to its ultimate consequences, the Legion principle of naming the post after the first inhabitant of the county to have died in the war justified the celebration of an individual of ill repute. Contrary to Chauncey Eagle Horn from the Rosebud Reservation or Matthew B. Juan of Sacaton, Arizona, two soldiers who had died in combat and been given their own monuments, White Bear had not even perished on the battlefield. As in the case of Charles Solis, the theme of Christian forgiveness was a major argument in the sanctification of the Indian war dead, here redeemed by his death in wartime from a life of petty crime. But the Indian identity of the reservation was another political argument to boost Sam White Bear's rise to the status of post's namesake. For purposes of recruiting members, the new post could not bypass the Lakota soldier. It had to make him into a hero.

The move had the added benefit of allowing the white-dominated post to claim the status of the "only Post to represent the Indian boys who served in the World War." This reinforced its status as a genuinely Western post; emphasized its connection to the Indian Bureau, some of whose employees worked in the same town and were members of the post; and, finally, was a concrete illustration of the spirit of comradeship that Legion members had claimed to defend since the end of the war. While the Sam White Bear post was far from being all-Indian and confined Indians to ceremonial roles (for example, sergeants-at-arms), it was also distinctly more open to Indian veterans than other posts that had taken Indian names, like the nearby "Otterman" post no. 94 of White River. Besides, it was only by welcoming Indian returned soldiers that the post could draw a symbolic benefit from its name in Legion conventions and media outlets on the regional or national scenes. Placed above the door of the Legion hall and reproduced on its flag, its uniforms, or its letterhead, the Indian name of these posts set their members apart from their peers, which were often richer, bigger, and closer to the regional and national leaders of the organization. While monuments demonstrated a post's ability to raise funds by focusing the energies of local communities, an Indian name guaranteed cash-strapped groups a brief measure of attention out of proportion with their status within the American Legion. No less than the more material possessions of the post, it allowed its members to exist in a national, even an international space where the war dead were honored, from Washington, D.C., to the American cemeteries in France.

Cemeteries and Monuments for the Indian Dead . . . and the Living

The Legion post was therefore the foremost agent in the nationalization of the Indian war dead in local communities, by a self-conscious effort at demonstrating the long-lasting effects of brotherhood in arms. It was mostly in Legion-directed ceremonies that Native

American war heroes were publicly recognized as having given their life to the nation. It was also through the locally based Legion post that Indian dead as a group were reconnected, via their living comrades, to civilian communities both white and Indian. And it was in Legion-prescribed rituals that the gravesites of such veterans were linked to the transatlantic archipelago of U.S. national cemeteries.

Before the war, Washington, D.C., had been known to only a few select Indian leaders, who traveled to the national capital to discuss tribal affairs with members of Congress, the president, or, more often, BIA officials. During the war, however, Indian soldiers passed through the city. While there, they may have visited Arlington national cemetery, a site of national remembrance created after the Civil War. They may even have paid homage to the two lonely American Indian figures buried there: Cochise's son, who died during a visit to Washington, and Ross McMullin, a Pottawatomi soldier who had fought in the Union ranks. In 1921, the decision to erect a Tomb of the Unknown Soldier similar to monuments erected elsewhere in Europe proved an opportunity to reinforce American Indian presence in this centrally located site of American patriotism. As in England or in France, the particular monument represented an opportunity to honor all fallen soldiers without seeming to honor one class or race above the others. In American society, where race had been an issue throughout the conflict, it seemed especially fitting. During the ceremony, American Indians were well represented. One of the eight pallbearers was a Cheyenne named Thomas D. Saunders. More importantly, perhaps, Plenty Coups, a Crow leader who had distinguished himself in Plains warfare and had scouted for the U.S. Army in 1876 and later on the reservation as well, was invited. Given instructions not to speak, he followed his own plan and took the stand.

Plenty Coup's speech was short and to the point: "I feel it an honor to the Red Man that he takes part in this great event today because it shows that the thousands of Indians who fought in the great war are appreciated by the white man. I am glad to represent all the Indians of the United States in placing on the grave of this noble warrior this coup stick and war bonnet. Every eagle feather represents a deed of valor by my race. [. . .] I hope that the Great Spirit will grant that these noble warriors have not given up their lives in vain and that there will be peace to all the men hereafter. This is the Indian's hope and prayer."

The speech was not revolutionary. Given by an old chief in full regalia, it rehearsed themes that were well known to his audience. The value of sacrifice, the bravery of "the red man" (a "noble warrior"), the expected gratitude of the "white man," the peace that should result from the fighting, the prayer to "the Great Spirit": None of these features could have caused much surprise among the other participants. But those were words and intentions that anyone could understand and, indeed, appreciate. More innovative, and audacious, was Plenty Coups's determination not to be a mere token and indeed to speak in the name of "[his] race" and "represent all the Indians of the United States." Marking the tomb with culturally identifiable Plains Indian artifacts like the coup stick and the war bonnet was a deliberate attempt to merge tribal and national commemorative traditions. It enhanced Plenty Coups's personal stature immensely. Finally, it sounded a dissenting note in a ceremony emphasizing the duty of citizens: Nowhere did Plenty Coups give a sign that he considered Indian soldiers' involvement other than a spontaneous expression of their warriorhood and a renewal of a long-held Indian tradition. Thus, marking the grave might indeed have been another "coup" for the old leader. It certainly appropriated for all Indians a monument erected in the national capital for the express purpose of ignoring the racial differences of war heroes.[12]

Plenty Coups's gesture also resonates with other funeral ceremonies across the country, which offered renewed opportunities for variation on the interplay of tribal, racial, and national identification made memorable by his performance at Arlington. For a fitting example, one need only look at two other Crows, Allison E. Stone and Stephen Chief At Night, two World War I veterans who were buried in "Custer Battlefield" national cemetery, in Montana. Commonsensical enough, given the Crows' scouting experience with Custer and the proximity of the cemetery to their own reservation, the choice of this location validated a common interpretation of the tribe's involvement in the world war: It was but a continuation of earlier commitments to defend their own country, and, to that effect, side with the United States against their enemies. The burial place of the dead thus confirmed well-entrenched local historical worldviews.

The European conflict was but another version of traditional warfare. The balancing center of Crow history was located in the Plains, as was the legitimacy of Crow leadership. Back on the reservation after his Washington trip, Plenty Coups was careful to bring this point home. First, he made sure that Marshal Foch, the supreme commander of all the Allied forces, would visit him during his trip to the United States so as to reinforce locally the position of international leader he had taken on in Washington (their encounter was immortalized in a photograph reproduced at the beginning of this chapter). Afterward, plans were drawn to commemorate the encounter with a memorial park, to be decorated with a German field gun sent by the French generalissimo—a plan, however, that never came to fruition. Second, in 1928, Plenty Coups donated his house to Big Horn County, hoping that it would be turned into a museum of the Crow nation. Plenty Coups died in 1932, and in 1941 the Kiwanis club of the city of Billings dedicated a boulder on his gravesite with a flagpole and a bronze plaque identifying "Plenty Coups, Chief of the Crows, 1848–1932." In this context, World War I dead and veterans appeared to be mere pawns in a game that linked Indian and white local elites, local and national commemorative places. Handled by leaders who, like Plenty Coups, had been anointed as tribal warriors, the memory of World War I was a stepping stone to go back in time where real Indianness lay: before the reservation era.[13]

The imitation and interplay of national and tribal traditions was not only apparent in national cemeteries where Indian war dead were buried. It was also in evidence in *imitation* national cemeteries, on or off reservation cemeteries. In 1925, further south, in Kansas, members of the Kaw (Kanza) tribe participated in the erection of a monument to "the Unknown Kanza Warrior." The idea came from the white community of Council Grove, which stood on former Kanza lands. An opportunity to emulate the Washington monument presented itself in 1924, when the remains of a Kanza warrior were discovered next to the spot where the monument would be built. Apparently, the originator of the project was a World War I veteran, Franck Haucke, a Legionnaire and collector of Indian artifacts. While unique in its transposition of the national monument to the local scene, it was also a typical memorial project in the Plains:

It harnessed the commemorative energies raised by the world war to bring closure (or rather attempt to do so) to the period initiated by whites' arrival in the region, one that they were prone to look on as a conquest. Accordingly, in August 1925, the remains of the "Unknown Kanza Warrior" were transferred to the basis of an obelisk—a favorite mode of commemoration for the war dead since the Civil War. Peter Taylor, son of Al-le-ga-wa-ho, the chief who had led his people into their new reservation territory in Oklahoma in 1873, pronounced the thank you speech. Unsurprisingly, he presented the monument as a symbol of interracial friendship but also as a landmark signaling the territory the Kanza had had to leave under white pressure. Applied to a nineteenth-century Indian warrior, the rhetoric of the Unknown Soldier became more contentious. Individually unidentified but tribally Kanza, the man buried under the obelisk was undeniably a reminder of dispossession. While Haucke or other white participants might have been actuated by the trope of the Vanishing American, the inauguration ceremony proved that the mere fact of commemorating their dead with living Indians supposed coming to terms with colonization as a process of territorial expansion and deportation. This type of local reinterpretation showed how a national commemorative form, the Tomb of the Unknown Soldier, could be appropriated by local societies. More importantly, perhaps, such appropriation happened in ceremonies that made sense of the monument in terms often quite different from what its actual shape or markings indicated. In the Kanza case, it powerfully reminded white settlers of the anteriority and the continuity of the Kanza tribe, thus channeling national phraseology toward the Kanza themselves. Interestingly, Indians didn't even need to confront whites to achieve this result. They could develop this claim from within the patriotism promoted by their neighbors.[14]

Competitive imitation was, however, a distinct possibility in the process of acclimatizing national cemeteries to reservations. Nowhere was it more clearly expressed than on the Fort Berthold (now Mandan-Hidatsa-Arikara, or Three Affiliated Tribes) Reservation. There the American Legion post was named after Joseph Younghawk, a veteran who died five years after the end of the world war. The reason for ignoring official Legion regulations was obvious to all: Joseph was the son of Younghawk, a warrior who, like Plenty

Coups, had scouted for Custer in 1876. Even more decisive was the fact that Younghawk the father had been chairman of the Old Scouts Society, established in 1912 on the reservation, after the fashion of the GAR, to preserve the identity and esprit de corps of the reservation's scouts and, most of all, to maintain the grounds of the cemetery where all tribal members who had fought and fallen for the United States were buried. Collective, well-ordained cemeteries had long existed at Fort Berthold, whose populations had a long tradition of sedentary life. In the village of Nishu, the cemetery initially reserved for scouts was created as recently as 1910, and immediately after the world war, it was opened to the war dead of the European conflict. In it, generations were identifiable only by the shape of their federal government-paid headstones and the sparse markings engraved on the stones themselves. While the uniformity of the graves might seem a sign of the bureaucratization of warfare and honors, it was also a clear indication that Fort Berthold heroes continued to be acknowledged by the United States, which was willing to pay for their burial. Because some of the soldiers buried there had been released without an honorable discharge, the Old Scouts cemetery never became a national cemetery. There exists, however, no clearer imitation by Indians of the collective mode of honoring soldiers initiated at Arlington in 1864. For all intents and purposes, the Old Scouts Cemetery was, from the 1920s on, the national cemetery of the Three Tribes or (the distinction is worth making) a national cemetery on Three Tribes land. When the location of the cemetery was flooded under the waters of the Garrison Dam in the 1950s, the war dead were transferred to higher ground and the cemetery was rebuilt in its new location. Nevertheless, the interplay of tribal and national loyalties became tainted with a feeling of abandon and betrayal: By then, the Three Tribes' loyalties had again been demonstrated in World War II, and the removal of the cemetery under duress came as crushing evidence of the unequal relationship linking the United States and scouts and scouts' descendants.[15]

The symbolic interplay between cemeteries on and off reservations could take even more material forms. In certain cases, caring for the graves of veterans literally meant shuttling men, rituals, and objects between cemeteries, thus symbolically linking on- and off-reservation locations. Four Indian veterans of the Great War were interred at Arlington between 1918 and 1930. Three of them happened to have died in the Washington, D.C., area. The fourth one was Joseph Takes The Shield Jr. Drafted in August 1917, he was killed in France the next year, on November 1. His body was repatriated only in 1921, but instead of going to Takes The Shield's home, on the Standing Rock Reservation, it stopped in Arlington. This was not the result of a strategy by the Army or the Bureau of Indian Affairs to appropriate an Indian war casualty. Instead, it was the soldier's own father, Joseph Takes The Shield Sr., who insisted in a letter to the BIA office in the nation's capital that his son should not be brought home but rather be buried in a "military cemetery." A former soldier himself, he simply wanted for his son the best and most honorific burial that the U.S. armed forces could offer. Joseph Sr. was no "assimilated" Indian, and we shall see how the ceremonies he funded on the reservation in memory of his son were an opportunity to perform traditional dances and to honor customs. But he evidently saw no contradiction in having his son buried in a massively non-Indian cemetery; even more, he made the trip to the capital with his wife to attend the reburial ceremony. Other tribal members later remembered their duty to honor the grave. In 1923, Martin Medicine, vice commander of the "Joseph Takes The Shield" American Legion post no. 232, based in the Wakpala district of the reservation, had a priest in Washington place a specially made tomahawk on the grave in Arlington (the weapon later made its way to the Vatican, whose services asked the help of Catholic missions in gathering war trophies). In 1936, a tribal delegation went to the national capital to place a bow and arrows on the grave, while in Wakpala, a replica of the monument was erected in Joseph Takes The Shield Jr.'s honor. Dances and songs were organized in his memory, as well as that of the "fallen chiefs" of Standing Rock. In 1970, a group of veterans hailing from the D.C. area visited his grave and rendered him military honors. Joseph Sr.'s decision in 1921 had sparked an admittedly minor but nonetheless real tradition of physically connecting family, community, reservation, and nation in a bid to keep alive the memory of a war casualty.[16]

All of these examples should warn us against the temptation of systematically ascribing Indians' appropriations of military and patriotic symbolism to subversion, especially when it comes to the treatment of war heroes. As the cases from Kansas, Montana, and the Dakotas show in their diversity, burial ceremonies could be used by Indians to remind whites of their existence, to assert tribal identities, or even to mark tribal territories. This was more a product of collaboration and peaceful interaction, however, than one of militant confrontation. It was from within patriotic forms such as the military funeral or the national cemetery and from within innovations such as the Tomb of the Unknown Soldier that Indians were most able to make whites hear the essential message that the war had carried for them: They were still in existence, not only as a race but also as distinct ethnic groups who carried histories and cultures that were very different from those of the United States proper and yet now included within its borders. Local monuments to war soldiers, and not just the war dead, made this abundantly clear.

No directive came from Washington and the Bureau of Indian Affairs to commemorate Indian soldiers in stone. Even in the national capital, the project to build a monument to Indian soldiers was simply a project to beautify a small area located behind the main building of the Department of the Interior housing the headquarters of the BIA. Indian commissioner Cato Sells saw an "opportunity at this time to commemorate in lasting art of a high order that which seems to attain epochal meaning in Indian history and progress," and on that basis apparently initiated the project. As was to be expected, Sells envisioned a monument to Indian loyalty that would go beyond mere commemoration of the war to celebrate adherence to the BIA's vision of progress. He explained: "I believe a fine artist could work into such a monument something more than the late military renown of the Indian volunteers; that he could symbolize somewhat the progress of the Indian race in the United States and give to the design a distinction of high historic value culminating in the unified loyalty of both Indian and white races to the principles of our common Democracy." Like the project to identify all Indian soldiers involved in the war, the Washington monument was never completed. It was simply too costly and had to be abandoned as early as December 1921.[17]

For the expression of Indians' views of recent history, the BIA's inability to complete a war monument in Washington may have been a blessing in disguise. The absence of BIA leadership meant that the commemorative field would be invested not according to national directives but closely following local conditions and, potentially, Native Americans' needs. While few, if any, monuments were erected without at least token white involvement and BIA approval, they were always an opportunity to discuss Indians' takes on recent and less recent history, rather than merely rehearse assimilationist doxas. The design of monuments was literally a search for meaningful symbols to represent the passing of time and the position of the world war in tribal histories. How best to represent, within a given budget, the collective interpretation of the Great War?

For the Oklahoma Osages, money was not an issue. In 1924, when they requested congressional authorization to spend upward of five thousand dollars on a monument commemorating their participation in the war, they were not likely to be turned down. Rich from royalties derived from oil discovered on their lands in 1910, the Osages could confidently imagine a monument that would link past and present and point toward a bright future. Once their request was allowed by the federal government, the tribal council organized a committee of two, one a "mixed-blood," the other a "full-blood," under the supervision of Franklin Shaw, the council member who had originated the idea of the monument. As the committee sat in meeting and mediated between council members and building firms, it became evident that celebrating the dead could only be one part of the project. John Palmer, the tribe's lawyer, himself a Sioux adopted by the Osages, said as much in his April 6, 1925, speech in front of the committee: "As a member of the tribe, I would like to see a distinct Osage memorial erected. [. . .] as Osages, we should get away from the ordinary memorials that are erected to the memory of the dead. We had in this case a tribe of people participating, doing what they could in the matter of carrying on the last war. We gave, among other things, some points that stand out as a credit of the Osages greater than can be attributed to any like population in the United States."

In the rest of his speech, Palmer made explicit what the counter-model would be. He would have none of the generic feathered Indians that one white contractor had proposed. His monument was complex and stately. First, in full Osage garb, a majestic statue would point to the West. It would carry a shield bearing the colors of the

American flag and inscribed with the dates of every single war the United States had been involved in since the revolution, as well as verses from the national anthem. Standing across from the statue, a bronze representation of the World War I doughboy would carry at its base the name of the thirteen Osage soldiers killed in action in 1917 and 1918. Between the two statues would stand an arch proudly announcing: "To traditions true, the Osages in 1917 offered up their lives, and their treasures for their country, for home and for the good of others." In accordance with Shaw's wish that the tribe "mak[e] history" with the monument, Palmer was in fact outlining how it could educate both the Osages and their neighbors as to its greatness. His plan displayed an understanding of the particular visual codes that would allow such a monument to reach whites' hearts. That Palmer was familiar with Washington and the halls of Congress likely played a part in this.

Full-bloods in the council did not take kindly to a project that seemed to equate too generously the present Osages with their illustrious ancestors. Palmer had to be defended by another council member who reminded his opponents that the monument was to be part of a "fight for the right," a topic about which younger generations needed to be encouraged. The size and cost of the project amplified the ideological conflict between tribal council members. The company the tribe hired to execute the project, Tonini and Bramblet, had made a reputation for itself in Oklahoma and neighboring states for designing and building county courthouses, including that of the Creek nation in Okmulgee, Oklahoma. Abiding by the neoclassical aesthetics still associated with power and stateliness, they imagined a massive colonnaded building on a raised platform, complete with a cupola and surrounded by lawns. They had Palmer's statues standing in two separate niches flanking the main entrance to the memorial. All funeral allusions were reduced to a single funerary urn, symbolically placed in the central axis of the compound, ahead of the building itself. Reflecting the larger trend to avoid ostensibly "useless" monuments that was felt on other Indian reservations as well, the tribal council, after accepting the design, decided that the memorial would host its own meetings as well as the inauguration ceremonies of Osage chiefs.

No such use would ever be made of the monument, however,

for it was never built. First the Commission of Fine Arts of the Secretary of the Interior rejected the project as too mediocre. Acknowledging the "exceptional opportunity to erect a beautiful memorial to the Osage Indians," it recommended that the tribe hire "one skilled in the art of sculpture and architecture, and who had feeling for the traditions and history of the Indians." Mired in red tape, the project didn't receive a new authorization until March 1929. By then a fall in oil prices had led to the tribe's change of heart: Tribal monies needed now to be spent on more material goods. Apparently embarrassed at having to drive the last nail into the coffin of such a patriotic endeavor, the BIA superintendent of the Osages could only claim, contrary to historical record, that one Osage only had been killed in action after all. Apparently too, he missed the larger meaning of a monument that the tribal council had once imagined as a monument to the living.[18]

The very cost and ambition of the Osage monument had prevented it from coming to life. Most tribes, however, didn't have this problem. Imitating official U.S. monuments was not within their reach, but they could turn to the mass-produced memorials put out by regional and national private firms. Two forms dominated: the obelisk, already encountered as part of the monument to the Unknown Kanza Warrior, and the "Spirit of the American Doughboy," the sculptor E. M. Visqueney's ubiquitous representation of the charging American soldier of World War I. Inspired by the Statue of Liberty, the "Doughboy" was bought by hundreds of counties and cities across the United States in the interwar period. In Oklahoma, the so-called Five Civilized Tribes, comprising the Cherokees, Choctaws, Chickasaws, Creeks, and Seminole, had one erected in their capital of Muskogee in 1925. On the "ready-made" memorial, they added the names of their war heroes, their tribes, and their former chiefs. On a less grand scale, this was precisely the program that Palmer had envisioned for the Osages.[19]

For less affluent tribes, even Visqueney's statue had a whiff of luxury. On the Standing Rock Reservation, it took fifteen years and the Great Depression, with its general fall in prices, for tribal members to finally get one. As early as 1919, the tribal council had imagined a memorial hall that it optimistically proposed to fund by raising a fifty-cent tax on each reservation denizen (veterans excepted). In a spirit of inclusion, the hall would honor white and Indian soldiers and a plaque list the war dead. The next year, the project became more ambitious, with some council members suggesting that the building host war trophies (the BIA was asked to help acquire German field guns), a history of the reservation during the war, or the photographic portraits of Indian soldiers. Renouncing the idea of the tax, the council resorted to war-tested methods and raised money at an "Indian dance," only to see the two thousand dollars collected vanish when it was embezzled by a Sioux employee of the BIA. After this initial failure, the project, bogged down in rivalries between council members or the families of the war dead, also had to face the staunch opposition of BIA superintendent E. D. Mossman. A declared enemy of Sitting Bull's former comrades in arms on the reservation (who wrote of "Sitting Bull, the rebel, the demagogue and the reactionary" who "fights against all things progressive"), Mossman feared that a monument to the war would only be an opportunity to revive the memory of the chief killed during the "Ghost Dance uprising." Like his colleague in Osage country, he found local projects grandiose and out of touch with what he saw as the modest contribution of Standing Rock Lakotas and Dakotas to the war effort. Instead, he suggested a smaller project located in the white-majority reservation town of McLaughlin. Going further, in a context where calls to rehabilitate the world-known Lakota leader were mounting, Mossman proposed his own monument to what he felt was the founding event in the reservation's history: the repatriation under military escort of the families and warriors who, after the Battle of Little Big Horn, had followed Sitting Bull into Canada. In 1932, this monument was erected. But Mossman could not prevent Standing Rock Indian leaders from collecting money at their annual fair for a monument to Indian soldiers and chiefs.

In a matter of years, the commemorative policies of Standing Rock began to shift. In 1933, Mossman retired, and as the New Deal reached Indian country, new opportunities flourished. In 1934, founded in part by the Works Progress Administration, an obelisk was put up in the village of Little Eagle, in the South Dakota part of the reservation. Not only were Indian chiefs listed after those of

Indian soldiers, but Sitting Bull was among them, a small but significant addition that discreetly evidenced the revisionist potential of
celebrating tribal identities through and alongside Indian heroism
in the Great War. The memories of the Great Sioux War of 1876, as
well as of the violent repression of the Ghost Dance movement, were
equally, if subtly, honored. Now even inter-district rivalries played
in favor, rather than against, commemorative enterprises. Prompted
by the example of their neighbors at Little Eagle, denizens of the
Bullhead district acquired a copy of the Spirit of the American
Doughboy and inaugurated it in style in July 1935. In the early 1920s,
local issues had rendered all but impossible the celebration of Standing Rock in the world war. By the mid-1930s, the insistence that
soldiers have their monument finally allowed local communities to
begin to bring out repressed memories going back to the era of the
Indian wars.[20]

As should have become clear by now, the desire to honor soldiers of the Great War and their predecessors was far from isolated
in Indian country. Nor was the movement to incorporate the recent
past in the commemoration of the war a purely Indian one. In the
part of the United States that lay west of the Mississippi especially,
in territories that had been recently colonized, the 1920s were a
time to celebrate the work of the pioneers, or the signing of the
Indian treaty that had allowed them to settle the area. Indians and
whites did not, in other words, live in different times. So obvious
was the convergence that in South Dakota, on the Cheyenne River
Reservation, the historical society of the state felt it necessary, in
1932, to participate in the inauguration of the local war monument.
The historical society selected a contractor it had used in the past
and left it to reservation denizens to decide who should be on the
monument. The latter planned for a plaque where the names of five
soldiers killed in action stood under and were dwarfed by a list of
twenty chiefs, "friends to the United States Government," in the
words of Dakota reverend and veteran Francis P. Frazier, who gave
a speech at the inauguration. Responsibilities appeared carefully
shared, with the Bureau of Indian Affairs deciding on its location
and settling, for political and educational purposes, on the area of
the reservation it most clearly controlled. In writing, local superintendent Walter F. Dickens explained to his superiors the principles

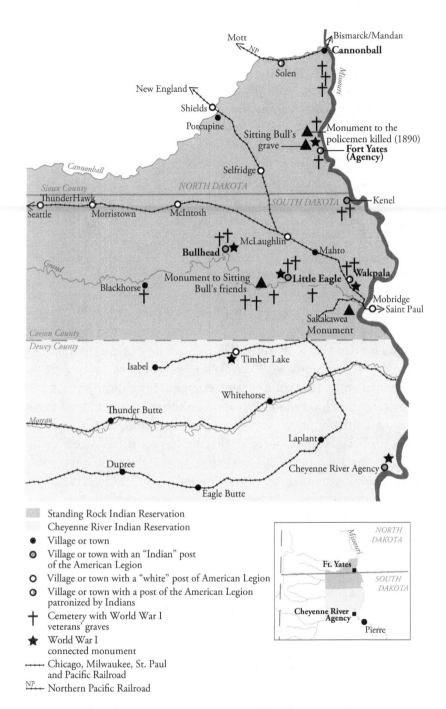

Mott

Bismarck/Mandan
Cannonball

NP

Solen

Missouri

New England

Shields

Porcupine

Sitting Bull's
grave

Monument to the
policemen killed (1890)
**Fort Yates
(Agency)**

Cannonball

Selfridge

Sioux County

NORTH DAKOTA

ThunderHawk

SOUTH DAKOTA

Kenel

Seattle   Morristown   McIntosh

McLaughlin

Mahto

Bullhead

Grand

Monument to Sitting
Bull's friends

Little Eagle   **Wakpala**

Blackhorse

Mobridge
Saint Paul

Sakakawea
Monument

Corson County

Dewey County

Timber Lake

Isabel

Whitehorse

Thunder Butte

Moreau

Laplant

Dupree

Cheyenne River Agency

Eagle Butte

Standing Rock Indian Reservation

Cheyenne River Indian Reservation

● Village or town

◉ Village or town with an "Indian" post
of the American Legion

○ Village or town with a "white" post of American Legion

◐ Village or town with a post of the American Legion
patronized by Indians

† Cemetery with World War I
veterans' graves

★ World War I
connected monument

┼┼┼ Chicago, Milwaukee, St. Paul
and Pacific Railroad

NP
┼┼┼ Northern Pacific Railroad

NORTH
DAKOTA

Missouri

Ft. Yates

SOUTH
DAKOTA

**Cheyenne River
Agency**

Pierre

Geography of veterans' activities on the Standing Rock Reservation

according to which he proceeded: "I personally approve of the type of the monument. It hasn't the appearance of a grave-stone. It is neat. We propose to put it on a conspicuous place somewhere within the school or Agency grounds, where it can be given proper care, and where it will be easily accessible to the public, and where it will not interfere with the landscape in any way."[21]

On August 11, 1932, orators flocked to the pulpit to give their own personal interpretations of the monument's meaning. All concurred in seeing it as a guide for the living, rather than a mere celebration of the dead. Lakota chief Joseph Warrior offered ecumenical praise for Indian chiefs who had fought to safeguard the independence of their people against American invaders as well as for those who thought it more prudent to negotiate and sign treaties. Warrior barely touched on the Great War but made sure to mention by name the four Lakota bands that had made up the original population of the Cheyenne River Reservation. William Williamson, the U.S. representative from South Dakota whose intervention had been necessary to get Congress to authorize the funding of the monument, insisted that the Sioux were civilized even before the arrival of the white man and added, in a twisted compliment alluding to African Americans, that Sioux had never let themselves be turned into slaves. They had already progressed far along the "white man's way" and taken up occupational pursuits that he hoped would become the norm in years to come. In a variation on the theme of the "union of the races," friendship and brotherhood, he linked interracial solidarity between chiefs and pioneers with his own childhood experience, growing up on a South Dakota farm among the Sioux. He finished on a note of praise for Indian soldiers, holding them up as role models for not only Cheyenne River youth but also for other members of the entire Sioux nation. Interestingly, Williamson had insisted in writing that chiefs and soldiers be honored by distinct plaques, a wish that went unheeded by the Lakota, more interested in emphasizing continuity than change. For South Dakota governor Warren E. Green, coming to Cheyenne River was an opportunity to remind his audience of the Arlington model and the Tomb of the Unknown Soldier. Specifically, he emphasized how the monument in the national capital should be regarded as emphasizing the color-blind nature of American citizenship. Himself a veteran, Roy Nash told his audience, in the name of the commissioner of Indian affairs, that Indian soldiers had simply done their duty and that the duty of those who had survived or were now old enough to follow in their footsteps was to pay their taxes. Peter Norbeck, a U.S. senator from South Dakota, praised the old Indian virtues of honesty, loyalty, bravery, and family spirit and promised to help the reservation's elderly in time of need but encouraged the young to do everything in their power to become self-supporting. George Puder, sent by a nearby white post of the American Legion and an ally of the Lakota in their efforts to build their own post, was actually the only one to talk exclusively about veterans. It almost seemed as if veterans had been but a pretext to discuss more portentous issues concerning the entire reservation community.[22]

The various stakes of participants in inauguration ceremonies couldn't have been more transparent. On the Cheyenne River, fourteen years after the end of World War I, recent war heroes had to make room for yet older figures, and the evocation of the dead was to serve the need of the living: reconciling the positions of former "friendlies" and former "hostiles," emphasizing continuity between the reservation period and the era that preceded it, instilling new duties. The different speakers' agendas were not necessarily compatible, but they converged when it came to historical awareness: All saw the war as an opportunity to talk of more ancient conflicts and, once this was done, to come back to Lakotas' current needs and to their future in the United States.

On the Cheyenne River or Standing Rock, monuments to the Great War helped give a physical center to reservation villages and sometimes attracted new monuments after World War II or the Korean War, or the Vietnam War, all of which gave concrete support to the belief that twentieth-century Indian soldiers merely reproduced immemorial "warrior traditions" carried over from before the reservation era. The social events that made them part of local life also emphasized that they were to serve as reminders not simply of patriotic values but of relationships between different times. Reservation Indians, all participants agreed, could not be "new men" devoid of a link to the past. If they were to make a place for themselves in the United States, it would be by following their own "way" in their new country—although what this way should be was a matter

of considerable debate. And because they proved important in bringing this discourse to light, World War monuments seemed to have
been conserved as well as, if not better than, their equivalents in
neighboring white communities.[23]

The insistence of Native Americans (and of their white neighbors)
on using monuments to World War I to talk about an earlier past
could be ascribed to a psychological law first put forward by Thucydides in *The History of the Peloponnesian War:* "though men always
judge the present war wherein they live to be greatest, [. . .] when
it is past, [they] admire more those that were before it." Yet, without
detracting from the greatness of the Greek historian, one would
probably be better advised to regard it as a historical phenomenon
in itself, rather than a product of universal psychology. In the case of
Native Americans, invoking former wars when erecting monuments
to the most recent conflict was a conscious strategy to influence the
present status quo and an attempt to repair some of the social and
cultural discontinuities brought about by colonization. Were heroes
of the Great War heirs to the "hostiles," the "friendlies," or both?
Because, by 1918, most reservations were located in areas only recently settled by non-Indians, such questions about the recent past
were shared by whites as well and were often, if not always, discussed
between colonizers and colonized. Some answers were conservative,
especially when they merely emphasized (Indian) loyalty or the need
to "unite the races" without explaining how this would play out in a
real world that placed whites above Indians in the social, racial, and
political hierarchies. In such contexts, the Indian dead were often
appropriated in patronizing ways. But Indian leaders and veterans
were not helpless, and they found strategies to commemorate their
dead that launched a fruitful dialogue with white ways of celebrating
wartime sacrifice and making local soldiers heroes for the nation. Imitation or appropriation of commemorative forms like the obelisk,
the headstone, the neoclassical building, or the statue and participation in American Legion rituals were never submissive attempts at
assimilation. Rather than a foil, the symbolic grammar of U.S. nationalism proved a resource to define and express local identities.
For Indians just as for their white neighbors, these identities had to
take into account the wider U.S. territory, its famous monuments

and landmarks, and the symbolic centrality of Washington. But inauguration ceremonies made it clear that, beyond world war veterans or chiefs of the past, it was themselves that Indian reservation
communities were intent on celebrating. And patriotism, with or
without monuments, proved a very appropriate opportunity to do
just that.[24]

CHAPTER THREE

Patriotic Gifts

WORLD WAR I prompted the telling of new stories and new views of the past. But traditional ways of committing events to memory did not disappear. In the West, on the Plains in particular, winter counts perpetuated a vision of history centered on individual bands. Among the Lakota, for example, the year 1917 was not systematically remembered as the year of the European conflict. When it was, the formulations that accompanied the year's pictograms depended on local events and local views as much as on a grand narrative of the war, whether national or international. That was the year when "lots of Indians joined army for war," "Flat-iron died," "Thunder Hoop died." The following year, 1918, could be a time of "war end celebration," the year when "Germany surrendered," or the year of "a big battle with the Long Feet." The annalistic nature of winter counts meant that this world event was inserted into a series of local happenstances, which automatically emphasized its specific meaning for the Lakota. Franco-German rivalry and the European theater of operations disappeared behind the history of the band, with its own series of conflicts with whites and other Indian groups. Events that would never figure in official histories of the war were regarded as crucial in local communities.

In the winter count of No Ears, an old warrior from the Pine Ridge Reservation, World War I was remembered as a time when much money was given to the Red Cross. Indeed, as early as 1917, whites frequently marveled at the vitality of Indian practices they thought had disappeared, and war-related dances and the gift giving that accompanied them were foremost on the list. After 1918, Memorial Day and Armistice Day ritual commemorations of the Great War brought to light activities that Indians had kept practicing ever since they had been forced to move to reservations. War did not create, or even recreate them. It did, however, make them patriotic and place them in a new context of competition between families and groups defined by ethnic and racial categories. Gift giving ceased to be relevant for Indians alone. Commemorating war tied local cere-

previous page: Frank Fiske, *Funeral of Ambrose Gabe at St. Elizabeth Wakpala, S.D.* (© Fiske Collection, 1952–1974, State Historical Society of North Dakota, Bismarck, North Dakota)

monies to national celebrations. As Indians' autonomous ways of collective remembrance were inserted in public and interracial ceremonies, extended families stopped being the sole or even the main focus of collective memory. Reservation districts, rather, and their white and Indian inhabitants were the environment where such a memory was built and contested, through shared rituals and disputed organizations. As donors, spectators, or honored guests, whites were now a regular presence in war-related ceremonies. They were, in fact, regular participants in a patriotic show whose main attraction and interest was giving—and receiving. Volunteering one's life on the battlefield had been the expected behavior during the war. Afterward, giving away one's property replaced it.

Patriotic celebrations and symbols such as the U.S. flag were thus appropriated locally by district- rather than reservation-based communities. In the process, the boundaries of groups defined racially ("whites," "Indians") were drawn anew. In some areas, the presence of both white and Indian veterans turned ceremonies into opportunities to promote the nationalistic fusion of the groups. But in other configurations they only helped to reproduce the already existing competition between them. Making a show of community itself, for oneself and also for others, celebrations that were centered on patriotic gift-giving readjusted the boundaries of Indian groups to the new, postwar realities of reservation life. Commemorations concretely pointed to the way Native Americans attempted to redress the balance of the unequal relationship that colonization had forced on them: by performing an extraordinary patriotism. They became a way for communities to enact, in the eyes of the rest of the world, the place they wanted for themselves in, and vis-à-vis, the U.S. nation as a whole.[1]

Giving as a Community Endeavor

To this day, giving and giveaways are very public affairs on Western reservations; indeed, they are the surest way of making an event public. Giveaways are shows that attract spectators, who, thanks to the generosity of a donor or a family, can always become participants and recipients of gifts. At the end of the nineteenth century already, this was common knowledge for Bureau of Indian Affairs employees, who tried their best to limit such events, or at least the value of the goods so generously distributed, as they would, in their opinion, only result in poverty and the prolongation of uncivilized customs. In 1917, patriotism made such restrictions problematic. Because goods were given away to support the war effort, for example to the Red Cross, the limits set on giveaways could be denounced by Indians as unpatriotic. When the conflict ended, Indians were not slow in turning what had been conceived by the BIA as an exceptional concession to the war emergency into a precedent. A telling example is the three-day celebration organized in August 1924 by Joseph Takes The Shield Sr., the father of a serviceman living in the Wakpala district of the Standing Rock Sioux Reservation. In honor of his son, Joseph Jr., killed in action on the Western front, Takes The Shield held dances, feasts, and public ceremonies on his own allotment in Thundershield. In the war he had given away a horse to the Red Cross. He again parted with his property (a plot of land in this case) to honor his offspring. Forest F. Bliss, the white "boss farmer" of the district, i.e. the local representative of the BIA, and an agricultural-instructor-cum-policeman, made no pretense of hiding his irony in the report he made on the ceremony. As Bliss understood it, vanity was Takes The Shield's sole motivation: "Joseph Takes The Shield the giver of the three day celebration will have to order larger suits as it kept him busy meeting tourists and friends, while his wife tried to help cook for the crowd." Other participants were likewise faulted for their supposed conceit: "Antoine Claymore was in his glory as he could have lots to say and seemed to be master of ceremonies. Joe Hairychin as chief announcer was in his prime and the words flew out of his mouth like a springtime freshet. Tom Frosted with his cabinet of highly dressed Indians was always in the limelight as he occupied a stool which raised him a little above the common Indian." But the ceremony was much more than the brainchild of a few select leaders: The entire local community was involved.

Eugene Bearking, also a BIA farmer but a Lakota, filed another report. He told of a rather massive event. Bearking counted 1,500 campers (300 of them whites) coming from three states, and 120 dancers who, having a difficult time confining themselves to the narrow limits of the dance arena, danced all day and most of the night in an exhausting competition that wore down the assembled drummers and singers. Bearking further noted that pricey beadwork had been exchanged to the amount of $15,000. Even more impressive was the outlay of food. Bearking denounced all of these testimonies of backwardness but could do nothing to prevent them. He had to admit that, as willing to receive gifts and hungry for the food they were given as were the Indian guests, they were even "hungr[ier] to give away." In this assessment, Bearking was not contradicted by the newspapermen from the nearby white town of Mobridge, who wholeheartedly praised the organizers of a celebration where whites, some coming from as far as New York, were enthusiastic participants and beneficiaries of this patriotic outpouring of gifts.[2]

The Takes The Shield celebration did more than impress on the public the image of Indian generosity. It deployed social distinctions in an Indian way. Dances and feasts separated men from women, the young from the old, couples from solitary dancers (adults and children), whites from Indians, strangers from locals—and sometimes brought these oppositions to a head: Alcohol-fueled disputes, especially between couples, were duly reported by BIA farmers. As befitted a patriotic ceremony, veterans were naturally set apart from the crowd, and an entire day, the last one, was specifically devoted to honoring them. *Wóyuonihaŋ*, the Lakota word for honor, connoted first and foremost reputation and distinction. Honoring veterans meant underlining their position as exceptional people, the best, *iyótaŋ*, with the implication that they would become dominant, chiefs in the community. In his report, Bearking made it clear for his white superintendent that veterans' families had no say in the matter: When their kin's name was called by the announcer and the drum, they simply had to give away property in honor of the ex-serviceman. Such was the power of the Lakota name that families still gave their children. Its value grew in proportion to the goods given by its bearer or rather, given in his name. The name thus tied a family's public generosity to an individual status. And not giving was considered stinginess, plain and simple. Behind a name, thus, lay a collective "face" that was kept by giving. The importance of the fact to all present resulted in the sheer "effervescence," to speak in Durkheimian terms, that characterized the ceremonies. Bearking himself spoke of this when he quoted an old man who summarily articulated the individual and collective significance of giving and emphasized its political significance as a temporary emancipation from BIA control: "I am very pleased with the giving away. It loosens up. Our farmer of Kenel has been very strict with us in giving away things but I see now where we can have pleasure of giving away things, through Joseph Takes The Shield doings."[3]

Bearking did mention one individual who refused to part with his property, an example that thus lets us understand better the pressure to give. Mark Walking Elk was, by Bearking's account, a "progressive," the owner of a "very nice little bunch of cattle, horses, pigs, goats." To be pressured into giving, he was reminded by dancers of the sick state of his wife, which called for generosity if supernatural powers were to come to her aid. There is no way for us to tell how many, like him, came and felt pressured to give without being able to muster the courage or find an excuse to refuse. We do know that not all present participated to the same extent in the ceremonies. Some danced, honored their relatives, and sported their best costumes. Others did not. Some stayed the three days, others just a few hours. But for all, gift giving was the measure of how they understood the articulation of individual, family, and collective identities. We do not need to endorse the dichotomy between progressives and traditionalists put forward by Bearking. While such a distinction had meaning for Indians as for whites, it does not sum up the distinctions created by giving. What patriotic celebrations did was not simply redraw the line between hostiles and friendlies: It also turned generosity from a traditional social value of Indians—in this case the Lakota—into an ethnic marker, a boundary on either side of which two ways of life, one Indian, the other non-Indian, appeared clearly defined and opposed. As was the case for war memorials, patriotic celebrations did not accomplish this work of identity building by excluding non-Indians but rather enlisted them in a competitive collaboration. This process was made possible not simply by reinventing traditional Indian practices but by tying reservations to a national patriotic network as well. The role of veterans' organizations in this process cannot be overemphasized.

Of course, the activities of organizations such as the American Legion on Indian reservations did not come about in a vacuum. On the Plains, especially, gift giving was never the sole affair of the individual. Organizations, warrior societies prominent among them, were in charge of regulating the circulation of goods among band members. Some of these organizations were still active, albeit in a fragmentary way, in the first decades of the twentieth century. Under Christian missionaries' influence, their activities had often been restricted to feasts and the collection of money for charity purposes, aligning them with the white clubs, with an emphasis on their honorary aspect. As soldiers left for war or came back, these organizations were summoned to honor and encourage them. But this new lease of public life did not last long, often because of the older members' reluctance to let in new recruits: Warrior society membership was predicated on the accomplishment of war deeds, which these old members assumed were no longer possible in a "white man's war." New, Legion-style veterans' organizations thus filled a void. But they were not limited to offering next-best substitutions for genuine cultural reproduction. Nor were they homogeneous spaces for cultural resistance, as some historians have contended. To understand their role, one has to remember that before World War I, social life on reservations had already been significantly reorganized around American-style organizations that had become a prominent focus of Indian life. Returned students' associations, district agricultural clubs ("farm chapters"), and denominational, church-sponsored men's and women's societies vied for the membership of Indians under the watchful eye of the BIA. Built into their rules and modes of functioning was an emphasis on cultural assimilation; a promotion of the nuclear, marriage-based family; and the family allotment as the primary site of production and economic as well as emotional investment. Even before Legion posts, it was the Red Cross that benefited from this reorientation of Indian social customs, especially gift giving, toward a greater similarity with whites.[4]

During the war, the needs of the federal government had been so enormous that Liberty bonds, already massively bought by Indians or in their names by the BIA, had not been enough, and giving to the Red Cross had been strongly encouraged. It had also afforded Indians a way to make their generosity a matter of public, rather than merely administrative record. Giving was embraced as a strategy to come directly to the aid of soldiers or even, on some reservations, to honor a vow to participate in Sun Dance ceremonies that had been forbidden since the 1880s. Indians were seldom given more than a purely honorary role in local Red Cross chapters. But these chapters were nonetheless the vehicle by which giving in public could be routinized again. They became sites from which a patriotic legitimacy would be extended to activities that were not sponsored by the Red Cross. A father, such as Joseph Takes The Shield Sr., could give in his son's name, during a furlough, or even in his absence; war dances could be accompanied by giveaways. State sponsorship of Red Cross events and the white community's approval of Indian generosity did not eliminate the BIA's campaign against ostentatious and massive gift giving. But it created the conditions in which it would be difficult for the BIA to deny to one man, acting on his own, what had been accorded to another, acting under Red Cross auspices. More importantly, it made Indian generosity a matter of national import, thus redirecting intra-community competition into an interethnic and interracial contest that linked each reservation society to a wider, country-wide political arena.[5]

That entire communities were to be involved soon became evident and was systematically reinforced by veterans' organizations. In the war, Red Cross chapters, with their emphasis on feeding and clothing servicemen, had been especially welcoming of women. American Legion Auxiliaries, while not direct heirs to the Red Cross chapters (they were often founded well after the Red Cross chapters had ceased functioning), reproduced the same pattern of segregated involvement for women. War Mothers and Sons of the Legion further formalized the role of family members in patriotic life within each community, alongside of men's organizations. Legion organizations similarly formalized the place of veterans' families and their attendant rights to participate in Legion activities, as well as patriotic sacred time, by sponsoring Memorial Day as a celebration of all war dead and Armistice Day as a tribute to all living veterans. More than an addition to the existing network of local associations, the Legion saw itself as the indispensable cement focusing and mobilizing local energies. Americanism was indistinguishable from service to the community, seen as an organic entity whose health was judged by participation in patriotic ceremonies. Community could be another name for patriotism.[6]

The focus on community as the goal and the means by which to promote the Americanist gospel led the Legion to multiply nonritualistic activities such as baseball or boxing tournaments, oratorical contests and scouting associations. Legion-sponsored activities put a ludic spin on patriotism and familiarized youth with the vocabulary of national belonging. All-Indian marching bands and baseball teams represented the communities from whence they came and brought them honor by their successes. Ideally, they became almost indistinguishably associated with them, going through the same ups and downs in the local, intertribal, and interethnic space in which they lived. This ambition to embrace and lead local life was also reflected in the presence of school pupils or religious representatives during Legion-sponsored activities. Indeed, in 1924 the first day of the Takes The Shield celebration was entirely devoted to religious ceremonies. Embracing the whole of social life also meant that the Legion did not limit its involvement to purely patriotic holidays such as Memorial Day and Armistice Day or the Fourth of July but sent Legionnaires to participate in most collective events on reservations. Legion posts thus blurred not only the line between patriotic and non-patriotic moments but also the line separating the Legion and the community it purported to serve, in effect giving a patriotic seal of approval to many gift-giving occasions.[7]

On reservations, where racial segregation was often as rigid a structure as in the South, the possibility of chartering "class posts" (based on occupational or racial criteria) greatly facilitated the insertion of the Legion in community life. Class posts were the product as much of racism as of Indians' desire to organize outside of the control of whites. While the South Dakota Legion did not have a single state-level leader of Indian descent before the 1970s, in Montana it was through the desire of the Crow that their Legion post was chartered in the 1920s with the express intention of not accepting whites. Here again, the Legion could draw on well-established social patterns. Missionaries had already emphasized, in church or school work, the necessity to hire Indians to foster participation and community pride—under non-Indian control. What was new about Legion "class posts" was how explicitly this separation between Indians and whites became the basis of activity and how it was tied to the need to represent not a tribe or a band but a community the likes of which were present throughout the United States, not just in Indian country. Ethnic (tribal) identity and racial (Indian) identity were now integral parts of the process by which patriotic norms and activities were supposed to help nationalize Indians.[8]

The Christian religiosity that the Legion shared with the Veterans of Foreign Wars was yet another feature of its activities that facilitated the organization's insertion into reservations' social networks and public life. Here again, the Legion could draw on earlier experiences, most notably that of the Grand Army of the Republic. In Minnesota or Indian territory, the GAR had already spread Christian-like rituals for patriotic funerals and ceremonies among Native Americans. In many fort communities also, it had been part of public life, propagating nationalistic sacredness but also American collective entertainment. By maintaining the possibility for Indians to join a veterans' organization that the GAR had inaugurated, the Legion allowed them to claim this sacredness for the heroized dead. In many places, American Legion posts merely propagated a standardized, systematic approach to such ceremonies. Regardless of their race, veterans were strongly invited to abide by the same rules of conduct (laid down in a manual of ceremonies), wear the same uniforms, fly the same flags, sing the same songs, and say the same prayers. They made this apparatus a requirement not just of patriotism but also, where veterans were concerned, of decency. Indeed, some posts were created specifically for the purpose of furnishing a community with the proper means for conducting former servicemen's funerals. The Legion ceremonial did not exclude other, more obviously Indian forms of commemoration, but it did provide a standard of harmony and decency that resonated with local as well as national norms.[9]

Organizing Giving

"Who gave the best horse? Who will store the post's flag? Who will keep the dead veteran's burial flag? Who will have the most beautiful grave?" After World War I, these sorts of questions frequently divided families during or near the time of Memorial Day or Armistice Day. Turned into objects, patriotism (and the war dead) could and did foster disputes between family members. Hoisted during patriotic ceremonies, the funeral flag materialized the patriotic nature of the bravery attached to the veteran's name as well as the tension between patriotic inclusion in the cohorts of war dead and families' attempts at keeping control of their deceased loved ones.

Photographs were another focus of attention, admiration, and envy. Taken in a studio before the soldier's departure, in civilian clothes or in uniform, in training camp, on furlough, they were not just stored, but hung on walls, especially if he had died in combat, as was the case for Isaac Looking Back, from Wakpala, whose picture, adorned with a gold star, was noticed by a social worker visiting his father's house in 1935.

In cemeteries, pictures appeared on individual and collective graves: Martin Yellow Fat's portrait, for example, was placed at the top of his tombstone in Kenel's Assumption Cemetery, under crossed rifles and a canopy resting on two American flags and above the inscription "Served with honor in the World War and was wounded in action [. . .] Son of Joseph and Maggie Yellow Fat." Photographs so publicly displayed were extremely rare and materialized the dignified pride that the families of veterans killed in action were encouraged to articulate with regard to their dead. Living veterans or soldiers could also benefit from the value attached to photographs as the substitute for an individual's presence. On August 7 and 8, 1942, World War I veterans supervised a Sun Dance ceremony in Little Eagle to honor the next generation's involvement in the new world conflict. They had the latter's photographs prominently aligned on a table in and around ceremonial tipis.

Photographs reinforced the personal nature of the ritual, linking the sacrifice of dancers to that of servicemen and to the meaning attached to the ceremony, dedicated that year to both victory and peace. The sacred context of the Sun Dance or the cemetery imbued photographs with a sacrality still in evidence in many of today's houses on the Standing Rock Reservation, where representations of Jesus and Mary are never far from walls covered with pictures of veterans from different generations. The envy that such displays could generate in other families is, however, a likelihood that the record does not permit us to substantiate much further. While the role of disruptive individuals in other, non-patriotic organizations emerges here and there, the evidence of conflicts opposing clearly distinct family groups as opposed to individuals is simply not there. What shows clearly, on the other hand, is the crucial importance of representing the community in front of others.[10]

For the Legion post to be able to achieve this goal, more than just respect for Legion rules needed to be established. Veterans needed to "keep the charter," as the phrase went—that is to say, maintain their accreditation by state and ultimately national institutions. This implied recruiting potential Legion members and, foremost among them, dedicated Legion leaders.

Indian posts, which were always small, needed to pay special attention to the size of their membership and the collection of their dues. Like all volunteer organizations, they spent a great deal of time simply recruiting new members or ensuring that the old ones remain involved. This job fell to the lot of commanders, in posts or in Auxiliaries. Ella Others, who helped found the Ponca Auxiliaries in Oklahoma, recalled how she was contacted by the post's commander even though she herself did not know she could be a member: "Tony Knight and his wife came after me to be a charter member of the Legion Auxiliary. I told them that I did not have anybody as a warrior or in service, but they told me I was mistaken and that my brother Newman Little Walker was in the service of the World War I and that I was eligible to be a member."[11]

Identifying and approaching potential members so as to ensure their participation, financial or otherwise, was the primary mission of commanders. It did not come easy, as the annual statistics of some posts demonstrate. In Fort Yates or Cannonball, for example, not one member continuously paid his dues between 1919 and 1945. Whether because of mortality or poverty, this meant a great range of fluctuation from one year to the next; the all-time low occurred in the 1930s. The problem was national, and the state representatives of the Legion encouraged local posts to launch yearly recruiting drives. There were years when recruiting became an end in itself in small, rural Indian communities that could not organize the various activities that were available to larger, urban posts. In 1933, this was precisely what mitigated the Legion's praise of local posts in Wakpala and Bullhead: While they granted them a trophy for their efforts at recruitment, they lamented the small number of other collective endeavors. The diagnostic identified a structural situation, still

valid today: Lack of funds restricted Indians to a limited number of
activities, which only made the role played by dancing and ceremonies more prominent. Money did not so much prevent activity as it
shaped it, focusing it on the most familiar and becoming a reason of
pride in itself.[12]

Dues, which amounted to $2.40 in 1919 and $3.50 in the 1930s,
could be enough to discourage membership or explain deferred or
cancelled payment. Time-tested strategies were mobilized by post
commanders to raise money and involve the community. Auction-
ing had been common during World War I; after it, Auxiliaries still
resorted to this tactic, selling blankets, pillows, or poppies. Patriotic
feasts were funded through collections organized during dances or
by having a drummer and a Legionnaire go door to door, asking for
a donation by calling out a veteran's name, then the name of his kin.
As evidenced in the Takes The Shield celebration, shame was the
automatic outcome of a refusal. Veterans themselves would publicly
make donations to their respective posts, as did Andrew DeRockbraine, from Bullhead, when he donated the prize money from his
rodeo activities in 1935. Municipal subsidies were not available for
Indian posts, as they were for white ones. While this meant that Indian posts could not count on a fixed portion of their budget in any
given year, it also served to promote a virtuous circle of Indianiza-
tion. Financial instability prompted the recourse to traditional fundraising techniques, "Indianized" the activities of the Legion, and
accelerated individual posts' institutionalization as normal features
of local life. Embezzling was all the more tragic for post life and was
apparently not an infrequent reason behind the failure of the American Legion to succeed in certain reservations. When and where this
danger was averted, giving in the name of patriotism could prove
sufficient to erect monuments (sometimes memorialized in winter
counts) and thus objectify the role of Legion activities as boundary-
making. Patriotic generosity was then reinforced as an ethnic trait,
recognized by whites. When the Kenel post gave thirty-seven times
its quota during the 1925 campaign for the Legion Endowment
Fund, the Legion magazine used the story to start a report on the
Legion's activities in the entire state of South Dakota.[13]

To raise money, the Legion post needed to insert itself within
existing social configurations and coopt local leaders. The danger of

embezzling only reinforced the need for good post commanders. They were elected every year on or around November 11, before the dance the fees of which would help fund feasts and parades for the year to come. Today's Legionnaires interviewed in North and South Dakota emphasize the central importance of one or two leaders' involvement in a post's activities. Before actual dollars are even collected, it is the expenditure of personal time by these leaders that "builds" a post, making it more than just a collection of individuals, a collective entity with its own reputation and the credibility necessary to ensure potential donors' cooperation. While current informants always seem reluctant to evoke political discussions between Legionnaires, they do emphasize the part played by these personal qualities and agree on the ideal image of a commander accepting his role as a burden placed on his shoulders by his fellow Legionnaires. Often chosen in close cooperation with his predecessor, the post's commander needed to be a leader of men and an organizer, able to set up an Armistice Day program in minute detail and to work, through his wife, with the all-important Auxiliary. His devotion to the job was measured by his willingness to pay for someone else's dues, if need be. A good orator, especially in "Indian language," he convinced easily. Modest, he embodied the traditional ideal of the "natural leader" who was also a "chief against his will," an ideal especially prominent among the Lakota where authority was often strongly related (at least rhetorically) to the reluctance to use it. Above all, the Legion commander was expected to give to the community itself a sense of its worth by fostering unity, harmony, and ultimately pride. Only then could a post be considered "strong."[14]

Many posts, white or Indian, seem to have shared this ideal of the devoted, modest Legion leader both reflecting and accruing his community's strength, but Indian posts had to contend with the specific problem of fostering a good relationship between World War I veterans and the warriors of previous generations. Death songs, war songs, and victory songs are still in evidence today in veterans' funerals and patriotic ceremonies and owe their longevity in part to their inclusion in Legion-sponsored ceremonies that started after World War I, especially on Memorial Day. As such, they testify to the overall success of intergenerational relations in post activities.

Among the Arikara of the Fort Berthold Reservation in North Dakota, the "Younghawk" post no. 253 explicitly replaced the Old Scouts Society of the previous generation who had fought alongside Custer at Little Big Horn. Among the Poncas, the dances of the "Hethuska" warrior society survived in the powwows organized by "Buffalo" post no. 38, an all-Indian organization founded in 1927. In Bullhead, on Standing Rock, Legion work was made possible by collaboration with warriors' societies that included some of Sitting Bull's followers; on November 11, 1929, four hundred Lakota came from the neighboring Cheyenne River Reservation to take part in these intergenerational activities.[15]

The commander's job was facilitated by the inclusion of family members in the post's life, a tenet of Legion work that allowed for the mobilization of extended families. Wives were not the only ones to join the Auxiliaries: mothers, sisters, daughters, and granddaughters also participated. Their role was not only decisive in the logistics of feasts; they also helped Legion leaders convince individual veterans to give a hand, or "show up." The vocations of guardians of commemorative rituals were born in the context of dances. At Bullhead, Agnes One Elk, the sister-in-law of veteran Straight Pine, was first involved in the send-off ceremonies given for some of her neighbors in December 1917. After the war, she became a mainstay of war dances, in charge of marking Lakota veterans with a black spot. So central was her presence that the powwow that developed around the ceremonies she participated in stopped at her death. The strong involvement of select individuals does not seem to have led to proprietary feelings. Takes The Shield's sponsoring of a celebration for his son in 1924 was clearly linked to the fact that Joseph Jr.'s name had been given to the district's Legion post and to his own honorary membership in the post. But no accusation of attempting to turn the post into his own personal organization surfaced. In Bullhead, where the post's namesake's father was also given honorary membership, it was only after World War II that a family emerged as the dominant one in post activities. "Keeping the charter" then became a family affair because a relative's name had been added to the name of the post. But after World War I, when only 11.5 percent of veterans were never members of the post, participation in Legion-sponsored events seems to have been equitably spread throughout the community. It left no trace of intra-group conflicts in the record. The importance of strong personalities meant that some would be elected leaders more than others, as is obvious from the few post records that survive, but turnover was the rule in Legion, as in other community activities. Voting procedures, while formally adhered to, were often but the official sanction of decisions collectively made by a few dedicated Legionnaires. Splitting a post, on the other hand, could mean the end of all post activities in a district, which, in turn, often meant losing the opportunity of being represented collectively beside non-Indians.[16]

Meeting Strangers, Giving Kinship

The patriotic ceremonies during which Native Americans learned to honor their dead and veterans from World War I were from the start national, even international ones. In 1919, the United States aligned themselves with European norms to set Armistice Day apart as the main date to commemorate the conflict. Before becoming the holiday honoring living veterans, Armistice Day was imagined as a way to unite the nation in preparation for new challenges, world peace and the international role of the United States. Republican president Warren G. Harding made this the focus of a speech on November 11, 1920:

> We fought for the one supreme cause which inspires men to offer all for country and flag and we fought as becomes a free America, and dropped the hatred, and stifled greed, when the victory for defence was won. We proved anew that there is a free and ample America, which does not ask, but freely gives. We were Americans in name before the World war made us American in fact, not a collection of peoples, but one people with but one purpose, one confidence, one pride, one aspiration, and one flag. We learned a lesson, too, of transcending importance. Righteousness and unfailing justice are not in themselves a guaranty of national security. We must ever be strong in peace, foremost in industry, eminent in agriculture, ample in transportation.

Once appropriated by the United States, the day of remembrance soon became a special day in local life as well.

A national celebration first proclaimed in 1919, Armistice Day was not declared a federal holiday until 1938, meanwhile being principally upheld by states, local communities, and Legionnaires. Just as the GAR had appropriated Decoration Day (the other name of Memorial Day) and pushed for its officialization in 1889, Legionnaires made Armistice Day their own date in the calendar. In the process, they redefined Memorial Day as more than the celebration reserved for their elders, turning it into an opportunity to pay an intergenerational tribute to all deceased U.S. soldiers. Memorial Day, Harding explained in 1921, "marks our recognition of those who, from our national beginnings, have deserved the most that the nation could give in gratitude and appreciation. It reminds us that in every generation from Lexington to the Argonne, our valorous sons have well deserved the highest tribute that a nation fortified, defended, preserved, could give to them." By taking over Memorial Day, the "nation" appropriated the sacredness and the family care that were essential components of the commemoration. Before the Great War, Memorial Day could, on occasion, see tributes paid by local communities to Indians allied to the United States. After the conflict, it was, in theory at least, the nation that assumed responsibility for mobilizing entire Indian groups.[17]

Locally, Armistice Day and Memorial Day programs varied in length and diversity from one year to the next and from one reservation to the other, depending on the particular activism of a post, its ability to mobilize, and the participation of churches or the BIA. They did, however, follow largely similar programs. Armistice Day clearly alternated between religious or solemn moments and more relaxed, even frankly entertaining parts. In the morning, the names of soldiers killed in action were first called out and militarily saluted. The living received a handshake. Prayers were given, songs sung, communion taken. Squads of Legionnaires saluted the flag itself. Speeches on military preparedness, self-sacrifice, and the flag were given in some sheltered space, usually a school, whose pupils were made to attend the ceremony. The afternoon saw the beginning of more entertaining activities: basketball or baseball games, movie sessions, hunting parties, or beauty contests could be organized. In the evening, the Auxiliaries proposed a communal dinner, which was usually followed by a dance lasting until the small hours of the night. Memorial Day followed a similar pattern but was preceded by another special day, Poppy Day, a time for families to clean up family lots in cemeteries and decorate them with paper flowers that were usually made and sold by Auxiliaries. On Memorial Day itself, the different cemeteries of the reservation were visited in a procession headed by priests, pastors, and Legionnaires. Schoolchildren followed them, as did the surviving veterans of Indian wars. Although they were intended as shows of patriotic allegiance and community conformity, both patriotic days were also heterogeneous moments, where the religious and the festive, planning and improvisation, the familiar and the stranger, Indians and whites could coexist.[18]

Ethnic boundaries were not reinforced as a side effect of the ceremonies: They were, rather, a central element of these manifestations of national loyalty, emerging from the very structures of reservation societies. Several cemeteries were visited because whites, living apart from Indians, were not buried with them. For one day in the year, processions connected places that were usually unconnected, at the same time that they underlined the social segregation driving their geographical separation. White and Indian Legion posts, which collaborated in the event, similarly allotted each other specific moments to lead and organized reciprocal visits. During the 1924 celebration mentioned earlier in this chapter, the Takes The Shield post was invited by the all-white post of the neighboring town of Mobridge, located on the outskirts of the Standing Rock Reservation. There, Indian Legionnaires presented a visiting Legionnaire from New York City with gifts of a tobacco pouch and a pipe. Giving, under such circumstances, was not simply the concretization of the discourse on the brotherhood of races. Next to the set of purely patriotic practices (songs, speeches, parades, tributes to the dead), generous patriotism promoted a set of interactions that did more than reinforce the language of loyalty, brotherhood, and submission—going as far, sometimes, as to turn it on its head. Giving transformed white settlers from rivals, debtors or creditors into partners with whom and through whom Indian inhabitants of reservations could reaffirm their own specific and legitimate identity. Indian participants in Memorial Day and Armistice Day ceremonies used patriotic moments to safely claim, for all to hear, the superiority that was denied them most of the year in their interactions with whites. Ethnonyms in particular, often a badge of stigma, became one of honor.[19]

Giving competitions developed within local, specific configurations. For Legion posts to play their role as promoters of distinct identities to the fullest, Indian veterans needed to be numerous enough to charter their own posts—if possible, several posts. In the spring of 1929, Standing Rock already boasted six posts and their Auxiliaries. The chronology of the creation of the different posts and the visibility of several recurrent individuals in their charters suggest a diffusionist story: An all-white post was created first on the reservation but was soon followed by the Fort Yates post, set up near the BIA agency at Fort Yates, and later by the other districts. The Fort Yates post naturally fell under the control of that administration, which was central to the life of the village. It placed itself under the patronage of the county's first war dead, Lakota Albert Grass, but made sure it closely coordinated its activities with that of the Bureau. One of its most active members was also its historian, the journalist and photographer Frank B. Fiske, the son of a U.S. soldier and an apostle of interracial appeasement and fraternization. His regular reports on Legion activities in newspapers made it clear how little room was left for Indian veterans in that particular post. The situation was more complex in two other villages on the reservation. Cannonball and Wakpala sat at opposite ends of the reservation but shared a connection to railroads and a mixed population of whites and Indians, farmers, small merchants, and artisans, all dependent on the sale of grain and cattle. Their "all-Indian" posts were truly more Indian in their racial makeup and their autonomy from the BIA, which became even stronger with the white exodus that characterized the Great Depression in the region. A third group of posts included isolated or outlying communities with no direct link to the railroad, or indeed to paved roads. In Kenel, and more clearly perhaps in Bullhead and Little Eagle, Legion activities mobilized Indian war veterans, representatives from the old warrior societies, and U.S. Cavalry Indian auxiliaries. Individual scouts, in particular, were recognized as "Friends of the Whites" and given honorary memberships in the local posts. At Fort Yates, the presence of both Indians and descendants of U.S. Army soldiers lent relevance to the Legion's emphasis on nationalistic fusion; in the rest of the reservation, more racially homogenous appropriations of nationalistic themes served, on the contrary, to reproduce the already existing competition between whites and Indians. Beyond its de jure openness to Indians and to Indians' self-organization, the Legion could de facto be used, by Indians as well as whites, to reinforce boundaries.[20]

Whites' demand for Indian participation in community celebrations was crucial in these developments. A few days after November 11, 1933, the *Mellette County News,* covering the Rosebud Sioux Reservation, casually noted: "The Indians of the district held a celebration down by the river and following the program up town, many drove to watch the dancing and other features of the Indian program. Several of the white soldiers joined in a sham battle which was followed by speeches by Indian leaders." Neighborly visits with a zest of voyeuristic tourism had been a mainstay of reservation life for whites since the end of the nineteenth century. Local fairs and Wild West shows set a standard for "western" entertainment that pervaded collective events no matter what the occasion or the race of the majority of spectators. Indeed, although primarily directed at whites, Wild West shows linked both groups' identities in shared and not always unequal rituals: Parades, sham battles, rodeos, and shooting and roping contests were yearly events in many towns on or near reservations. Like Frontier Days or Pioneer Days, shows, fairs, and rodeos were entertainment and commemoration all in one and bound Indians and non-Indian, white communities into a mythified past, that of the first years of their installation in the country, the "Conquest." For the show to serve its purpose (authenticating the identity of settlers as semi-heroic pioneers, forging ahead of civilization into savagery), "true Indians," preferably in traditional garb, had to be invited. "Citizens' clothes" were dropped in favor of clothing more befitting "savages' dances" like the scalp dance, all to the great despondency of BIA agents, who were rarely a match for the sheer pressure of whites to let Indians participate in their celebrations. The Fourth of July was a prime opportunity for whites and Indians to meet, indeed to visit each other; it was also a clear precedent of the mixture of patriotism and Indian dance that became central to Armistice Day and Memorial Day after World War I. On the Sac and Fox reservation of Iowa, the local powwow was even sponsored by the state's historical society—at least according to an infuriated Indian Affairs superintendent.[21]

The financial underpinnings of such encounters could hardly be missed. Indians often came to white fairs in pursuit of a wage, and whites patronized Indian celebrations for a free show. Money was always a strong part of the "patriotic situation" of these local, biracial communities. In 1922, for example, *The Tomahawk*, the newspaper of the Ojibwa reservation of White Earth, Minnesota, deplored "a growing disposition to neglect" in the celebration of Memorial Day; a few years later, in 1925, it blamed the impossibility of putting together a decent Armistice Day program on the poor financial circumstances of most reservation inhabitants. In November 1928, *The Mellette County News* of Rosebud regretted that the same celebration was "less important than it should be" and prophesied the rapid demise of a holiday that commemorated a conflict in which the United States had lost much less than Europe, and that consequently would soon interest no one but veterans. But in 1935, the *Corson County News* covering the southern portion of the Standing Rock Reservation announced the upcoming celebration of Armistice Day in the white town of McLaughlin as "the first [. . .] in many years." Indians were not the only ones to tighten their belt and practice patriotic austerity. Their investment in patriotic ceremonies closely followed that of whites, because they shared similar, albeit unequal living conditions and because they were participants in one another's celebrations—where money was always an essential consideration.[22]

Meeting at patriotic celebrations was in itself ground for competition and mutual education. For Indians, in particular, Armistice Day and Memorial Day were opportunities to correct white misconceptions about themselves. It often started with the first thing that was exchanged, or rather, given: food—and table manners. As told by Joseph Wheeler, a Wichita from Anadarko, Oklahoma:

We always used to gather at the cemetery, people come from Anadarko, they used to come out there every Decoration Day—American Legion. Whole bunch of them set a table on the ground. We don't eat on the table, we just sit down. We tell them, white people, you get to learn how to sit down. We watching one guy, he run a car shop, you know. I guess

he looked down the other way, he saw something you know.
Oh, got a fork. He stuck one of them, make them about that
big you know (about the size of a small tamale) call them
corn dumplings. Got pumpkin in there, pumpkin with it.
Sometime get walnuts, wild walnuts, you know. Just put it
in there. Mix it in there, you know, with dough. And man,
he ate it. He got him another one. Soon as he got through,
he said, "I want to meet some people who's got a recipe for
this." Maybe some woman's cooked it, somebody cooked it,
he wanted a recipe for it. But it took a lot of work.[23]

Reminding whites of Indians' military prowess was also a favorite.
As master of ceremonies on November 11, 1927, Albert No Heart,
a prominent member of the tribal council of the Standing Rock Reservation, minced no words for white visitors. He flatly declared the
Indian "the best soldier in the world." Thomas Frosted, his colleague, specialized in speeches on the meaning of the flag to Indians
and their right to call it their own. A former scout and policeman as
well as an informal recruiter for the war effort in 1917 and 1918, he
used patriotism to struggle against what he perceived as the BIA's
deliberate attempts at undermining his status, especially his rank as a
chief. In some of his most sweeping declarations, affirming the value
of Indian participation in the war became a way to boost his personal status by attacking the hypocrisy of civilization itself. On one
particular Memorial Day, he "explained in a few words the symbolic
meaning of the monuments which mark the resting places of the
dead. He added that he believed that the Indian today were making
better use of Christianity than the white people from whom they
had received it." General indictments of "whites" under the guise of
patriotism and Christianity were thinly veiled attacks on "the whites
who live next to me" or even "you whites who are listening to my
speech"—because whites were in attendance, and one, Frank B.
Fiske, took note of the speech and printed it in his newspaper.[24]

During patriotic celebrations, aggressiveness could be physical
as well as verbal. Sham battles were fought that blurred the line between tributes to the dead and conflict between the living. Sometimes they reversed the narrative of Wild West shows, whose organizers liked nothing better than to tell the story of Indians' defeat at

the hands of whites after the temporary Indian victory at "Custer's Last Stand" or Little Big Horn. Sham battles, in fact, had been a feature of Sun Dance ceremonies even before they appeared in the West during Wild West shows. When practiced in the fall, on Armistice Day, they took on a wholly different meaning from that which they had had in pre-reservation days, when they were contests waged between Indian men. As Alfred B. Welch, a white veteran closely involved in patriotic activities on the Standing Rock Reservation, noted, during sham battles such as the one he helped organize in 1922, the desire to make these shows as realistic as possible called for not a little violence against men and beasts—and for white participation:

> During the day I had put on a sham battle with some Germans [settlers on the reservation]. The Germans were old men of the Dakotah and were fine actors. The action was a simple, flanking movement, which the Indians could all understand and they were terribly excited about it. After the fight we feasted. I had watched them prepare the dogs. They killed them by swinging them around by the hind feet and dashing their heads upon a stone. [. . .] The hair was singed off over a fire and the meat was cut up and boiled with tipsina and rice. They, however, fed the ex-servicemen on chicken, hard bread, bananas, coffee and some fried beef. The dog went to the older people who sat in a circle outside the lodge. The prisoners were last, amid much glee. [. . .] In the PM we had another sham battle and I turned the prisoners over to the women. They handled them roughly, throwing them to the ground, cutting off their buttons, etc. In the evening the women put on a scalp dance with scalps of the enemy on poles.[25]

A few years after the fact, the Sioux of Standing Rock reenacted the battle against the German Empire, this time on their own turf but still with live ammunition. They did not accept just any whites as partners: Turning an international conflict into an ethnic one, they fought "local Germans," immigrants hailing from German-Russian villages who were their neighbors and sometime economic partners as well as the buyers of their lands. The symbolic castration they made them suffer at the hands of "the women" turned patriotic celebrations into counter–Wild West Shows. Compensatory violence was not indiscriminate retribution, however. It was a game on the borderline of the intolerable. Men were now the only ones to bear arms. Women could no longer physically castrate enemies or scalp them— the scalps present came from earlier conflicts. German "war souvenirs," especially helmets, replaced scalps just as buttons substituted for testicles. Helmets were even distributed by the BIA, and, like photographs, figured prominently in some veterans' homes and in early pictures of victory celebrations. Violence was very real, limited, and pointed. While one could get hurt, indeed lose an eye, in a sham battle, as happened to veteran Sam Foster of Little Eagle in 1926, such direct violence remained accidental and far less significant than the symbolic violence equating neighbors with enemies and summoning the history of the Indian wars by enlisting an old warrior's participation, in the middle of a celebration that proclaimed interracial brotherhood and the end of old grudges.[26]

Whites themselves were not oblivious to this side of the ceremonies. They often insisted on the gospel of brotherhood and loyalty, as did Frank B. Fiske when concluding his Memorial Day report with the following words: "The whole program at Fort Yates showed a deep feeling of patriotism among whites and Indians alike and a spirit of appreciation of those who have passed to their reward in behalf of their country that is seldom witnessed in small communities." But others did not ignore the implicit or explicit challenges involved in Memorial Day celebrations of Indian participation in the war. On the Rosebud Reservation in 1921, a columnist reminded his readership that Indians had not fought the war alone—nor had they been alone in organizing Legion activities: "While the majority of the boys from Todd County were Indians, a number of white boys made excellent records in the Army or Navy and they are now very active in American Legion work." Doubts regarding the exact nature of Indian patriotism continued to be expressed. On Armistice Day, a visitor to Standing Rock wondered about the extraordinary display of patriotic symbols and prudently concluded thus: "and all seem patriotic."[27]

Despite the violence and the occasional doubt, patriotic loyalty began, as early as the late 1920s, to be defined as a characteristic Indian personality trait. A 1929 press release of the American Legion announced: "Few people in America take patriotic occasions so seriously and participate so unanimously." In 1938 the WPA Guide to North Dakota embraced this opinion as well: "The Indians are intensely patriotic, and it would be hard to find a fair, tribal council, or any other meeting over which the flag of the United States does not fly." Indian patriotism was no longer a curiosity but a given of local community life in the Plains. Whites accepted it, emulated it, even imitated its concrete manifestation. While circumscribed to families, small groups maybe, the imitation of Indian practices on Memorial Day at Standing Rock signaled that the symbolic reaffirmation of Indian identity through patriotic participation could indeed influence whites. In the northern district of the reservation, the very Germans who had been roughed up in sham battles developed the habit of covering their dead's graves with food offerings and paper flowers, just like their Indian neighbors. So peculiar was their assimilation of Indian customs that their own relatives living off the reservations called them *Indianer* (German for "Indians"). A spectacular example of how far Indians could go in reshaping ethno-racial boundaries, the case of Standing Rock German Russians is representative of the prime importance of multiracial and multiethnic participation in patriotic rituals. For each group, patriotism was a way to define oneself in relation to the other, even when the boundary between groups was being crossed through exchanges of gifts and sharing of customs. No rite threw more light on this dynamic that the adoptions of non-Indian veterans or military personalities.[28]

The practice of adopting white Americans was among the most formal interactions to be integrated into patriotic rituals on and around Native American reservations. A rite in and of itself, it had served in Indian-whites relations in pre-reservation days. Early on, it had been repurposed to formalize white missionaries' insertion into bands' life. With the progressive demise of Indian military power, the feathered headdress that came to symbolize adoption for whites carried less noble or friendly associations. Perceived as somewhat ridiculous spoils of war, the regalia and the name bestowed upon the adoptee could now be the butt of jokes among whites. Such appropriations and some Native Americans' reluctance to submit to such ridicule did not, however, erase the initially diplomatic aspect of a ritual that turned a stranger and potential enemy into a relative.

Legion officials tried early on to exploit the publicity potential of adoptions. In 1921, responding to visiting Field Marshal Ferdinand Foch's desire to meet Indian veterans, they organized a meeting with true and tested "Friends of the Whites": Crow chief Plenty Coups and Marcellus Tomahawk, a former Sioux policeman involved in the killing of Sitting Bull. Both adopted Foch in abridged yet detailed ceremonies. White reporters gently mocked the proceedings, but Indian sponsors insisted on the duties Foch accepted by becoming an adopted Indian. Red Tomahawk was particularly explicit. For him, Foch's adoption was but the reactivation of an old alliance between the French and the Sioux that went back to the seventeenth century and had been renewed on French battlefields in 1917 and 1918. Red Tomahawk admonished the French generalissimo. Above all, he must promise to take care of the remains of Indian soldiers buried in French cemeteries:

My Brother [. . .] You are French. We knew your people a long time ago. You were the first white we ever saw. [. . .] I am glad to see you today and to shake hands with you. We are friends. You were in trouble once. You asked us to help you out. We sent our best young men to help you fight. They went away across the ocean waters. We were afraid then and many people cried. [. . .] We helped you. My young men carry papers which say they did something brave over there. They struck the enemy for you. Some of them wear your rope [the fourragère, a French military award] around their shoulders. We fought your enemies for you and we left some of our braves in your ground. That ground is mine now. [. . .] I want you to promise me this: That you will never let any one desecrate that ground where my young warriors are lying. I don not want any one to plow up their bones. I do not know what the ground looks like, but I am afraid that their bones will be scattered.[29]

At this level of interaction, adoption was indeed tantamount to diplomatic negotiations. But even outside of such exceptional and much publicized ceremonies, adoption still carried weight on Plains reservations, especially when it was conducted by veterans. Despite white mockery, individual Indian names kept being bestowed on individuals. If possible, they were tied to past displays of bravery. As they came back from war, servicemen were given new names by older warriors and in turn received the privilege of naming children themselves. So important was that role in naming ceremonies that the veterans' role transcended ethnic and linguistic boundaries. Verna Mayhemotah's father, an Arapaho veteran from Oklahoma, was regularly invited to perform that function for Cheyennes installed on the same reservation as his people. He accepted the invitation, as the honor of naming was shared by both sponsor and sponsored. Often, the name was but a distant evocation of fighting. Charles Howard, of Wakpala, named a child "Blue Roan," in memory of a horse he had given away during a ceremony. Thomas DeRockbraine, of Little Eagle, called another child "Among the Smoke," in a more direct allusion to trench fighting. On the Rosebud Reservation, George Big Owl took on the yet more explicit name "The One Calling Out" to commemorate a night spent in a foxhole, unable to respond to the call for help of a wounded friend. The practice of linking one's child's name to a memory of the war could even spill onto his official, Anglo name: Martin Medicine, also of Wakpala, named his own son "Marne" to commemorate the second battle of the same name in the spring of 1918. In a few years, names gained by veterans or bestowed by them became part of the onomastic reservoir of each reservation. They rarely hesitated in taking this practice to patriotic ceremonies and adopting their white comrades, already their brothers in arms.[30]

Alvin M. Owsley, the national commander of the American Legion, was made an honorary member of the "Ojibway tribe" in 1923. Adalin W. Macauley, the national president of the Legion's Auxiliary, was adopted by Osage chief Bacon Rind in August 1927, a few months after President Calvin Coolidge himself had been adopted on the Pine Ridge Reservation. Paul V. McNutt, another national commander of the Legion, became one of the Jemez Pueblo of New Mexico in 1929. The same year, the Crows adopted the commander of the Veterans of Foreign Wars in Montana. In 1930, Standing Rock leaders adopted O. L. Bodenheimer, McNutt's successor. In 1932, Bodenheimer's replacement, Henry L. Stevens, became an honorary Blackfoot. In 1933, Mrs. Alford S. Blackburn, the president of the Auxiliary, was made a member of the Shoshones. The routinization of the procedure may have compromised its seriousness in many an Indian's eye; it did not compromise, however, the ritual's relevance as a boundary rite. As much as some Indians and whites could mock the artificiality of some of these proceedings, they did not abandon the idea that authentic rituals remained possible, if restricted to Indians themselves and a limited number of whites. The annual forays into Indian country of non-Indian veterans also supported the maintenance of another pre-reservation custom: intertribal competition. The successive or simultaneous adoptions of leaders such as Foch by different Indian groups were not only the result of an external demand. They made sense in terms of the rivalries that preexisted the arrival of Whites in the West and could be seen as a minor but vigorous theme of adoption ceremonies. The rite, in other words, was not purely and simply absorbed into practices that Indians had no control over. Whites were adopted in front of other Indians or in response to their previous actions.[31]

And whites answered in kind. Interracial diplomacy was apparent in invitations extended by Whites to Indians. The Bismarck Auxiliary regularly invited Annie Two Bear, another Standing Rock resident and Albert Grass's mother, on Armistice Day, because her son had been the first resident of North Dakota to be killed in action. Entire groups traveled on occasion. All-Indian bands were invited to major patriotic events, even to presidential parades, as were drill squads. By 1917, both activities already had long roots in Indian education, as music playing and military exercises had been mainstays of boarding school education since the 1880s. Recast in the post–World War I context, they not only testified to Indian civilization or mastery of originally foreign practices; they also served as a standard of community vitality and excellence. Far from being one-time occurrences, these trips in and out of Indian country reveal a system of exchange that went beyond folklorization and were a direct effect of the acclimatization of patriotism to Indian country inhabitants, both white and Indian, and their needs. Indians and whites might live miles apart and ignore each other all year long, but on patriotic occasions, they met and traded gifts. The gift of kinship was probably the one most sought after.[32]

Patriotic Giving as an Identity Trait

The war had been a time when a collective, racialized identity had been ascribed to Native Americans. Whites had made all Indians into natural-born warriors, for propaganda and recruiting purposes. The funerals of war dead had allowed for the controlled reinsertion of these savage warriors into biracial communities on and around reservations—turning these events into celebrations of peace that formally ended the hostilities on the frontier. The routinization and ritualization of patriotic celebrations on Memorial and Armistice Days further stabilized the new identity of Indians as America's foremost patriots. Through giving in particular, Native Americans consolidated their reputation and had their patriotic fervor recognized by non-Indians as an identity trait. Local ceremonies did more than just prove the validity of the claim. They took it out of the realm of racial stereotypes into actual interactions between individuals and groups. As a result, it was not just the "Indian race" that was designated as essentially patriotic; local communities also identified with their tribal ethnicity or even with the name of the bands that had founded them. National symbols and Indian ceremonies deployed in an interracial context were adjusted to serve this new purpose.

On the one hand, the exchange of food, gifts, names, or even blows supposed different types of modification for Indian ceremonies. Rites could be shortened to fit a program. Violence was euphemized to fit the moral standards of Christianity. Alternate foods were sometimes used. As Lakota and Dakota veterans gathered on Armistice Day 1930 around the Standing Rock Reservation's superintendent and leaders like Thomas Frosted, they did not perform the dog dance that was common under similar circumstances, during which puppies were killed, boiled, and consumed and war deeds publicly recited. Instead, the veterans of Fort Yates danced around a cake. The substitution was simple, if not apparent to neophytes. Because Americans did not consider young dogs a delicacy, or even proper food, the substitution paid tribute to the taste of the dominant culture in the person of the superintendent. It could be read both as an acceptance of non-Indians' standards or as an ironic nod to their dietary restrictions. It did, at any rate, produce a tasteful, legitimate Indian identity in a patriotic context. As happened with adoptions, the inclusion of whites resulted in adjusted rituals and set apart unmodified proceedings as genuine or "authentic." Forced into the dilemma of embodying natural-born warriors without actually enacting warrior rites, veterans produced two sets of rituals—for the dog dances did not stop. Rather than hybridity or assimilation, the scene at Fort Yates demonstrated the participants' sensitivity to the realm of the possible and to the place-based propriety of rituals: Dog simply could not be eaten in front of the superintendent and his guests. But whether displayed on a comic or on a more serious note, tribal customs could be part of patriotic ceremonies.[33]

The alternation of serious and "for show" Indianness was especially evident in the powwow, a cultural formation that would become a prime site for expressing reservation Indian identities. The powwow appropriated the juxtaposition of sacred and mundane interactions present in Armistice Day. Powwows took over the practice of contests, inherited from fairs, and applied it not just to rodeos, foot and horse races, tugs of war, and beauty queens but to dancing as well. They also appropriated the honoring rites that were an integral part of patriotic celebrations. The Grand Entry of dancers, generalized after the Vietnam War but already present after World War II, is strongly colored by the seriousness of Memorial Day processions behind the U.S. flag. Today still, veterans lead the parade behind the U.S. flag and American Legion post flags and preside over an inaugural display of patriotic rites. Military salutes, flag anthems, victory songs launch powwows while the names and military history of the veterans heading the parade are made public by the announcer who also takes care to emphasize for the audience the value of sacrifice. Only then can the dances properly begin. Several long-lasting powwows point to the 1940s as the time when, through the cooperation of World War I and World War II veterans, this Indian reworking of patriotic rites took shape. At the time, the Ho-Chunks started their powwow on Memorial Day, while the Kiowas selected Armistice Day for their own celebration. On Standing Rock, in the Bullhead and the Little Eagle districts, two community pow-wows started being organized in the late 1940s on June 28, for the former, and July 27, for the latter. On these dates, the communities had inaugurated their monuments to World War I. The Ponca pow-wow started even sooner, organized by the "Buffalo" Legion Post no. 38. Throughout the Plains, the injection of patriotism in Indian dances served neither assimilation nor cultural resistance but rather a complex refashioning of local, tribal, and Indian identities in which "borrowed" elements soon lost their foreign color while "Indian" rituals were reorganized.[34]

Nowhere is this process more in evidence than in the uses and interpretations of the U.S. flag that became common in Indian country in the interwar years. In the nineteenth century, the American national emblem appeared in Indian country as a battle standard and, as such, was put to very different uses. It could stand as a trophy taken from an enemy or as a present, conferred by the U.S. upon allies and carrying with it the prestige attached to diplomatic encounters and sacred objects. Chiefs were buried with it, at their own request or when they received a military funeral. Reservation life complicated the status of the U.S. flags for Indians. On the Pine Ridge Reservation in 1874, the erection of a flagpole by the BIA was considered almost a casus belli. Beginning in 1889, BIA schoolteachers were encouraged to unambiguously tie the flag to the values of obedience and submission and to Indians' inclusion in the United States. On Fourth of July celebrations, Indian dancers flew the flag conspicuously above their tipis to prevent any misinterpretation of their meetings as occasions for hostility. Ambiguity was still apparent in the decade that preceded the Great War. In June 1915, Crow Ghost, a resident of the Cannonball district on the Standing Rock Reservation, reminisced for Alfred B. Welch about the flag that one of his grandfathers had received from Colonel Leavenworth before a joint expedition against the Arikara in the first decades of the nineteenth century. Crow Ghost was very conscious of the high value of this family heirloom; it was associated with a specific military event, "a great thing [. . .] and all the people know about it." Although he remained somewhat vague on the subject, he also underlined the flag's power: "He said that if [Welch] would make him a flag like his grandfather used to carry he would hold it high in the air when there was a war and sing for [Welch] if [he] was ever in danger upon the battle field."[35]

The flag's pattern, commonly used in beadwork on the Plains, retained a supernatural quality. Appropriating it, in one form or another, could be a way, even before World War I, to gain personal prestige. Red Fish, one of Crow Ghost's neighbors, understood as much when in 1915 he fashioned a Sioux flag, also called a "Seven Fires Council flag," in reference to the Seven Fires constituting the Sioux nation. The U.S. flag, or rather American flags in general, provided him with a wealth of symbols and a pattern to arrange them. He borrowed the stars and stripes and the blue canton in the top left-hand corner and reprised the North Dakota flag's eagle holding in his claws symbols of war and peace—with an Indian twist: Instead of an olive branch, he put in a pipe and a tobacco pouch and also added a bow to the bundle of arrows. The flag, Red Fish explained, was a reply to Joseph K. Dixon's 1913 "Wanamaker Expedition" to Indian country. Dixon had intended to have all the tribes he visited sign a pledge of allegiance to the U.S. flag. Instead, Red Fish designed the Seven Fires Council flag. His efforts signaled that the U.S. emblem was as much an inspiration as a foil, and anticipated a conceptual effort to rethink Indian nations using American and Indian symbolism together that would become common after World War I.[36]

During the conflict itself, the flag could not but serve as an anchor for patriotic unanimity. Under pressure from peers and teachers, boarding school pupils were strongly encouraged to regard the emblem as a materialization of the nation and of Indians' duty toward it. Charles Roy Morsea, a third-year student at the Hampton Institute for Native and African Americans, gave the following speech in 1918 in front of fifteen hundred people, including four hundred soldiers of the 372nd Infantry regiment at Camp Stuart near Newport News, Virginia:

> To the *Stars and Stripes*, my father has been loyal, both in the past and the present. During the Spanish-American War he entered that great army and did his part in Cuba and the Philippine Islands. To-day he is across the water doing his

bit, and there are probably about 5,000 of the red race over
there fighting that the world may enjoy the brotherly love
that now exists all over the United States. My mother is in
the Red Cross service, thus leaving me at Hampton alone;
but may my prayer be granted that soon I will be able to do
my duty by the flag. Our country has only one flag—the *Stars
and Stripes*. It is the flag of freedom—the flag of free men.
Let us as citizens of this country give our bodies, our spirits,
and our hearts to the acts that will make us true American
citizens.[37]

Morsea could not have expressed the meaning of the flag in a more
orthodox way. His words mimicked the "Balch" formula, which ironically had been inspired by the German Empire: "We give our heads
and our hearts to God and our country; one country, one language,
one Flag." Starting in 1892, under Francis Bellamy's influence, the
formula was used as a response to the pledge of allegiance. Flag rituals pointed to the national emblem as a thing to be defended. One
was called to the colors or answered the call of the flag. More than
a thing, indeed: Under various names (Old Glory, Stars and Stripes,
the Star-Spangled Banner, the Red-White-and-Blue), the U.S. flag
was a person, just as the federal state was Uncle Sam and the country
the Good Old U.S. of A. The automatic association between loyalty
to the Republic and loyalty to this living entity was one of the most
powerful ways to generate consent among both whites and Indians.
The meaning of the flag was omnipresent in patriotic celebrations
and was repeated *ad nauseam* from the first days of military service
through training, the front, demobilization, and returning home.[38]
    Wartime patriotism did not encourage the totalitarian disap-
pearance of the individual in an abstract symbol but rather created—
or recreated—a personalized relationship with the flag. Morsea's
mention of his parents meant that the gift of oneself to the national
emblem could be justified by one's family's values or history. The
public utterance and subsequent publication of the speech show that
such justification was authorized and even encouraged. The mention of the "red race" and its contribution, another learned formula,
made sense in a racialized projection of the diversity of the U.S. population (and the world) that was common before, during, and after

the conflict. But red also had specific connotations in many a Native American language, whether it pointed to the earth as its main association or to blood, life, and courage. As a component of the U.S. flag, it could be reinterpreted as easily as could the other components of the pattern: the stars, the stripes, and the three national colors.

Victory celebrations were a prime site for this type of recomposition and reinterpretation. On November 30, 1918, in Cannonball, participants asked themselves the same question: Should the U.S. flag be included in the Indian ceremony? For the younger men in attendance, manipulation of the flag would provoke whites' anger and should be avoided. Older men insisted on the opposite: "They said that the U.S. flag must be organically (*okiheyan*) a part of the old Indian emblems since the white people coming to this island had become the successors of the old Indian governments, being more wise and efficient (*iokihi*) on world-wide scale, as was shown by the success in the present war."[39]

Through faulty help in translating the speech, or through his own mistake, Aaron McGaffey Beede, the white pastor who reported the debate in a paper intended for scientific publication, mistranslated the Sioux word *okiheyan* or *okiheya*, which connotes inferiority or subordination as much as integration. In the interpretation proposed by the older men, the flag was clearly associated with Sioux' status as "first Americans." By virtue of its red and white stripes, it reminded whites of their own status as "successors" of Native Americans in the country. Instead of flying the flag alone above the sacred tree that constituted the center of the victory ceremony, Cannonball elders decided to fly under it a smaller "Indian flag"—"an emblem of our race," they said, that they would thereafter use in all ceremonies. A petition signed by the reservation's tribal council later endorsed that proposal and forwarded it to the BIA.

Thomas Frosted was present at the celebration. His detailed interpretation of the meaning of the "Indian flag" closely resembled what, only three years before, Red Fish had first proposed:

> It is a flag, and yet it is not a flag in the sense that the U.S. flag is a flag; for, as you know, a nation has but one flag, and the minds and the hearts of all the people of a nation are devoted to the nation's one flag similarly as they are devoted

to the sun, the great benefactor of all people on the earth. You see that the main part of this flag is red, which does not mean that the red is superior to the blue and the white in the flag in the smaller part, but it means that the Red men were the first people here on this island. The color red signifies the earth and all that grows out of the earth—the people, the food which is provided by Nature for people, and the food which people learn to cultivate for themselves. The color blue signifies the sky above the Earth with all its unmeasured boundaries, its everlasting power, and its kindly wishes for the Earth and all that is on the Earth. The color white signifies that by action of the Earth and the Sky here comes a future world for all beings great or small. [. . .] The Red men freely gave [white people] the cultivated plants and food that they already had for their own sustenance, food-plants well adapted to the soil and climate of this island. And with wisdom superior to ours in cultivating foods the white people have made the food-plants that the red men gave them the chief factor in providing food for a great and powerful nation.[40]

In Frosted's account, men and crops were equated as productions of the earth, a rhetoric (and a belief) that reinforced the representation of the "Indian race" not only as autochthonous but also as naturally equipped to feed new arrivals. The myth institutionalized in the Thanksgiving holiday thus received a political, less neutralized interpretation, and the original gift of food, his next words further explained, called for reciprocation. In the same light, the U.S. power was "unique" and superior but not supreme: Sun, Heaven, and Earth still held sway over it. The Sioux flag that articulated these concepts functioned as both a commentary on the U.S. national emblem and a cosmology of power. It tied recent events and gifts of food or life to original encounters and exchanges and contained clear demands for the enforcement of an egalitarian contract between the races: "We note there are two stars on this flag, one representing the white men and one the red men. And this does not mean the joining of these peoples in this great war merely; it is intended to mean the union of these two races in one great nation with determination fixed and strong hearts pledged that each people on the earth, great or small, shall be free from the clutch of the Kaiserites [Germans] and shall possess their homes in safety." The special relationship binding Sioux and Whites was to be founded on right, security, and freedom. It justified the possession by the Sioux of a special flag, a privilege based on autochthony that Frosted denied other ethnic groups.[41]

Innovative interpretations of the flag were of course deployed in a controlled environment. After World War I, the U.S. emblem continued to be extremely visible in churches and schools throughout Indian country. Closely associated with salutes, parades, and recitations, it was a common sight throughout reservations. But above all it was systematically associated with music. The old "Star-Spangled Banner" song, officially recognized by President Woodrow Wilson in 1916, became a national anthem in 1931. Patriotic and military songs such as "My Country, 'Tis of Thee" ("America"), "Tenting Tonight," and "Over There" resounded after "Taps," rifle shots, and drum rolls at every war-related event. This sonorous presence of the nation and the flag reinforced and embodied prescribed feelings: love, triumph, hope, anger, pride, resolution. Songs sung in English (a language many Native Americans were still not comfortable with in their daily lives) were to be listened to or sung with reverence. After World War I, behavior in the vicinity of the U.S. flag became ever more codified. In 1919 still, teachers could encourage their students to yell at it as a form of salute. The code published in 1923 by the American Legion National Commission on Americanism made such behavior unthinkable. Silence was now the proper attitude in front of the flag. Men in uniform were to offer it a military salute, the rest of the audience to take their hats off. The flag was now officially "a living thing," and veterans were its official guardians, encouraged to enforce the respect it was due. Beginning in 1929, the flag would even have its own day, on June 14.[42]

For all the insistence on propriety by institutions both public and private, behavior at patriotic celebrations was by no means uniform. Around the flag, men and women of all ages, persuasions, and denominations congregated in a semi-religious atmosphere where the Creator appeared, fugitively, in rapid prayers and blessings. For some, salutes, salvos, and other euphemistic allusions to the violence of war prescribed by the Legion code must have been but a curiosity;

for others, a boring obligation before the important part of the event, namely the dances. The Legion's censure often went unheeded. After World War I, in Indian country, the flag remained an emblem to wrap oneself in (to the outrage of some white visitors), as it had been since the nineteenth century. For many a soldier's or ex-soldier's family, however, flag rituals enacted the direct connection that the war had created between the serviceman's relatives and the U.S. state. In 1924, Joseph Takes The Shield Sr. and his wife paid tribute to Joseph Jr.'s grave in Arlington National Cemetery before visiting the BIA offices in Washington, D.C., where they requested a U.S. flag "in memory of their son." For other families too, the stars on the flag had since the war been associated with sacrifice. Flags had hung in front of tipis during recruitment drives. "Service flags," on which silver stars represented active servicemen in the community, were reproduced on tipis. They brought home the association of individuals with a prominent feature of the national emblem that was made only stronger by the subsequent use of "gold stars" to designate soldiers who had died during the hostilities. The veteran's burial flag pushed this association to its limits by fusing the respect due the nation with that due one's deceased relative. On the Plains, it was flown during patriotic events by family members and could only be taken down after the simulation of an act of bravery. The power of the flag was similarly invoked in Legion fundraising activities, when post officers approached veterans with a flag in their hands to collect dues. Both multiplied and individualized, inserted in objects and ritual sequences, genealogies, histories, and teachings, the flag became not just a metonymy of patriotism but also a fundamental resource in a local, Indian political economy of memory. Freed from its former status as a "white flag" protecting Indians against aggression, it became the ultimate representation of Indians' paradoxical "difference within conformity"—a symbol of their identity as super-patriots and an embodiment of sacrifices made in the war and reproduced during patriotic celebrations.[43]

Patriotic celebrations thus revealed the simultaneously competitive and imitative construction of identities that participation in World War I had made possible for Indians and whites. Just like their non-Indian neighbors, Native Americans had to make sense of symbols and ceremonies that tied the expression of their identities to a hierarchy linking community, ethnic group and race, and the nation. Living "under the flag" had but a few years before the war been equated with living in the shadow of laws that were as inextricable as a "spider's web." After the conflict, this shadow became protective, fertile even. The "President's flag" or "Great Father," "Grandfather," or *T'uŋkášilayapi* was now a positive force in Sioux lives: "The President's Flag will stand for ever/Under it, the people will grow," ran the lyrics of a "Flag song." Indians could come to the aid of the flag and the president, stand by them and defend them: "Grandfather beseeched me/(to help Him) so I destroyed the German and I also took his land," ran another song. This transformation happened through the repetition of practices among which, as we saw, gift giving and giveaways played a decisive role. In a patriotic context, giving was not simply an ethos or a habitus. Made necessary by the extraordinary demands of the war effort, giving was later used by Indians to celebrate their own identities and even question the colonial relationship that tied Indians to an inferior position in their own reservations. Instead of receiving their pittance from a benevolent Great Father, they gave generously not only to their own but to whites as well. Giving away goods, animals, and money made it possible for veterans' families to transform their relative's individual bravery into social capital for themselves and cultural capital for their larger community. Patriotism practiced during and after the conflict as a gift of one's self, one's relatives, or one's property became a personality trait that even whites acknowledged. Once imagined only as "warriors," Indians were now "patriots," even quintessential ones, in a sense that held at bay the savagery associated with the former term. The national project of merging all differences in the patriotic melting pot, so apparent in school patriotism, became a local project that articulated small and big fatherlands, the reservation and the nation, through rituals that sometimes shored up, sometimes questioned socio-racial hierarchies. The symbolic work accomplished by veterans and their families resulted in both Indian interpretations of American symbols and the repurposing of Indian rites (adoptions, dances) for life in an American context. As the embodiment of Indians' generosity, the U.S. flag became an ethnic symbol. It carried transparent political demands for more rights and more equality with whites, but it could also smooth over differences, whether between reservation groups and the federal states, between local whites and tribal groups, or even between veterans and their own communities. For veterans were far from pawns in the hands of their families and elders.

CHAPTER FOUR

Bad Boys, Forgotten Heroes

W AR HAD BEEN a powerful way to discipline the nation in general and Indians in particular. In contorted and idealistic bureaucratic phraseology, commissioner of Indian affairs Cato Sells publicly defended this fundamental principle. "I regard," he told his employees in the first weeks of the conflict, "the hour as opportune for moulding and converging all natural human instincts and ambitions toward the honor of equal opportunity and loyal service in the affairs of a great self-governing people." For all defenders of assimilation, the war looked like a golden opportunity. After the guns fell silent, patriotic celebrations could seem a way to prolong its effects. At Memorial Day and Armistice Day, BIA agents continued to present veterans and their families and communities with ideal representations of their position and their role vis-à-vis one another and vis-à-vis the nation. Veterans were not passive recipients of these efforts. In retrospect, the years or months away from reservations in the "white world," which many of them tried to prolong after the conflict ended, could appear to them as a parenthesis, a time of freedom, from BIA control at least, that ended as soon as they set foot again on the all-too-familiar ground of reservation life.

It was not simply that veterans were back under the supervision of the Bureau of Indian Affairs. Families and elders were equally prone to reassert control over former soldiers. Honoring veterans was an opportunity to reaffirm community bonds and bolster Indians' status vis-à-vis whites. But celebrations could also be rituals to manage fears and distrust toward the veterans themselves. The fear concerned young men who had been away from home and had learned to wage violence and adopt, even flaunt unconventional behaviors. They had gotten (more) used to challenging authority, individually or as a group, had drunk alcohol, had sex outside of wedlock, or asserted their own worth compared with those at home who had not helped the war effort by risking their own lives or donning the uniform. Veterans, in other words, might not content themselves

previous page: Frank Fiske, *Albert Grass Funeral Cortege, Cannonball, N.D.*
(© Fiske Collection, 1952-6394, State Historical Society of
North Dakota, Bismarck, North Dakota)

124

with the symbolic gratification that their own communities were so ready to grant them, and the latter were aware of it.

In many cases, faced with control and distinction, the effects of which were sometimes indistinguishable from one another, veterans fought back. They relied on a hard-won mastery of patriotic and citizen-soldier ideologies. Coming back home with a greater awareness of their rights, both individual and collective, they, in essence, built a group identity for themselves, challenging the norms imposed on them by non-veterans or using them to gain greater control of their lives. There was more than honor in the status they received. There was conflict. And there was scandal. Some of it remained local, opposing veterans to other members of their communities, or to the local agent of the BIA. But the wider national scene, on which veterans' rights and status were also debated, was never far removed. As veterans learned how little their status could mean in the often depressed economy of reservations, they soon began to harness the symbolic resources they possessed to challenge the place they were assigned. Expectations of veterans' exemplarity were their bane. They were also a resource when, turned on their head, they served to question the morality of the treatment they were receiving at the hands of their countrymen. In the process, veterans forged for themselves an identity as forgotten heroes.[1]

Playing Truant

Military service in World War I provided Indian veterans with precious little technical capital to reinsert themselves in the reservation economies. Those who had served in the Medical or Transport Corps had acquired skills they could hope to transfer into the peacetime job market. Several used the vocational education received in boarding school to get into technical positions in the armed forces. Joseph J. Gurnoe (Red Cliff Ojibwa) trained as a machinist at the Hampton Institute in Virginia and joined the Navy, an itinerary that seems to have been common among Eastern boarding school students. William Schenandoah, an Iroquois from Hogansburg, New York, joined the Navy before the war, and during it was assigned to the nascent Air Force, where he remained even after the war ended.

Andrew Bellecourt (White Earth Ojibwa), Robert Big Thunder (Wisconsin Winnebago), and Morris Wheelock (Wisconsin Oneida) used their experience with motor vehicles during the war to become truck drivers after it ended. More generally, reflecting the effect of the war but also a generational trend, many veterans were among the first inhabitants of their reservations to drive—and own—a car.[2]

Postwar itineraries as specialized technicians were not common, however, for Native Americans. With 85 percent of Native American recruits serving in infantry regiments (according to the Eddy report) and a significant portion of them having limited command of oral, but especially written, English, the prospects of the majority were simply that they would return to the agricultural jobs the BIA had prepared them for. Nor was the immediate postwar period a propitious time to pursue academic or technical training. For many Indian veterans, similar in that respect to many non-Indian veterans, war had been an opportunity to get away from school in the first place. Those who had joined underage (11 percent of those who had made it to France, according to the Eddy report) were especially unlikely to return to school after leaving the Army. Steve Youngdeer told the principal of his school as much before he left for a war in which he would be killed: "Your letter was received today and I will kindly answer you this evening. In regard of you asking me of my returning to school. I don't hardly think I will return to school, as Uncle Sam has supported me enough. I was at Carlisle 8 years since 1903 till last June except 1908–09. But some how or other I more interested in athletic sport than I did in my school study. I think I can support my self the rest of my day to come by working."[3]

Youngdeer's thinking was in line with that prevalent in the United States after World War I. One generation ahead of the G.I. Bill, veterans from 1917 and 1918 had few rehabilitation opportunities open to them. For the wounded and the disabled, the Federal Board of Vocational Education offered some prospects under the guise of "rehabilitation."[4] A few programs allowed veterans to acquire the technical know-how necessary to regain the social position they could have hoped for before the war. Getting a university education or joining the ranks of the middle class were not objectives for the programs' inventors. A few individuals managed to attend universities as part of their rehabilitation. Only those who had prior knowledge of academia made use of this opportunity. Chester C. Beaulieu, an Ojibwa "mixed-blood" from White Earth already familiar with school life, studied law at the Sorbonne in Paris, France. Fred Mahone, a Hualapai from Arizona, studied for a few months at Valparaiso University, Indiana, before dropping out. In Beaune, France, Morris Wheelock was selected for training preparatory to West Point Military Academy. Plagued by clinical depression after his time fighting in the trenches, he had to relinquish the idea. It was only in 1921, after working in road repair, hospitals, and construction, that he finally availed himself of the program for disabled veterans set up by the Veterans Bureau and trained as a professional musician at the conservatory of Green Bay, Wisconsin. Walter S. Sevalia, an Ojibwa veteran who had been one of the first Indian soldiers to be widely touted as a war hero by the BIA, experienced firsthand the difficulty of claiming educational benefits, even for one with his stature. After a year of high school, Sevalia joined the University of Wisconsin in February 1922, hoping to train in motor design. It was only a few months before he became the object of a negative evaluation by his supervisors, who found him "not of the university caliber." After two and a half years of rehabilitation, he was instead invited to enroll in a technical school that would provide him with a shorter—and cheaper—formation. Perhaps on account of this report, Sevalia did not attend the follow-up meeting with his university supervisors. In 1930, he had become a boat pilot, taking tourists around for a living in Sault Ste. Marie, Michigan. Sevalia had been in a better position than most Indian veterans to benefit from the very limited educational opportunities open to them. Belonging to the 18 percent of soldiers who, among the 93 percent that answered the questions in the Eddy report, made it above fourth grade, he was part of a distinct Indian elite. That he couldn't make it in academia despite this advantage was not simply a testimony to his personal limits. Indians were just not expected to benefit from non-agricultural rehabilitation programs.[5]

Expectations were indeed quite low. While educators and officials did anticipate educational benefits for Native American veterans, they limited them to what they regarded as behavioral improvements. Familiarity with the "wider world" had always been a major reason for taking Indians out of their surroundings and placing them among non-Indians. Outing programs, such as the one started at the Carlisle Institute, in Pennsylvania, at the end of the nineteenth century, were based on this very principle. In practice, however, both BIA officials and Indian veterans seem to have been content with the latter simply returning home. Rarely was regret expressed. When Lynn Eagle Feather, a Lakota from Rosebud, chose to get married instead of joining the Agricultural College of Brookings in his home state of South Dakota, the superintendent of his reservation fatalistically acknowledged that "the young man seems to be inclined to live the life of an Indian and nothing else." Not knowing the exact number of veterans they had under their control and receiving no specific instructions regarding them, local BIA agents had no means of challenging this trend and showed little desire to do so. In a national report on the American Indians during the war, the national office cruelly held up a Cheyenne soldier as an example of the "wonderful transformation in him for the better" the war had brought about. Gassed, shell-shocked, and wounded, the unnamed veteran had come back with the most precious gift of all: discipline. Associated with ideas of self-confidence, politeness, linguistic proficiency, patriotism, and familiarity with the world outside the reservation, discipline summed up official expectations toward Indian veterans. Indian Office agents differed little, in that regard, from other officials dealing with veterans in the rest of the country: Reintegrating ex-servicemen, whether wounded or disabled or neither, implied bringing them back into the fold as fast as possible and with as little cost—and fuss—as possible.

Several Indian veterans appeared to have been willing to give just this image of themselves. Charles Little Chief, from Standing Rock, professed to have been "glad I was in the army for I learned good many things which I wouldn't have learned if I stayed home." Joseph Filario Tafoya, a Santa Clara Pueblo wrote back to his BIA superintendent in May 1918 that he was "doing well and doing the best I can to my share. I'm expecting for a promotion in early date." In August, he added: "I am in good health and enjoying life and all my duty. [. . .] The farther I step, the nearest I get to the real service I am here for, and more I feel as a Real American." In 1919, looking back on his war experience, he declared: "I have learned to take good care of my health, military rule and discipline. I have learned the different lives of difference nations and people and their tongues just enough to get along. I have the experience of the soldiers life and hardship in the camp and on the battle field. [. . .] I have the experience of hiking to the front through mud and rain, water up to the knee." The expectations of Indian veterans and BIA officials alike clearly influenced one another in a dialectical relationship that left little room for protest or defiance in the years immediately following the war.[6]

Even more than a decade after the conflict ended, veterans could still be held up as role models, evidence that the war had changed Indian recruits for the better. On Standing Rock in 1930, Straight Pine, a veteran living in the isolated district of Bullhead, was commended by the local boss farmer of the BIA. The Lakota veteran, the farmer told his superior, had sold his cattle before the war and had returned home with nothing but a few horses. But Pine, an active Legionnaire, had worked as a cowboy, accumulated a small amount of capital and acquired a cattle herd. Moreover, he had taken to farming and now sold hay to his white neighbors for a profit. According to the boss farmer, Pine was even willing to contribute wisdom confirming the orientations of the Bureau: "He says that there is a good living on the farm for anybody that will reach out after it, and I will say that he is reaching out." Veterans like Pine could be used to demonstrate the success of the Bureau. They also showed how little the agency's expectations had been modified by the war: Local and central agents expected nothing else than a return to normalcy after the parenthesis of the war in Europe.[7]

The fact was that the BIA knew little about "its" veterans, if only because they were often long in returning on reservations. As late as 1925, the superintendent of the Crow reservation had no idea where most of them had gone and had to organize *in absentia* a ceremony in their honor. In 1926, the superintendent of the Ojibwa reservation of Lac du Flambeau complained that he had "experienced considerable difficulty in securing [. . .] information [on the reservation's ex-servicemen] owing to the fact that even the brothers of some who served are unable to give me their present addresses and whether they have family or not." The situation was similar in some Pueblo villages, or on Standing Rock, where a 1922–1923 census mentioned but a third of the total number they should have identified. Of those surveyed, 70 percent were married by then, probably the most likely motivation for returning to the reservation. For a good part of the 1920s and to a certain degree in later decades, Indian veterans of World War I were migrants. On the one hand, many had left no wife and children behind when they joined. Neither had they had to quit jobs, lucrative or otherwise. On the other hand, they were familiar enough with English and the "white world" to be able to make their way off the reservation, whether for a few months or a few years after they were discharged. Thus Elmer Red Eagle, a Lakota from Fort Peck, spent a few months in Chicago "to have fun" and, according to a family tradition, returned home after having had a child with a Chinese Chicagoan. A city stay only prolonged the "time out" period that followed the Armistice for American recruits in France or in training camps stateside. Reasonably well-off, at least by reservation standards, many Indian veterans were able and willing to make use of their time in the service after the Armistice, and for at least a few months after their discharge, to enjoy the freedom of which their BIA-earned education had often deprived them. In New York City, the minor surge in the American Indian population prompted by the war made headlines and helped boost local Indian organizations. Speaking to anthropologist H. Scudder Mekeel in 1930, William Fire Thunder, a veteran from Pine Ridge, likely used his own experience to talk about "the need to organize homes in big cities for Indians to live with Indians and have jobs [. . .] like a German, Italian, or other community in a big city." Urban life, experienced in France or the United States, was for all a notable experience of their military service and the initial months after their return to civilian life.[8]

Being away from the reservation did not mean "spinning off," leaving behind tribal life and assimilating into the mainstream of American society. On the contrary, some groups' proximity to major cities encouraged temporary stays or even regular commutes between reservations and urban areas. This was especially true of the Iroquois or of Californian tribes. For others, especially those most intent on leaving the reservation, the move was more momentous and difficult. Even for someone like Oscar White Weasel, a Lakota from Cheyenne River, who had come to "think the white man is better than the Indian" and apparently desired to assimilate fully, wartime service did not provide enough of a break to start him on the path he so ardently longed for. Growing up fatherless under the tutelage of an alcoholic man who regularly beat him, White Weasel was sent to a boarding school, which he was able to leave only in 1916 when he joined to National Guard to serve on the Mexican border. After nine months in the service, he joined the Army in 1917. When he returned home in 1919, his mother had died from the Spanish influenza. He gave this as a reason for joining again. In 1924, after serving on the Panama Canal, he returned to civilian life in Washington, D.C. This time intending to make a life for himself on the Cheyenne River Reservation, he returned home to marry. Despite having seen "taxes [eat] up [his] deeded land" and laboring under asthma he thought he had contracted in the war, White Weasel lived ten years as a farmer, raising chickens and pigs with a fair amount of success. As the Great Depression set in, he had to rely on relief, work on roads, and try his hand at raising cattle before finally getting a job off the reservation. With the onset of World War II he moved to Springfield, Missouri, then closer to home and later Fort Meade, not far from Rapid City, South Dakota, where he worked in a military hospital. It was only when he retired, in 1963, and at the request of his wife, who wanted to see her grandchildren, that he went back to the reservation, where he died in 1979.

Marriage and retirement added to the Great Depression to make reservation life both extremely difficult and unavoidable. Yet urban life was also a crucial part of White Weasel Bear's existence, one that military service in World War I made possible and perhaps even desirable. The very fact of leaving the reservation and BIA control means that we have few ways to document this type of experience for Indians. For many, like Paul Bald Eagle, from Pine Ridge, little was known except that he was "said to be living in Philadelphia." But this absence is significant in itself: For many, war and the immediate postwar years were often years of "playing truant," not returning home to the regulations of reservation life. All boasting about "wonderful transformations" aside, BIA agents were acutely aware of the fact and of the risk it entailed for their own control over reservation communities.[9]

Seeds of Disorder

In the assimilationist tradition most BIA agents were steeped in, the foremost risk posed by young men returning to the reservation was the phenomenon known as "going back to the blanket." It went beyond donning "Indian" clothing. While the blanket symbolized Indian tradition, going back to it meant, especially for students returning from off-reservation boarding schools, renouncing the training they had been provided with and readjusting back to reservation life, with its communal values, lack of jobs, and relative distrust of the non-Indian world. For BIA agents, losing young people to "the blanket" meant that the costly effort of educating Indians into non-Indians, one that had been pursued with great obstinacy by the Indian Office since the 1870s both on and off reservations, had been in vain. Although it had collective aspects as well, a central part of assimilation involved a process of individualization. Civilizing Indians meant forcing them to adopt a type of social and economic life centered on the monogamous, nuclear, land-owning family that was supposed to have made the success of the white American way of life. Imposing legal marriages and legal possession of land, with the corollary possibility of passing land down from parents to children, required considerable investment from the federal government. From the 1880s onward, its agents had to insinuate themselves "from cradle to grave" in every aspect of their wards' lives to make sure this program was implemented. War and patriotic celebrations compromised this work via a feature of mobilization that had been one of the first targets of the assimilationist program: dances.[10]

Participating in dances was for an individual the ultimate sign that he or she had gone back to the blanket. Indeed, few other activities short of actually waging war against the United States could have been as offensive to assimilation as dances. Branded as pagan by missionaries, they were also strongly associated with military activity by BIA agents and U.S. soldiers. In the Plains, the Sun Dance and later the Ghost Dance, in their various tribal guises, were widely looked upon by government agents as hotbeds of dissidence and "hostility." Severely limited by military and police intervention supported by official rulings, Indian dances did not, however, disappear in the reservation era. On the contrary, they became one of the few focuses of collective life that were not directly sponsored by white authorities. The Grass or Omaha Dance, originally a fixture of the Ponca's Hethuska warrior society, became common in Indian gatherings throughout the Plains, focusing activities ranging from collective meals to naming ceremonies, welcoming visitors and gift giving. New dances joined this nucleus. One of the reasons invoked by the BIA for banning them, or at least controlling them, was their supposed effect on Indians' morality with partner dances attracting the most violent opposition even though they clearly imitated white practices. The emphasis on national holidays such as Independence Day, Washington Day, or Arbor Day was not only part of a program of Americanization. It was also intended as a way to channel Indians' propensity to get together to dance and, in the process, waste the time and money that should have been employed in farming and becoming civilized. A widely held hope on the eve of World War I was that Indian dancing had successfully been restricted to only the oldest class of reservation Indians, while youth had been no less successfully directed to white and therefore "healthier" forms of entertainment. The hope rapidly proved unfounded.[11]

As veterans started coming home, and newspaper after newspaper, both local and national, harped on the victory and scalp dances that their families put up, BIA agents began displaying uneasiness. They even feared that a "return of the repressed" was in the making. It was not enough to sponsor holidays, or even Memorial or Armistice Day, to organize readings, the singing of anthems, or patriotic contests. Patriotic ceremonies themselves could become holidays for "reactionaries," composed as they were of a mix of "pagan dances" and programs organized by returned soldiers' associations. New regulations had to be devised. In the spring of 1923, Commissioner of Indian Affairs Charles H. Burke sanctioned the local efforts of BIA agents to control dances that, in line with the wider moral outrage at the "dance craze" in the non-Indian world, they insisted on seeing as lewd displays of naked bodies and unbridled sexuality. Circular 1665 recognized dancing as "not inconsistent with civilization" but declared it damaging "under most primitive and pagan conditions." With the latter involving, among others, "the reckless giving away of property," the new regulation was encompassing enough to give local agents all leeway to enforce severe dancing regulations. Restricted to one a month and limited to people over fifty years old, dances were reaffirmed as a prime target of the civilizing work of the Bureau. Controlling dancers with a veteran background became an objective in itself.[12]

BIA agents had good reasons to believe that they would have to dispute this control with older Indians. As early as 1919 they were confronted with a level of resistance and organization that testified to many reservation groups' determination to use the prestige of the uniform to fight back against anti-dancing regulations. Honors given to veterans by their neighbors and families were always means to reinsert them in Indian-controlled relationships. And there were plenty such honors to go around. Just as their departure had been an occasion to reactivate old ceremonies, veterans of the Great War were given attention and presents in a way that had been customary for their parents or grandparents when they came back from war. In the Plains especially, it was not unusual for people to hand a veteran a silver dollar on the street in the first weeks after his return. Among the Sioux, he received choice pieces of meat at dinners organized between dances and was offered a seat apart from the crowd. He was honored in the Grass Dance, in the Scout dance, and in certain partner dances like the Sioux "49" dance. In accordance with an age-old tradition, he only (and older warriors) was allowed to pick up a feather when it had fallen off a headgear during a dance, on condition that he would tell one of his war deeds. At Armistice Day, entire communities saluted veterans and shook their hands. At Christmas, they were the only ones authorized to light the fire in the church's stove. When they died, the plate they used during ceremonies could be used only after their memory had been honored.[13]

In Wakpala, on the Standing Rock Reservation, the emphasis on continuity between warriors and veterans of the U.S. armed forces resulted in a specific design to designate the year 1918 on the local winter count kept by Paul Allen Eagle Horn, the father of a World War I veteran. While the year 1917 was straightforwardly represented by the depiction of an American doughboy in uniform, complete with hat and puttees, the year 1918 was symbolized by the same soldier carrying two lances, a symbol of Sioux warrior societies. Inside family circles, the Great War rekindled traditional conceptualizations of war as well as of the place of veterans within their communities. Non-veterans themselves were not shy about explaining the fact to visitors from the outside world, as one of them demonstrated in his answer to an American Legion journalist: "The warrior has always been held in high regard among the Indians, and so with us the World War veterans are especially honored. They are distinguished, set apart, in all Indian activities."[14]

Few facts were as undisputed in Indian country and even beyond as the special place of Indian veterans within their own societies. But such unanimity masked the manipulations necessary to allow veterans of the U.S. Army to act as a stand-in for warriors who had often distinguished themselves against this very body. One need only look at the vocabulary used to designate them to get a sense of the symbolic adaptation that Indian societies had to impose on themselves to bridge this gap. While the term *veteran* was of course ubiquitous on all reservations, each Indian people developed its own vocabulary to describe the veteran experience. In Lakota country, the word used for veteran was *akíčhita*. Sometimes designating a messenger, specifically one who carried a message of a supernatural nature, *akíčhita* was especially used to describe an elite within the warrior societies that used to regulate life in camp or during the buffalo hunt. Wary of losing their status and function, many *akíčhita* became BIA policemen in the years that followed relegation to the reservations. Another layer of meaning was added to the word by the fact that, because they showed the same kind of group discipline, U.S. soldiers were also designated as *akíčhita* in Lakota or Dakota. An *akíčhita*, from 1918 on the preferred term to translate "veteran," was not, in other words, simply a *zuyá wičháša* or *ikíčhize wičháša*, a warrior, but a bridge between Lakota and white ways of waging war. Identifying veterans with *akíčhita* came with a general euphemization of soldiers' activity during the war. While the role of defender of their tribes had always been inscribed among the attributions of warriors, World War I considerably reinforced that aspect. The rape of Belgium, the Zimmermann Telegram, the sinking of the *Lusitania*, allowed pro-war Americans to frame America's entry into the European conflict as a defensive gesture, and the move was promptly followed in any Native reservations such as Standing Rock whose Indian leaders imagined their involvement as a fight against freedom-hating "Kaiserites." In the process, *akíčhita* could be imagined as defending interchangeably Indian land or the U.S. territory, Belgium or democracy, the U.S. Constitution or treaty rights. Warriors, in other words, were reimagined, not just resurrected.[15]

Equating warriors of old and veterans was especially difficult for groups split into opposing factions by the onslaught of American colonization, with one urging moderation and negotiation and the other defending a more militant approach. In the nineteenth century west of the Mississippi, service in the U.S. Army was often the clearest dividing line between allies and enemies of the United States. While the desire to maintain a warrior status might have played an important part in military service after the end of the Indian wars, memories going back to the era of division and intertribal conflict continued to define individual and collective identities on many reservations. Among the Crows, a continuous involvement alongside American forces made it easy for orators like Plenty Coups to emphasize military service as a Crow tradition and turn what was originally a survival strategy into a century-old commitment on the side of "civilization." On the White Mountain Reservation in Arizona, home of the Chiricahua Apaches, the world war had in certain cases the exact opposite effect: It helped renew old hatreds and rekindled old rivalries. This was especially the case for veteran Sam Kenoi, son of an Apache scout in the U.S. cavalry, who held Asa Daklugie, Geronimo's nephew, responsible for his mother's death in deportation. The Great War was distinctly an opportunity for Kenoi to mimic his father's itinerary. Joining at a ripe age (he was over forty years old), Kenoi took special pride in the fact that, among his enemies, none had had the courage to enlist. He rejoiced in the fact that Daklugie, who sometimes boasted of having served in the Spanish-American War, immediately shut up when Kenoi evoked his own service in 1917 and 1918. For Kenoi, conflicts from the past were not extinguished by the war but renewed. They were like plants that continued to grow: "I say this much about it. The white man plants corn. But he puts two kernels in the ground. One good kernel will yield, but one rotten kernel will kill the good one if you put them together. So, as smart as the white people pretend to be, there's one time they planted a good kernel with a rotten one. The shadow of the shameful way they treated these faithful Indians and United States Scouts still lies over us." Kenoi's logical next step after returning from war was to take his fight into the tribal political arena.[16]

The political and sometimes factional nature of the conflicts that pitted reservation members against one another in the control of veterans' prestige was evidenced in other ways on other reservations. After having first appeared to validate the assimilationist agenda, many Indian veterans soon gave signs that they would not be as docile as expected. At a victory celebration in the Cannonball district of the Standing Rock Reservation, Claude Killspotted, a tribal council member and local leader known as a devoted Christian and an equally devoted dancer, seized the opportunity to remind veterans of their duties and "told the young soldiers that they had learned much about discipline and the value of obedience. They must not forget these lessons, but must be better men and show good examples to the other people who had to stay at home." The message was addressed to both veterans and the BIA. Well aware that federal agents would look with anxiety on the possibility that veterans had come back as troublemakers, Killspotted asked them to demonstrate that this would not be the case. In doing so, he also tried to assert his own influence over them. He was not alone. A few moments before he started his speech, a group of old warriors made it clear that dances would be a time when veterans would have to demonstrate their commitment to one set of values or the other, for "about a dozen old warriors entered the dance and, at least three young men, wounded in France, also took part for the first time. Later in the evening these young men were told that they were entitled to enter this dance at any time or place, but they must first prove that they had been wounded in action."[17]

The call of old warriors on young veterans to take part in dances should not be regarded as simply "traditional" but as a strategy fitted to the reservation context. It was meant to ensure that service in a non-Indian army would not result in a loss of connection to the "old ways." The appeal to "discipline" was a similar attempt to maintain established hierarchies in a context where Indian communities had lost most of their traditional control over their own warriors. In the Plains, telling of war deeds in front of fellow warriors was enough to assert an individual's claim to bravery and status as a warrior. Such a method of validation was now partly out of reach for Native communities. In World War I, the fight had taken place abroad, out of sight, and the only proof of an individual act of bravery was a citation written in English (or worse, French) by a non-Indian officer who in most cases would never set foot on the recipient's reservation.[18] Honorable discharges, citations, and medals were now the only and very bureaucratic proof of a veteran's deeds. On them depended not only tokens of appreciation by the veteran's family, friends, and neighbors but his access to health care and pension. Certain old warriors reacted to this by simply denying their young followers initiation into warrior societies; such was for example the case in Bullhead, on Standing Rock, where they were said to have refused to recognize trench warfare as manly enough to warrant induction. The argument, if real, was decidedly specious. But it speaks to the uncertain status of veterans in some communities.[19]

Doubted and Stigmatized

While they disagreed on the ideals veterans should embody, the BIA and elders on Indian reservations agreed on one fact: Veterans needed to be controlled as much as they were to be honored. And more often than not, doubt and stigma could replace distinction. Several factors conspired to build the image of the "bad boy" veteran. Ambivalence about the exercise of violence among populations that were by the time of World War I steeped in Christianity might have played a part, as well as older representations of the danger represented by young men marked by death and blood. But the very age of the new warriors was also a problem. As their frequent designation in English implied, the immense majority of them were mere "boys" and were collectively known under this label. They were individuals young enough to fight but insufficiently settled, often unmarried. To many of their elders, they needed to be protected against themselves, and communities needed to be protected against them as well. Behind the ideal of the citizen-soldier or the warrior fighting for his nation and his community, reservation societies were confronted with real veterans, in all their diversity, some drafted, some volunteers, some confined to training camp, others marked by their combat experience, some who worked in the Medical Corps, others in the trenches. New distinctions appeared among those had been in the war, and they were promptly materialized on the face of war monuments, whose makers scrupulously distinguished between the dead and the living but also between those who had seen the front lines and those who hadn't.[20]

Military pensions, an otherwise clear sign that a veteran had earned the attention of the nation, could also be seen as driving a wedge between veterans' relatives. Their amount varied depending on whether or not the veteran had served overseas. Getting a pension could tear families asunder instead of reinforcing their prestige and bolstering their financial status. So could the war risk insurance through which American political leaders had sought to prevent veterans' future claims for compensation. On Standing Rock, Joseph Takes The Shield Jr., Wakpala's hero, divided up his ten thousand dollars between his sister Angela and Cecilia, whom he regarded as his daughter but who was legally the child of another reservation denizen. After Joseph died, no agreement could be found between would-be beneficiaries. While Joseph Jr.'s plan received the support of reservation superintendent Eugene D. Mossman, the Veterans Bureau rejected it and transferred the entire amount to Joseph Sr.'s account. Pensions could also arouse the jealousy between families, especially when World War I veterans used their acumen to get them for their parents as well. In 1935, shortly after Francis Bullhead had managed to get one thanks to the help of Usher L. Burdick, the senator from North Dakota received a letter whose author bluntly stated: "If the Bullhead claim is allowed, [. . .] I don't see why mine should not be considered." As late as the 1960s, pension recipients could see their rights contested in no uncertain terms by jealous neighbors. Such a letter about Jacob Shoots Near, a veteran who died in 1968, reached the local Veterans Service Officer shortly after his death. In it, his widow was described as a money grabber who didn't need the money. The letter had no recorded effect on the awarding of the pension. But its very existence demonstrates that at least some individuals did not hesitate to have recourse to the authorities to see a perceived wrong redressed.[21]

We don't know if these rivalries and jealousies ever extended beyond letter-writing. We are much better informed on another, even clearer sign that veterans did not always live up to the ideal of community heroes: alcohol. Excessive drinking had long been blamed on Native Americans. As early as the seventeenth century, towns and governments had attempted to restrict the sale of strong liquor to the indigenous inhabitants of the continent. Regarded alternately as a cause of war, the origin of Indian depopulation, and the foremost explanation for their poverty, the sale and consumption of alcohol had been repeatedly criminalized throughout the nineteenth century. Missionaries especially had made a point of organizing temperance societies and instilling among Native Americans the idea that drinking was a moral sin. Until World War I, however, its consumption was not associated with any particular class of the American Indian population. This changed with military service in 1917 and 1918. Regardless of individuals' degree of inebriation or frequency of consumption, veterans began to be associated with the stigma of drunkenness. In the long run, the association between war service and alcoholism would serve to describe the World War I generation as affected by the trauma of combat. Native American traditionalists especially were prone to retrospectively ascribing this origin to the social problems they saw veterans of World War II or Vietnam struggling with. In the 1920s, no such conceptualization was available. Drinking simply signaled to whites and Indians alike that veterans were not only to be honored but needed to be forced into line. They would not, however, surrender without a fight. In Lac du Flambeau, the BIA superintendent made it clear to the central office that some of "his" veterans opposed vigorous efforts to his desire to discipline them: "Your office will note [...] that some have given me considerable trouble during the past year because of infraction of law; others are staid and sober minded in at least as far as their light permits them and are desirous of doing the best they can for themselves. [...] None of them that I can find belong to the Legion and with but one exception, I do not think any have kept up their insurance." Out of reach, rebellious and unaffiliated to the one organization that was supposed to regulate their collective existence, veterans were also drunken delinquents.

The accusation did not distinguish veterans much from other young men of the same age, who saw the same stigma attached to their "time off" behavior by both their white and their Indian neighbors. Neither did the accusation of licentiousness of promiscuity. But in 1929, in Bad River, another Ojibwa reservation, veterans were singled out by local leader Sam F. Denomie for their apartness, which Denomie saw as an excuse for immorality: "The overseas boys and those that were called into the training camps, there were 49 of them, formed a special organization for their special use, a perfectly healthy and clean organization. They rented a building to meet in and things were all right for a while, but they got to boozing there, and they are boozing there right now. You can go there any night and find boys and girls, old men and young girls, dodging around behind the building; there is no light there and it is perfectly shameful."

The apocalyptic vision of generations mingled in sin under the cover of darkness turned the Legion post (perhaps "John A. Sky Jr.," post no. 150 in Odanah, Wisconsin) into a devilish den. Veterans were more than troubled youngsters: They destroyed communities under the guise of patriotism, sheltered behind the walls of their normally respectable organization. On Standing Rock, an Indian boss farmer, Asa Littlecrow, made the same point: "Return soldiers are disturbing elements on Standing Rock Reservation, disregard all rules on reservation. We all realized that the soldiers boys give their lives to their country and while they are on overseas duty the citizens and Indians at home help their utmost to support the soldiers, and when they return we show them a good time, but in spite of that they even run away with another men's wife and break rules on reservation." Veterans, in other words, were taking advantage of the tolerance that their neighbors were at first willing to grant them. They abused it. For Eugene D. Mossman, they were at the forefront of the sexual laxity that had engulfed the Standing Rock Reservation after World War I. Native anthropologist Ella C. Deloria herself blamed the only case of incest she could think of on the reservation on the impact of the war. Whatever the specific causality they invoked, whether they blamed war, alcohol, or individuals' perversity, observers agreed that the World War I generation was a troubled one. Age was the problem, and World War I veterans would be all too willing, as they reached maturity, to fault veterans of the following conflict for the very same kind of behavior they had themselves been accused of. Yet there was more than intergenerational labeling going on: Alcohol consumption, and all the attendant behavior, was indeed a major way for veterans to distinguish themselves and to claim rights that other Indians were deprived of. It made sense as part of a behavior exhibiting freedom, in line with mobility, interracial socializing, and fighting for special rights.[22]

Pride and Humiliation

On reservations, claiming freedoms not allowed to others was indeed a common attitude of many Native veterans. If behaviors as diverse as drinking, "running around," talking back to BIA superintendents, and boasting of one's patriotism and heroism can be regarded as part of the same ethos—and they were by contemporaries—they pointed to a pattern of rebelliousness that came close to summing up veterans' collective identity. Alcohol in particular, always a symbol of reservation life's restrictions, had been consumed during the war by fellow soldiers. It stood for manliness, independence, and comradeship. Collective drunkenness was associated with the boastful telling of war deeds, and the many wartime episodes when it had been consumed, on furlough, after or even during combat. Drinking was a learned behavior, and veterans carefully cultivated the positive associations it brought to memory, inasmuch as most "good" memories of the war were connected to its consumption in one way or another. Sam Kenoi, among others, was particularly eager to remember nonmilitary "exploits" accomplished under its influence. Among those, sex or hints of sexuality, especially with French women, were a subject of frequent "commemoration." The joke of "babies left behind" abroad would be a link connecting different generations of veterans throughout the twentieth century. In 1928, the Society of Oklahoma Indians published in its newspaper an article inviting its readers, among them veterans, to reminisce on the "romance of a doughboy with maiden in sunny France." Evidently, such fantasies were not specific to Indian veterans. They had been part of a general American approach to wartime service in France as exotic and potentially titillating. Veterans on Standing Rock might have been far removed from the portraits as sexual predators that Asa Littlecrow drew of them. But enterprising sexuality and disregard of traditional boundaries separating sexes and races were nonetheless part of their collective image.[23]

Indeed, veterans were not content with drinking or propagating legends about their sexual lives. They actively claimed the right to be freed from the usual restrictions, especially in the case of alcohol. Particularly difficult in the 1920s in the midst of national prohibition, the claim began gaining traction in the 1930s, when the discrepancy between on-reservation restrictions and off-reservation free access to alcohol brought to light the discriminatory nature of the alcohol ban for Indians. The Legion hall, with its occasional bar (off reservations), became a focus of both drinking and claiming the right to drink. But the stigma did not abate: As veterans received their "bonus" in the 1930s, and sometimes "drank it" or used it to buy cars, they again became the object of criticism. Distrustful of their budgeting abilities, white observers denied them the right to use their money freely and insisted on seeing such expenses as a car as luxury items—even though transportation was a central problem of reservation life, as indeed of rural life anywhere in the United States. In other cases, they blamed veterans for drinking instead of looking for jobs. In July 1929, John Longmarsh, a Winnebago veteran, was intent on reversing the logic at play in such accusations. The commander of his Legion post, Longmarsh freely admitted to his drinking to a visiting U.S. senator and then regretted the ensuing trouble with the police. He did not, however, apologize for being out of work despite having been trained as a stone setter and demanded that the federal government find him a job. His superintendent denied him a letter of recommendation because of his drinking, but Longmarsh protested: The BIA agent should have acknowledged that it was joblessness that had made him drink in the first place. As the senator snappishly replied that unemployment was no excuse for drinking, Longmarsh launched into a jeremiad many other veterans had used: "Well, during the World War, when our country was in danger, they did not look at it that way, they took us regardless of whether we drank or not, and then when we go and risk our lives they send us back and we can find nothing to do to make a living and they are through with us."

In the context of depressed reservations on the eve of an even greater depression, Longmarsh connected the draft, alcohol, unemployment, veterans' preference, and the collective identity of his fellow veterans and Legionnaires in ways unexpected by the authorities. While we have no way to determine whether or not alcoholism made its mark on the World War I generation, the web of associations connecting alcohol to most other areas of veteran activism is remarkable. At a time when alcohol consumption was associated with sin and crime, Indian veterans could also boldly regard it as a war-connected right that had as much to do with officially sanctioned veterans' preference as it had with illegality. Connecting it to the uncertain legality of drafting Indians was a powerful rhetorical move to question the self-righteousness of veterans' accusers. It also made sense of individual trajectories, contrasting the violence of mandatory military service with the stigma of joblessness and abandon, thus opening the way for denouncing the scandal of the veterans' situation in the United States of the 1930s.[24]

Talking of alcohol often opened the way to talking about frustrated rights in general. Among other biographical themes, Native veterans were especially prone to remembering the difficulties they encountered upon returning home from war. The winter of 1918–1919, with its massive Spanish influenza epidemic, was a special focus of rememoration. Two percent of the Native American population died at the time, and many soldiers came home to find a least one parent dead from the flu. Such was the case of Jesse Cornplanter, a Seneca from New York. Anthropologist William N. Fenton, who wrote Cornplanter's biography and collaborated with him throughout his lifetime, particularly noted how Cornplanter chose to remember his traumatic return home as an event that Seneca warriors had often reported on in previous wars: Thinking they had reached home, they would find the charred remains of their villages and their families gone. But Cornplanter went further than his ancestors: He questioned the reasons why he had, against his father's wishes, volunteered in the Great War. At the same time, death in battle, he said, would have been preferable to losing his parents, brothers, and sisters to the flu. In an article published by the local press ("Indian Chief Returns from France to Find Kin Claimed by Death"), whites seemed to agree with this tragic representation of Cornplanter's war experience: "Much has been written of the loyalty of descendants of foreign-born parents and the exploits of the heroes have been no more pronounced in self-sacrifice than the deeds of Chief Jesse Cornplanter of the Cattaraugus Indian reservation," who was wounded and promoted on the battlefield only to come home to his new status as an orphan.[25]

The white press was less prone to criticize the rush on Indian lands that high agricultural prices had stimulated during the war and the forced granting of U.S. citizenship to veterans. This was, however, another event that remained durably associated with the end of the war on most Indian reservations and that veterans did not easily forget. Plowing and cultivating more land had seemed eminently patriotic in the wartime. It was also particularly congruent with the desires of many non-Indians in and around reservations to "free up" unused Indian land and make it marketable. In theory, this should also have resulted in lessened control from the BIA. Yet this was rarely the case, if only because inherited (or "heirship") lands remained under the control of the Indian Office, and with them the supposedly "emancipated" veterans, who were disproportionately concerned with the granting of citizenship. On Standing Rock in 1922 and 1923, 86 percent of veterans present were citizens, two-thirds of whom had become citizens between 1917 and 1919. In most cases, their military service was listed as proof of their competency in managing their own affairs, an essential requirement for attaining citizen status. Because the land of an emancipated Indian became taxable, citizenship was frequently accompanied by loss of land, as land was sold to pay for back taxes. Veterans like George Sleeps From Home, who hailed from the Kenel district of the Standing Rock Reservation, even remembered being especially targeted by such an operation. In 1943, reminiscing on the past to better prepare the return of the World War II generation, he looked back on his first years as a veteran: "I would say that most of this patent-fee Indians did not know what they were signing at the time. As to the ex-service-men, the Indian police ordered all the Indian ex-servicemen to the agency to sign up. Some disobeyed orders and still retain their allotments." But Sleeps From Home himself was among those who had obeyed, and he always regretted it.

In certain cases, even shadier dealings allowed white guardians of Indian veterans to gain control of their wards' properties. William Hickman, a Choctaw alumnus of the Chilocco boarding school, remembered that his guardian had forced him to sign a will in his favor before going to war. The practice was so common in Oklahoma that the state historian, Grant Foreman, finally took it upon himself to denounce it to the BIA. Outright dispossession, however, mattered less than the perceived—and scandalous—conjunction of return from home, granting of citizenship, and loss of land.[26]

Such widespread associations were compounded by a phenomenon white veterans would have recognized as intolerable as well: the impossibility for Native veterans to have preferential access to jobs. In the 1920s, the Army remained the most likely way for Native American veterans to recycle their hard-earned skills and find a job based on their wartime experience. Some managed to get valuable technical training there, but few kept their rank. Contracts were limited to three years, and for veterans like James McCarthy, a Tohono O'odham, staying in the Army was more a way to keep "seeing the world" than a professional career. It merely delayed the return to the jobless environment of reservations.

The moral and legal recognition of "veterans' preference" held greater promises. Starting in 1919, it granted honorably discharged soldier veterans priority in federal jobs. On reservations, this privilege became connected to the long-standing claim of Indian populations that they should be given priority in hiring in the local branches of the BIA. But military service proved an unequally efficient way to claim a job. Several niches opened up in federal employment the 1920s. Under the patronage of a Peoria civil servant in the BIA, Charles E. Dagenett, a member of the Society of American Indians, a handful of veterans managed to regain positions lost during the war. Alwin Hawley, a Haskell Institute alumnus and an "exemplary young man" according to his superiors, worked at the BIA's Chicago Warehouse in 1917. After his return from France, as he dabbled with the idea of working in the private sector, Hawley contacted Dagenett and managed to be hired on his own reservation at Fort Peck,

Montana. Schools were another sector where veterans, most of them former students, were valued for their knowledge of military drill and discipline, and physical fitness. After his service in the Navy, Joseph J. Gurnoe became a teacher of physical education. Others were hired as aides and disciplinarians.

Working as Indian police was another job connected symbolically and technically to at least some military duties, and it had, for many Indian peoples, the benefit of an ancient association with warrior duties. But positions as Indian policemen were limited in number, and cutbacks in the 1920s did not help. Policing did not provide Indians with steady employment, and veteran status was often far from an overriding criterion for jobs that fell under the patronage of the local BIA superintendent. On Standing Rock, Henry One Feather, himself a policeman's son, managed to make BIA employment a regular source of income throughout the 1920s and 1930s. Trained in mechanics, carpentry, painting, and farming, he alternated work on his land and temporary positions as janitor for the BIA agency, handyman at the BIA school in Fort Yates, night watchman, road hand, and policeman before taking advantage of the work relief programs of the New Deal era. His case was not an isolated one: On other reservations too, patriotism and skills acquired in the military were not enough to solve veterans' employment issues. Even when they claimed preference, most veterans were restricted to odd jobs, repairing roads and buildings or filling janitorial positions.[27]

The Patriotic Presentation of Self

Confronted with limited opportunities and unyielding control, Native veterans started presenting themselves as betrayed and ignored. Their position was complex, for the moral right they had to the attention of the nation was closely connected to citizenship, in many cases the root cause of their predicament. Theirs was therefore a problem of adapting to the specific context of the reservation rights that were, by their very nature, to be universally applied to all American veterans. This turned veterans' public utterances into balancing acts, moments when they needed to articulate the conformity of their itineraries to the patriotic norm, emphasizing sacrifice, suffering, contempt for slackers, and willingness to volunteer, while also negotiating access to financial compensation, health care, and jobs that were extremely difficult to come by on reservations' isolated territories. This required training and gave each individual veteran's self-presentation utmost importance. To claim anything, a veteran had to act and talk like one.

The first months of service brought this point home soon enough. Perhaps more than combat, which many of them didn't see, military service was an opportunity for inexperienced young men to learn how to face gigantic bureaucracies armed with the sole weapons of patriotic rhetoric and pen and paper. Beginning in January 1918, the BIA had authorized the Young Men's Christian Association and the Knights of Columbus to draw up a census of Indian soldiers in training camps, so as better to protect them against the evils of camp life and discrimination. Young soldiers were after all the leaders of tomorrow. But in the tents put up by these organizations, more than Christian indoctrination took place. On YMCA letterhead, soldiers wrote home to their families and friends, to their schools, and to the BIA intent on defending their rights. From Camp Sevier, in Greenville, South Carolina, Ernest Red Feather (Rosebud Lakota) complained of being mistreated and thrown in jail. For the first time in his life, perhaps, he attempted to use his belonging to the group of "the only real Americans," as he wrote, to attempt to be released, going as far as to compare his condition to that of German prisoners of war. With about a third of all Native Americans not yet U.S. citizens in 1917, other soldiers were more interested in figuring out under which law they had been drafted. Camp life was a good moment for someone like Todd Harden Smith, also from Rosebud, to make inquiries as to his rights: "I would like to know all about the rules of an Indian becoming a soldier." The first months of the war had seen several tribes protesting collectively against the draft. In camp, the protestors were sometimes small groups but most often isolated individuals requesting BIA intervention.

Getting their information from one another or from their fellow white soldiers, Indian recruits learned about their rights piecemeal but tried to use them as soon as possible. What were they entitled to, as soldiers and as Indians? What were their duties? How far were they supposed to obey? Answering those questions meant coming to terms with the related facts that, at least for the duration of the service, their lives had been nationalized and that "national" rationales were the most likely to help them get what they wanted. Loyalty toward teachers, schoolmates, schools—all groups that the young soldier was supposed not to "let down" by proving unequal to his new task—was rapidly construed as a stepping stone toward loyalty to the nation in general. Whether they were confronted with the bureaucracies of the secretary of war or the secretary of the interior and the BIA, Indian soldiers swiftly learned to use the common parlance of World War I doughboys. Their talk of "sacrifice," "right," "fairness" and "justice," "doing one's bit" for "one's country," going "across" to fight "the Hun" or "the Boches" as "real Americans" was not simply a way to get their message across. It became part of their public identities, a legacy from the war as tangible as discharge papers and body wounds.[28]

In wartime, forceful affirmation of patriotism and anxious attempts to get released from the service had been common among Indian soldiers. After the war, memories were recentered on the idea that military service had been a duty that most had simply gone along with. In one of the rare instances where one can guess at this most personal of evolutions, William Menz, from Standing Rock, answered two questionnaires on his service, one in 1920, the other in 1921. In the first one, he emphasized the "good cause" of fighting for freedom. In the second, "duty" had become the only justification for enlisting. Peter O. Barnaby, from Flathead, Montana, wrote letters for an entire year from Camp Lewis in Washington state; Long Island, New York; and finally "somewhere in France," asking to be released from the service. "If you only knew," he wrote, "how it feels to be the only Indian in the Co. I don't think I'm being treated fair." But in the climate of 1921, Barnaby found he could do little else but claim that "I didn't have to go, but I wanted to go. I wanted to go and fight for the flag." Constraint had to be taken out of the picture, replaced by consent and patriotism. In the postwar years, mobilized by their communities in patriotic ceremonies as model Indians, veterans could not waste time on nuances. Their discourse had to emphasize the pride of wearing the uniform, even the willingness to reenlist if necessary.[29]

Letters written in wartime could evoke the violence inflicted and suffered by the soldier. In letters from the front, especially, violence surfaced. Thus did Welch Teesateskie, an Eastern Cherokee from North Carolina, euphemistically admit: "I had some awful times." John Morgan, an Ojibwa recruit, described, in a vein that was not rare in soldiers' correspondence, how shocked he had been by a French landscape where "everything was smashed on the battlefields and dead men horses and trucks laid here and there which was put out of use." "Warrior traditions" were unequal to the task of coming to terms with shelling and other manifestations of industrialized warfare. In a song composed after returning home, Andrew Black-hawk, a Winnebago from Wisconsin, did not hesitate to confess to fear: "Early in the morning the bullets passed by us so thick, and I am scared." Amputated limbs, tuberculosis prompted by gas attacks, and depression (called "neurasthenia") were not edited out of the letters. Even on reservations, the idea that the war had been a calamity was openly expressed by people like this "old man of the Teton-Dakota on the Standing Rock Reservation" who refused to volunteer ethno-botanic information for anthropologist Melvin R. Gilmore, complaining that "we have enough misfortune already, counting the war and the epidemic of influenza, without inviting further disaster by such sacrilege." But after the war, rare were the veterans who, like William B. Newell, a Mohawk, an alumnus from the University of Syracuse, a pastor, and, during the war, an interpreter to General John J. Pershing, denounced the "atrocious propaganda, the damnable lies told about the German soldiers during the World War, simply to rouse the hatred of the Allied forces to a point where they would spill their blood in fighting them." By contrast, Newell emphasized the idyllic nature of social life among Iroquois before the advent of the white man, describing the Iroquois Confederacy as both the first democracy and the first league of nations. Newell also wrote that Iroquois ways inspired U.S. democracy and that his people promoted health and had invented freedom of religion, freedom of expression, women's suffrage, divorce, and birth control. But his Christian denunciation of the evils of war was more isolated than his promotion of Indian values.[30]

Even rarer were denunciations of racial discrimination in the service. The centrality of ethnic and racial representations during recruitment and induction had meant that a significant number of

Indian recruits had likely suffered from what historian and Vietnam-era veteran Tom Holm designated as "the scout syndrome." Unfamiliar with the notion but all too familiar with its manifestations, William Fire Thunder, from Pine Ridge, denounced it to anthropologist H. Scudder Mekeel in 1931. Because of their perceived natural-born skills in tracking and ambush, Indian soldiers were often selected for patrol or night duty. Firethunder's experience is borne out by the Eddy report, which found that 102 individuals, or 8.8 percent of the sample studied, had served as scouts during World War I. After the war, however, specific complaints regarding military service per se were drowned out and jingoistic proclamations, such as that of this Native American Marine, became commonplace: "I of course like any other American Warrior couldn't stay at home while others facing the bullets." Denouncing "slackers" who had dodged the draft became an integral part of veterans' identity, expressed in ironic songs like that of the Pawnees: "Our beloved flag went across the ocean and came back./Are you really glad to see it back again?" Indeed, the fear of being called a slacker had been a distinct part of the desire to enlist. Andrew Beechtree, an Oneida from Wisconsin, who worked in the automobile industry before the war, admitted as much twenty-plus years later when, reminiscing on his enlistment, he simply stated that he had felt lonely after his friends enlisted and feared they would call him a slacker. For someone like Kiutus Tecumseh, a descendant of the famous Shawnee chief who was particularly active in the defense of Indian citizenship, not being a slacker and its corollary—being a veteran—were indeed indispensable qualifications for any Indian intent on tackling the most necessary task of all: taking on the Indian Bureau. From a constraint to a duty to a requirement for public action, military service needed to be reframed if it was to become what many Indian (and non-Indian) veterans hoped it would be after the war ended: a source of rights. And many veterans understood this.[31]

The Scandals and Rewards of Veteran Life

For Indian veterans who lived on reservations, establishing patriotic credentials mattered in several specific contexts. When talking to outsiders, displaying patriotism helped identify Indian veterans with other American veterans. It bolstered their claims for equal rights and compensation. On the reservation, it was a common tactic of those veterans who wanted to escape the scrutiny of the BIA without being branded as radicals, rebels, or reactionaries. As soon as they came back, many Native veterans started questioning every aspect of bureaucratic control on their respective reservations, sometimes gesturing toward the use of violence, symbolic or otherwise. Roy G. Coffey returned to Pine Ridge and found out that his brother-in-law had died before paying for a horse Coffey had sold him. Coffey wrote the superintendent, threatening the BIA agent with a suit if the "damn horse" wasn't paid for soon. Profanity, learned and heavily practiced in the service, had no place on the reservation, and the superintendent threatened Coffey back with a fine. Characteristically, veterans worked their conflict out through letters: habits of protesting on paper, acquired in the war years, came in handy on reservations. As in Coffey's case, many veterans protested against the controls placed on their finances. On the Crow reservation, veterans requested free use of their accounts at the BIA agency. The superintendent then complained that "some of our young men who have bank accounts in this office are under the impression that the regulations governing the handling of Individual Indian Money permit of turning over their entire bank balances to them upon request because they are returned soldiers." His protest had little effect on veterans. Not content to claim their money, some even criticized the sacrosanct principle that all Indians, and veterans first among them, should receive citizenship. The very possibility that such a move would result in loss of land was not lost on them.[32]

Refusing citizenship was a tricky move, for it was the foundation of veterans' rights and of their ability to claim help outside reservations from white veterans and white-majority veterans' organizations. If veterans had any claim to being especially oppressed by the Bureau, it was based on the citizen-soldier principle, which, applied to Indians, meant that individuals who had demonstrated their loyalty in times of war deserved the full measure of citizenship after the Armistice. The scandal of "reservation life" needed to be denounced as a personal wrong suffered by patriots in spite of wartime promises of equality and freedom. On Standing Rock, John Red Bean, a Santee Dakota who had left BIA boarding schools for the Canadian

Army before deserting and reenlisting in the U.S. armed forces, served in France and was demobilized in February 1919. Back home, he discovered that his mother and sister had died of the flu. A few months later, he minced no words in a letter to the commissioner of Indian affairs. Because it articulates themes that were to become ubiquitous in public utterances by veterans in later years, his text warrants lengthy quotation:

> I had my discharge and came back to civilian life. Rather say in Reservation Life, as we are not citizens and taken care us by the government and wished to say something about this as we entitled to received our full citizens. As we went across the Ocean and do our bit for our country and now we got home safe and we loose some of our best friends as now I am I civilian life and still in government life. And it's the same as soldier life we need pass to leave Reservation and they told us we a Trust Patent Indians as long as we are not citizens of the United States by Regulation we are entitled to it as they told me I will obey the Rules and Regulations of the Reserve for which I object as I take a chances on my life to do something for my country and I did. So am I entitled to obtain my paper or where I will get out from or applied for. As I don't like this Reserve life. And why they don't stop the Indian boys from being drafting as the Indian Department always talked about the Trust Patent Indian and they could not do as what they please. I kindly wished the give us liberty and do as we please, to go where we want and etc. I wished this matter will be pushed on for the Indian soldiers boys who were in France as I am in need of citizenship papers.

Red Bean's flow of demands and complaints couldn't have been more incisive. He denounced the double standard of Indian patriotism and citizenship, specifically pointing out the concrete consequences of "reservation life" (or "reserve life": his Canadian stay might be showing here), a life of "passes" and "rules and regulations" that looked an awful lot like wartime restrictions. So incisive was he, indeed, that five months later his wish for a freer life was granted. Instead of a "trust patent" he received a title in fee simple for the land he owned on Standing Rock—a passport to U.S. citizenship that he obtained without having to claim it under the Act that, less than a week before, had granted citizenship to all Indian veterans who officially requested it. By 1920, Red Bean was in Canada. His was a successful itinerary of going to war, coming home, and claiming and gaining rights that less than a decade before had been reserved to a small reservation elite. Red Bean's desire that he and other veterans "do as we please"—an undeniable attribute of the manhood for which BIA agents professed to train Indians—was favorably looked upon in the immediate postwar years, and he was among those that took advantage of it. Raising scandal could bring immediate rewards.[33]

In other cases, denouncing the scandal of veterans' trampled rights started as a losing battle, the better to become a part of veterans' identities. This was especially the case of veterans who, in the 1920s, tried to have their war-related ailments acknowledged by federal agencies and veterans' organizations. Before the war, Jesse Cornplanter had collaborated with anthropologists like Arthur C. Parker and had been familiar with the non-Indian world. He had even worked in the automobile factory of the Willys-Overland Company in Toledo, Ohio. In 1918, left without a family on his native reservation in New York state, Cornplanter went back to Toledo but found only temporary employment. This was in part because of depression and the consequences of gas attacks suffered during the war. Cornplanter sojourned several times in Veterans Bureau hospitals, moved to the Allegany reservation, then to Buffalo, where he managed to stay until the beginning of the 1930s, surviving on odd jobs, the salary of lectures on Indian culture, and help received from white friends like Joseph Keppler, a white cartoonist who was also a collector of Iroquois artifacts and an ardent defender of Indian causes. Cornplanter actively tried to be granted a pension for disability, at first without success. Sickness and hardship prompted the beginning of a painful awareness for him. As he told Keppler, "My case has been a hard affair—due to the reason that I did not take prompt action when relapse first set in. [. . .] I did not know where to apply." He had had a chance to rise up in the ranks at Willys-Overland, but "I like a fool enlisted." In a January 1926 letter sent from a soldier's home in Dayton, Ohio, and signed "your Indian veteran," Cornplanter further told Keppler how the American Legion and Veterans Bureau had turned their backs on him and decided his depression and tuberculosis were not service-connected, despite medical opinion to the contrary. "In order to be entitled to any kind of help, I had to humiliate myself." Later he explained: "They just refused me aid, denying my rights for being Indian and referred me to State charity and Welfare, who also did the same, on account of not being resident and me a Native 100% American, good enough to volunteer for service and being disabled, also being in past a legionnaire [. . .] I am fed up. [. . .] all I can say: there is something wrong [. . .] But I did my little bit like a man. In a way, deep down in me, I am proud of the fact, whether I die a pauper or get my just due."[34]

The suspicion that it was his Indian identity that prevented Cornplanter from benefiting from the attention that was his due became part of his identity as a cheated veteran and foolish patriot. He easily pinpointed the origin of his problems: "I am suffering now from that patriotism feeling that blinded me back in 1917–1918." It was altogether another issue to deny that his war experience held any form of benefit. On the contrary, Cornplanter thought that "army life has taught me the meaning of duty." But his health issues were soon compounded by economic hardship. With the onset of the Great Depression, return to the reservation to avoid the expense of "city life" was a solution he didn't take to kindly: "For me living on the reservation is a detriment, just a set-back. No place for one with ambition. I prefer being elsewhere."

By the end of the 1920s, Cornplanter finally started cashing in on his hard-earned patriotic credentials. He received his first loan on the government certificate that would allow him to claim, in 1945, the "bonus" granted all veterans in 1924. In 1931, he managed to see his handicap recognized and received his first monthly check from the Veterans Bureau. Soon, however, his monthly allowance took a big dip with Depression-era federal cutbacks, and he found it necessary to turn to charities or even New York's representative in Congress, before being allowed to take advantage of certain New Deal programs. In 1938, he published a book of Iroquois legends illustrated by himself, thirty-five years after his first endeavors in the field. His war ailments made him slow as well as irritable and, by his own account, dependent on alcohol. "The dog-gone war ruined me,"

"I am still fighting the war," "I've never been the same man since Sept. 29, 1918," he wrote Keppler, referring to the day he was gassed. For Cornplanter, getting a new disability rating remained a lifelong endeavor. In the words of his friend, anthropologist William N. Fenton, it had, by the end of his life, become a career in itself. Despite his conflicts with the American Legion, he never renounced his membership and later joined the Disabled American Veterans. His identity was profoundly tied up with his sense of unrequited and "foolish" patriotism in 1917.[35]

Few Native American veterans' "careers" are as fully documented as Cornplanter's. But in his dogged fidelity to the American Legion and determination to keep trying to make sense of a war experience that became more and more difficult to justify as time passed, the Iroquois veteran was not isolated. Even when they shut their doors to them, bureaucracies dealing with veterans' issues were essential to veterans' sense of self and distinction from non-veterans. Hospitals and soldiers' homes such as that from which Cornplanter wrote became especially important to veterans. For Indian veterans, they made available services that were all but nonexistent on reservations and very hard to gain access to anywhere else. They even created a distinct veterans' geography around reservations. Ex-servicemen from Standing Rock could thus go to the Hot Springs Battle Mountain Sanatorium in South Dakota; to the veterans' hospital in Fargo, North Dakota; to the Army hospital in Helena or the VA hospital in Harrison, Montana; to Fort Riley, Kansas; and, in Minnesota, to Fort Snelling, St. Cloud, or St. Paul. Martin Medicine, a veteran from Wakpala, went to one of these facilities in 1935 for a simple appendectomy. Many like him felt they were better treated in there than in the regular BIA hospitals. Moreover, veterans' hospitals were places where ex-soldiers could engage in interracial relations with white veterans but also, in states with large Indian populations, in exclusively Indian relations. After getting married on the Pine Ridge Reservation, Thomas Bad Cobb, a very young veteran, was sent to the Hot Springs sanatorium for a heart condition. There he met an Indian woman at a fair and started a romantic relationship with her. While BIA judges sued him for adultery, they decided not to be too hard on him, as the young veteran showed "considerable promises." Despite its origin in sickness and suffering, the medical mobility of veterans was another way to claim the freedom and rights they had earned in war.[36]

This last point should also help us put into perspective claims that Indian veterans suffered from a special kind of oblivion and distinguish between claimed and felt injustice and what little of the reality of injustice is still accessible to historians. In 1925, the widow of the same Lieutenant Eddy who had surveyed Indian veterans for their scouting skills wrote the American Legion to denounce the abandonment of "First American" veterans by federal agencies. In good "Friend of the Indians" fashion, Edith H. Eddy was evidently trying to play on the old trope of the "vanishing American." But contrary to her claims that Native American veterans were forgotten by federal authorities, there is evidence that as early as 1923 the Veterans Bureau made sure they were getting the same kind of services as their non-Indian colleagues. In the winter of that year, following the nomination of General Frank T. Hines to reform an agency that had become mired in controversy, the Veterans Bureau organized tours of reservations in the Plains and the Southwest. In Minnesota, the Dakotas, and Montana, the touring team was composed of a general practitioner, a specialist in trachoma and tuberculosis—diseases that were extremely widespread on Indian reservations—and a representative of the Veterans Bureau who helped Indian veterans fill out claims for health care or pensions. According to the Bureau, the team met with considerable success. Their visit was in part justified by racial stereotypes: While not all agreed that Indian veterans bore their trauma any differently from non-Indians, practitioners still blamed a tradition of remaining "stoic" in the face of hardship and hiding pain and wounds for Indians' unwillingness to claim compensation or even check their mail for information on their rights. This was a misinformed view. But this program of the Veterans Bureau testified to the creation of a relationship between Indian veterans and the federal government that was, for once, mostly unmediated by the Bureau of Indian Affairs. Started in the 1920s for some, the relationship with the federal medical services was often rekindled in veterans' declining years. On Standing Rock, Alphonse Bear Ghost, from Cannonball, was a patient of the Veterans Administration hospital in Fargo in 1971. In the 1960s, Guy Chapman, from Fort Yates, spent part of his retirement years in the home for ex-soldiers in Lisbon, North Dakota, as did Joseph Grey Day, also from Cannonball, who, writing in December 1963, had nothing but praise for the institution, enchanted as he was at the "modern heated rooms, laundry every week, and meals," and thanking his county Veteran Service Officer for filling out his application. Just like Cornplanter, these veterans, who were particularly active in the 1920s in claiming rights for veterans, could feel vindicated. They were not systematically short-changed by the system.[37]

Individual examples can do little more than reinforce the idea that the ability of Native veterans to claim privileges varied according to their case and throughout their lifetimes. They are evoked here to give an idea of the variability of their conditions—a variability that was often all but lost in public claims by veterans and non-veterans who claimed to speak in the name of them all. Having become familiar in the war and in the immediate postwar years with the expectations and rewards that were associated with their status, veterans quickly learned to fashion their discourse to make the best use of this status in reservations, in a time of often grinding poverty. They developed an ability to use the stereotype of the super-patriotic Indian veteran to struggle against the oppressive aspects of reservation life or their own status as would-be models for Indian youth. This meant insisting on the specific injustices they had suffered in the war or upon returning home. This also meant making use of their own organizations to develop a social life that allowed them the freedom they were denied under BIA control. While not all made this into a "career," most learned to articulate specific historical and personal sequences (enlisting, getting citizenship, losing their land) and politically laden feelings: pride in their ethnicity or race, being owed something by the nation, rebelling against the scandal of dispossession and refused benefits. The war did not mark their itineraries only as "time off" or "time away" but also a time of political education. It brought a sense of rights, debt, and loyalty that could be mobilized by veterans as they struggled to create identities for themselves as tribal members, citizens, and members of the U.S. nation. In this configuration, actual combat meant much less than it used to in warrior days. Native veterans' status needed to be made sense of within a relationship with the state. This supposed a careful balance between conformity and rebelliousness, fidelity to their home communities and to the rest of the country. Specifically, they needed to prove the compatibility of their war-earned rights with treaty rights, so important on so many reservations. Because most of them lived on reservation, they also had to frame their problems as part of the major political struggle of their time: fighting off the Indian Office.

CHAPTER FIVE

Patriotic Rewards,
New Freedoms

T HE TIME PERIOD opened by the end of World War I could appear full of possibilities for Indians desirous of questioning their political position in the United States—but also full of risks. The Paris Conference of 1919 settled the war in Europe, created the League of Nations, and worked as a major forum for "small nations" wishing to claim the Wilsonian principle of self-determination. Many Indian activists were eager to use the principle to reform Indian affairs at home. They called for the end of wardship for their fellow Indians and demanded the demise of the Indian Bureau. At the same time, many of them had also become aware that claiming U.S. citizenship unrestricted by BIA regulations, one of the strongest claims pushed by Indian activists on the national political scene, could have negative effects on Indians' rights. Officially a war waged by free citizens against imperial subjects, the European conflict had legitimized the imposition of citizenship on more and more Indians. To non-Indians, their loyalty in the war seemed to demand it: Indians had acted as citizen-soldiers and deserved to be granted the full rights attached to this status. Citizenship, however, brought taxation, and taxation resulted in loss of Indian land. With the end of the conflict, enemies of Indians' collective rights showed clear intentions to continue this policy, and used the idea that the nation owed veterans a debt to unmoor them (and their land) from Bureau protection and further Indians' assimilation.[1]

In this context, Native veterans and patriots were placed in an ambiguous position. They could claim rights as deserving members of the nation, but they risked losing much in the process. Indian veterans, like their white comrades in arms, soon organized to be granted special rewards for their military service. In the United States, the idea that the nation owed a debt to its ex-soldiers had been articulated with special force since the Civil War. As the country joined the European Allies in the Great War, Congress anticipated future ex-servicemen's demands and settled for what they regarded as the most economical option. With the War Risk Insurance

Act Amendments of 1917, congressmen guaranteed that soldiers' families would be entitled to a $10,000 life insurance policy, provided their relative in the service had paid his monthly dues. Specific aid in the form of pensions and services would be given, but only to the wounded and the disabled, as well as to the families of war dead. For Coolidge, Harding, and Hoover, the three Republican presidents of the 1920s, military service was a duty that entailed few if any rights, and fiscal conservatism represented the ultimate rationale for any policy regarding veterans. The American Legion, outraged by what it regarded as a betrayal of the moral contract binding the nation in its dealings with veterans, mobilized. Its leadership and rank and file united to get the federal government to grant veterans an "adjusted compensation." Veterans, as deserving citizen-soldiers, were to be paid back the salaries they lost by serving in the armed forces of the nation, or rather the difference between these salaries and their measly Army pay. In 1924, all honorably discharged veterans were issued a certificate testifying to the compensation owed them. Under the new legislation, however, this was to be paid them in 1945 only. In the meantime, they would only be allowed to get a grant from the Veterans Bureau, the amount of which was limited to a maximum of 22.5 percent of their total "compensation." Indian veterans were part of the fight. That same year, all Indians born in the United States were granted citizenship.[2]

Claiming patriotic rewards without claiming citizenship, or claiming citizenship without losing Indians' special rights: This was the delicate balancing act Indian patriots were required to maintain. It meant redefining the privileges attached to citizenship and military service and connecting them with privileges, rights, and customs (such as treaty rights or Indian dances) that non-Indians rarely regarded as patriotic. Imagining solutions to this problem and inventing patriotic rights in the process required political activism of a new kind, one that bridged Indian and non-Indian rights and discourses, transcended reservation boundaries, and explored the intersection of universalistic soldier-citizenship and the particularistic condition of being Indians in the United States. The 1920s were a testing time for Native patriots and a testing ground for this new strategy. In the process, they asked troubling questions: Could Indians be freed from BIA supervision? And with what consequences?

Patriotism suggested new answers to what was, after all, the core of the "Indian problem."

The Republican Synthesis

Beginning in the 1860s, self-appointed "Friends of the Indians" addressed the need to locate Native Americans in the U.S. body politic as "the Indian problem" or "the Indian question." Along with the "problem," they formulated as a "solution" the complete cultural and political assimilation of Indians. Indian wars and Indian reservations were but temporary delays, even stepping-stones for a project that envisioned the eventual demise of Indians' collective life and separateness. "Friends of the Indians," banding together in influential societies and clubs such as the Board of Indian Commissioners or the Indian Rights Association, stood in an ambivalent relationship with the Bureau of Indian Affairs. They monitored it, criticized it, but also justified its existence by claiming the need to protect the Indians from unscrupulous whites and from themselves. Foremost among their concern was the Bureau's handling of the rights that Indians had acquired by treaty. Could those be compatible with U.S. citizenship? Were Indian claims based on treaties to be handled administratively, or did they require judicial intervention? Could the Bureau be part of the solution, or was it part of the problem?

To ascertain the limits of Indian citizenship or of BIA trusteeship, many "Friends of the Indians" did not hesitate to turn to the courts. One major venue, however, was closed to Indian groups from the start: the U.S. Court of Claims. Announced in 1863, the impossibility of suing the United States severely limited Indians' ability to claim redress against the BIA afterward, as they needed to acquire special jurisdictional acts to be able to access the Court. Between 1880 and 1918, only thirty such complaints were filed. After World War I, however, momentum built to adjudicate Indian claims once and for all, and Indian claims were allowed in the Court of Claims on a much more liberal basis. Between 1918 and 1946, they reached a total of two hundred, the number accruing by a range of five to nineteen a year. "Friends of the Indians" regarded easier access to courts as a demonstration of the nation's sense of honor and justice. They also saw it as the only respectable way to remove a major stumbling block on the road to solving the "Indian problem." Adjudicating treaty claims went hand in hand with promoting citizenship, including voting rights, and assimilation into the U.S. body politic. Invoking Indians' loyalty during the war provided the high moral ground for such endeavors. Indians, however, developed their own interpretations of the relationships linking military service, treaty rights, and citizenship rights. As observations made in Sioux country demonstrate, Indians could take claims based on treaty rights into directions unanticipated by their "Friends."

The Sioux Jurisdictional Act was adopted on June 3, 1920, less than two years after the end of the war. The Act allowed representatives of the Sioux Nation (the legal name covering the bands of the Western Sioux, or Lakota, with whom the United States had signed treaties as early as 1815) to sue the United States for the recovery of a very specific and valuable territory: the Black Hills of South Dakota. Reserved for Indians under the 1868 treaty of Fort Laramie, the Black Hills had been taken under duress through another treaty in 1877. As early as the 1890s, councils had been held on Sioux reservations to obtain compensation for the Black Hills. Twelve reservations were concerned in the United States. On the eve of World War I, organizing such councils had become an important political activity on many of them. The movement did not abate during the war. In the midst of the conflict, representatives of the Sioux Nation held councils and looked for a tribal lawyer to uphold their cause. Reservation denizens involved in the claims process also began to conceptualize military service as the guarantee that Sioux demands would be addressed. Some, on Pine Ridge, later remembered that they had refused at first to enlist, as they were bound by treaty not to take up arms against whites again. This was an interpretation of old peace treaties shared by many Native Americans throughout the country. On Pine Ridge, according to one testimony, communities had agreed to let their sons ignore this clause and enlist without going through medical examination, but on very specific conditions. The federal government was to give pensions to all tribal members and agree to the return of the Black Hills. In April 1918, Sioux delegates at an inter-reservation council on the Crow Creek reservation further declared: "We have proven ourselves faithful citizens, defending our common country with our white brothers with our young men and money. Surely we deserve some justice and liberty—the liberty and freedom for which we are all fighting." They were ready to take advantage of Sioux loyalty and patriotism to push for the final adjudication of their claims in U.S. courts.[3]

Harry L. Gandy, the Democratic representative for South Dakota, made no mention of the war in his speech in defense of the Sioux Act. Speaking only of "right" and "justice," he nevertheless used the moral context of the immediate afterwar period to justify an act the benefits of which he hoped would be a definitive settlement of the vexed question of Indian ownership in South Dakota. To the Lakota on the Rosebud Reservation, Gandy insisted that he defended the bill as part of an agreement with the Indian Office. The agreement involved allowing the BIA to offset its expenses for the benefit of the Sioux from the overall amount of the compensation sought from the U.S. Court of Claims. In practical terms, Gandy was pushing for a policy that would come to be regarded as termination: Settle Indian claims so as to give white settlers a firmer ownership of their lands, end special Indian rights based on treaties, and bring an end to the collective existence of bands, tribes, and reservation groups. Gandy's motivations were probably even more complex, if one is to take into account the electoral considerations that likely went into his thinking. As William Williamson, his successor, explained in 1920, any candidate in federal elections in South Dakota needed to take into consideration the fact that at least a portion of the Sioux in this state were voters. Some of them were explicit about their intention to trade votes for help in the Black Hills suit. In June 1923, one month after the Black Hills claim had been filed, Williamson himself visited the Rosebud Reservation. There, he participated in a celebration of Indian Day and courted Indian voters. He also discussed the Black Hills issue and publicly expressed his support for the idea that representatives of the Sioux nation should come together in a general council in 1920 to better pursue the claim. Like his predecessor, the South Dakota representative made use of patriotism to couple the promotion of Indian rights with ultimately assimilationist goals. Patriotic occasions were ideal to voice calls for justice. But such calls could not be made without tackling the most prized measure of political justice: the franchise.[4]

After World War I, treaty rights, voting rights, and patriotism appeared indeed closely associated with one another. Locally, if not nationally or at the state level, participation in the war made it possible for Indians to use the right to vote on an unprecedented scale. One of the most concrete consequences was their heightened ability to strike alliances with white politicians. In the case of North Dakota in the 1910s, Indian males who desired to vote needed to prove to the state that they had relinquished their "tribal relations," a concept that encompassed traditional Indian ways of life, ignorance of the white world and white customs, and collective ownership of land. Renouncing a perceived Indianness was paramount if they wanted to acquire effective voting rights. On election day, non-Indian election officers were in charge of assessing the severing of individual Indians' "tribal relations," and the situation left ample room for discrimination and arbitrariness. In 1918, in the county of Sioux, North Dakota, which covered the northern half of the Standing Rock Reservation, the issue was raised during the war as part of a larger contest to determine the location of the county's seat, four years after the county itself had been organized. Two towns competed for the title: Fort Yates, already the seat of the BIA, and Selfridge, a white railroad town with high ambitions of economic development. As early as 1916, a local newspaper, *The Sioux County Pioneer,* called on Indian voters to bring their opinion to bear on the issue, preferably in favor of Fort Yates. Hundreds were concerned, since the BIA had started delivering certificates of competency entitling them to citizenship. In 1918, Fort Yates won the vote by 106 votes. Supporters of Selfridge immediately contested the 56 ballots coming from the voting precinct of Rogers Creek, peopled with Sioux whose lands were still under the guardianship of the Bureau of Indian Affairs. Martin Swift, a county official, filed a complaint, arguing that these individuals could not be citizens and vote. The local court did not agree with Swift: The status of their lands should not deprive Indians of their voting rights even though they remained wards of the federal government.

The county court's decision did little more than confirm what was already going on: Indian voting was taking place on a large scale in North Dakota, whether Indians had been formally granted citizenship or not, and politicians at the local and state level took note of the situation. It mattered, however, that judges used participation in the war as a major rationale behind their decision. The trial court had acknowledged the fact that Standing Rock Indians had been "very active in war activities during the world war, many of them going to the army." Obviously, raising money, supplies, and material was regarded as an important part of patriotism, but only military service was specifically mentioned. Not only had these Indians demonstrated their loyalty and transformation into good American citizens; they had even proved the equal of "white settlers." As their level of education, farming activities, land ownership patterns, and relationships with whites testified, they were, for all intents and purposes, civilized and out of "tribal relations." Despite still being under the tutelage of the BIA, they were entitled to the full measure of citizenship, and their vote could not be rejected. In *Swift v. Leach* (1920), North Dakota's Supreme Court unambiguously confirmed this vindication of the compatibility of voting rights with specific Indian rights and regulations.[5]

Indian activists were well aware that their concerns, for long the exclusive purview of the BIA, could now be addressed through the vote and that patriotism provided a powerful rationale for doing so. Out of the several organizations born after the demise of the Society of American Indians, one in particular was intent on harnessing the Indian vote: the National Congress of American Indians. Not to be confused with the organization of the same name founded in 1944, the Congress was launched by Gertrude Bonnin in 1923. Bonnin was a Yankton Sioux activist married to a BIA employee (also a Yankton) who had served as a captain during World War I. In 1919, she urged the U.S. government to honor the blood spilled by Indian soldiers and grant Indians the same rights of self-determination as the United States had seen fit to grant European peoples, along with unrestricted U.S. citizenship. Throughout the 1920s, she fought relentlessly to loosen the BIA's stranglehold on reservation politics and encourage Indian voters to make their voice heard. In this most Republican of decades, the Grand Old Party was the target of choice for Indian activists like Bonnin, and it proved not a little responsive to Indian demands.[6]

Whether at the state or at the national level, Republicans sought to take control of the Indian vote. Even before North Dakota's Supreme Court had rendered its decision in *Swift v. Leach,* local Repub-

licans attempted to court Indian voters and tout Indians' patriotism
to gain their attention. Locally, their eagerness to promise Indians
rewards for their loyalty may have stemmed from the difficult position they found themselves in at the beginning of the 1920s. In North
Dakota in particular, Arthur C. Townley's Non-Partisan League
claimed the important farmers' vote, and Indians could justifiably be
regarded as a voting bloc to mitigate Republican defeat. At the national level too, Republicans made deliberate efforts to tie official
recognition of the loyalty of Indian recruits in with electoral politics,
even promoting the idea of a patriotic contract binding the tribes to
the Republican-controlled federal government. This started in 1919,
when, heeding the combined encouragements of the American Legion and of "Friends of the Indians," the Republican Congress
passed a bill entitling Indian veterans to claim all the rights of citizenship. This was a symbolic gesture, for most of them were already
citizens by then. Soon, Republicans went further. While their patriotic alliance with Indians is often taken to have culminated in the
passing of the Indian Citizenship Act on June 2, 1924, its true epitome actually took place a few weeks later.[7]

On June 28, 1924, the Coolidge administration issued each officially recognized tribe a certificate of recognition for services rendered during the Great War. The document was the brainchild of
Alfred B. Welch, a white veteran of the Spanish-American War and
World War I who was regularly involved in Legion activities and
patriotic celebrations on the Standing Rock Reservation. A committed Republican, Welch had been chosen to fill the position of
postmaster in the neighboring city of Mandan. He convinced his
superior, W. Irving Glover, third assistant postmaster general, that
Indian patriots deserved recognition. In North Dakota, the certificate was issued in a ceremony that was an opportunity to honor many
groups of patriots: veterans of the world war and former scouts having served under Custer; reservation populations in Standing Rock
and Fort Berthold, where Welch had acted as a recruiter during the
war; and chiefs like Thomas Frosted, who became the official guardian of the certificate on his own reservation of Standing Rock. Gifts
were exchanged between Indians and the Republican administration,
as they had been since the Lewis and Clark expedition from 1804 to

1806. The U.S. president, in particular, received presents through his representatives.

A direct link between the highest authority in the land and the tribes was thus symbolically reestablished. It bypassed the Bureau of Indian Affairs, whose representative on Standing Rock bitterly complained of having been kept uninformed throughout the process. On all of the reservations where such a ceremony was held, the issuance of the certificate served to imbue old symbols with new sacredness, and heavily mobilized the U.S. flag. In Pueblo country, village governors reminded Americans of the power they had been granted by the Spanish and after them by U.S. presidents. In support of the claim, they produced a cane given them by Abraham Lincoln. Among the Osages, the ceremony saw the organization of an "Osage soldiers peace dance" inspired by earlier Osage ceremonies. After 1924, the dance was held on October 14 (the day when the certificate was presented) and Armistice Day. The U.S. flag and the certificate itself were prominently displayed. The ceremonies powerfully contributed to fostering the myth that Indians had been granted citizenship as a result of their participation in World War I.

The political calculation was unmistakable. Throughout the country, BIA reservation superintendents, aware of the ceremony's implications, did their best not to seem to lend a hand to electoral scheming. On the Crow reservation, afraid of appearing to be courting votes for the incumbent administration, the BIA superintendent intentionally postponed the ceremony so that it would take place after the national elections scheduled for November 1924. By the end of the 1920s, the enlistment of Indian figures in Republican electoral efforts and the creation of electoral committees for Republican presidential candidates on reservations were routinized. Plenty Coups, who endorsed Coolidge among the Crows of Montana in 1924, or Thomas Frosted, who headed the Standing Rock committee for the election of Hoover and his vice-presidential candidate, Charles Curtis, were eminent symbols of this alliance.[8]

And the alliance made a mark on Indian policy. Far from being a merely practical combination, it supported a redefinition of the meaning of citizenship for Indians. The act of June 2, 1924, granting citizenship to all Indians born in the United States did not subordinate citizenship to the relinquishment of tribal rights. It thus confirmed a trend started in 1916 with the *United States v. Nice,* a U.S. Supreme Court decision that declared that Native American citizens could remain wards of the federal government. By 1928, Republicans were the first major political party to include an Indian plank in their national political platform. It formally guaranteed respect for the treaty rights of Indians. After the war, merely mentioning treaty rights would not automatically result in an Indian being branded as reactionary or backward. In the U.S. Court of Claims, in the congressional halls, or at the White House, Indian special rights now seemed well recognized—if only as a temporary measure before full assimilation. Patriotism had not won the vote for the Indians, but it had shaped the context in which it was possible for Indians to use the franchise without renouncing their special rights and their collective identities. This was especially efficient in the case of the Sioux. Turning to the Iroquois or the Eastern Cherokee, we should also acknowledge that the redefinition of Indian citizenship that patriotism seemed to permit had definite limits.[9]

The Dilemmas of Citizenship

The synthesis of treaty rights and patriotism that culminated in the 1924 presidential certificate ceremony and the 1928 endorsements of Hoover's candidacy was not an all-powerful tool to reform Indian policy. State legislatures were not as responsive as the Republican Party. In New York state, the case of the Iroquois or the Haudenosaunee speaks to the continued tension between treaty rights and U.S. citizenship in the 1920s and to the limited power of claims of patriotism to diminish these tensions when money, not simply recognition, was at stake. In North Carolina, it was the potential of patriotism to upset the racial status quo that set a limit to the extent of the rights that Indian patriots could claim.

Of all the Haudenosaunee, the Wisconsin Oneidas suffered perhaps the cruelest fate during the war. As early as June 1917, they were forced to accept citizenship and lose their land and complained that whites "beat us out of our property while our young men were preparing to go overseas to fight the Germans." Other Iroquois tribes tried to look for positive ways to harness patriotism. Requested to register and uncertain as to what they should do, Iroquois groups in New York state followed the advice of Seneca anthropologist Arthur C. Parker and declared war on Germany, thereby maintaining the fiction of a bilateral alliance between the United States and the Iroquois. Displays of patriotism did not, however, end pressures on Iroquois lands in New York state. In 1907, a landowner on the Oneida reservation had mortgaged her property and lost it to a white lender. State courts had legalized the procedure. In an attempt to get redress for the land lost, Iroquois claimants insisted that the case be adjudicated in federal court, where Indian disputes belonged. By 1919, this had become "the New York Indian Problem": Did Indians living within the boundaries of the state fall under its authority or were they exclusively dependent on the federal government to clear up complex issues of ownership and sovereignty? That same year, the state legislature set up a dedicated commission to investigate the issue. The commission researched the state's archives and called upon Iroquois memories to testify to the relationship that the once powerful confederacy had built with the United States. Edward A. Everett, a state representative, chaired the commission. In the very first lines of his final report, he declared his intention to solve the "Indian problem" in the state to the benefit of the Indians, in line with "the spirit of the United States towards the world war." After four million Americans had been mobilized in defense of European countries, it was now time to mobilize for the Indian cause "in a spirit of fairness." "I am firmly of the belief," Everett added, "that the spirit of justice awakened by this terrible world war will last until the Indian problem has been settled in justice to the Indians and in such a way that every white man living in the United States can look the Indian in the eye and declare that he is really and truly the brother of the white man."[10]

In the report, recognizing that moral arguments carried only symbolic weight, Everett made good use of history. His view, supported by the numerous testimonies of prominent Iroquois witnesses, was that participation in World War I represented but the latest in a series of Iroquois interventions on the side of the United States. Iroquois had always been the allies of the young nation. Indian experts insisted on this most consistently. According to Chapman Skenandoah (or Skenandore), an Oneida boarding school graduate and a veteran of the Spanish-American War, "The Oneidas, as a nation, was the only nation that never fought against the 'Stars and Stripes.'" Furthermore, tribes were the equal of states: "Whatever Uncle Sam says, I and the State has to comply." For Joe Johnson, another Oneida representative, all soldiers coming from his tribe were volunteers, by contrast with whites who had to be caught like "a fish." Their loyalty demanded federal attention. "We wanted to help the government in which we lived. We were not citizens by any means and when it came to buying bonds, we went to the full extent of our pocket books." Iroquois' status as Americans was based on thousands of years of occupation in the region. Oneida in particular and Iroquois in general could not be forced to accept a status, either as foreigners or as U.S. citizens.[11]

Indian witnesses were aware that they were treading on shaky ground. Skenandoah in particular seemed willing to accommodate U.S. insistence of citizenship, but only in the long run: "Speaking about putting Indians on equal basis, I surmise we should become citizens. But, as far as putting Indians on the same footing, that is impossible." Chief Lyons, speaking for the Onondaga, invoked the tutelary figure of Washington and replaced subjection with alliance and brotherhood: "George Washington guaranteed he was going to be our brother and made this Constitution of the Thirteen Colonies accept and agree. Every time our Brother gets into trouble, we get up and help him. We believe that is our Brother. What our people done when you fight against the British? We got up and fight too. What when you had trouble with Germany? How many Indians volunteered to enlist? Not a single one was crying when he went on war path. He was just as happy like when he gets up in the morning for his breakfast. What our brother he guaranteed us that is what we stand by today."[12]

Recourse to history allowed Indian witnesses to explain why they thought loyalty in the war could not possibly be regarded as a reason for unilaterally imposing citizenship on the Iroquois. Military service was their duty not as citizens but as allies of the United States, especially the federal government, and they had maintained their alliance against all odds for the better part of the previous 150 years. This, in turn, meant that only the federal government should be consulted when discussing legal issues, especially land issues, on Iroquois reservations. Everett himself was convinced. Iroquois were an allied nation that had never renounced its territorial claims in New York state. Treaties signed with them remained in force, as did treaty rights affecting hunting, fishing, and lands. As early as March 3, 1920, the United States Circuit Court of Appeals for the Second Circuit apparently agreed: It denied the state its jurisdiction over Indian lands, and the U.S. Supreme Court did not contradict it.[13]

Even within the commission where he presided, however, many disagreed with Everett's stance. Some, like Doctor R. W. Hill, speaking for the state's Charities Department, accused Everett of being backward-looking. For Hill, Everett's call for justice and admonition to defend Indian rights in order to uphold "the honor of the state" was little short of disingenuous. Indians were not to be told that they owned the better part of the state of New York: That would encourage them to stop working and stop walking the road to civilization. They would not get "equal opportunity" within the state and would end up being unduly distinguished from white citizens with whom, after all, they shared many biological connections. Exercising their rights and doing their duty as citizens was the only road to happiness for Iroquois. This was Hill's viewpoint, and it was far from isolated. Everett's efforts failed. His report, published in 1922, was promptly buried by the New York state legislature.[14]

The Iroquois did not stop trying to have their participation in the war recognized by the United States as part of a tradition of alliance. No Iroquois on the U.S. side, however, managed to get the same kind of recognition as their famous brother in Canada: Levi General. An Oneida-Cayuga chief known by his title of *deskaheh*, Levi General was a major proponent of Iroquois specificity, one especially intent on using loyalty in the war to bolster his case, one also who was willing to step on to the international scene to do so. Rooted in Canadian conditions, however, his case testifies, by contrast, to the specific situation of U.S. Indians.[15] The moral and emotional force of General's appeal to international arbitrage stemmed from the specific conditions prevalent on Canada's Iroquois reserves in the 1910s. As in the United States, World War I proved an opportunity for the Canadian government to accelerate the colonization of Indian land. With the Soldier Settlement Act of 1917, modified in 1919 to include Indian reserves, Native veterans were offered the possibility of claiming for themselves a portion of tribal lands. As had been the case in New York state, such land when mortgaged was liable to appropriation by non-Indians. But in Canada, such moves were compounded by a direct attack on traditional chiefs, spearheaded by Indian ex-soldiers. On the Six Nations Reserve in Ontario, veterans signed a petition against the hereditary status of tribal government positions and demanded the holding of elections. In 1920, an "Indian Act" launched a full-scale campaign to force citizenship on Canada's Indians—at the very same time that, in the United States, reformers of Indian Affairs were beginning to doubt the validity of this policy.[16]

The brutal confrontation between veterans and non-veterans was unusual by U.S. standards, as was Canadian Iroquois' appeal to an outside authority. As their delegate, Levi General first appealed to the British crown. Even if Canadian Iroquois had not been granted a status as allies during the war, General traveled to London to enlist the king's help. He went further and presented his case at the League of Nations, in the hope that the new international organization created by the Treaty of Versailles would recognize the Iroquois nation as a full-fledged member. Neither effort was successful. On October 7, 1924, the Royal Canadian Mounted Police raided the traditional council house of the Six Nations Reserve. Convinced by a report authored by Andrew T. Thompson, a Canadian officer who had recruited Iroquois for service in France, the Canadian government claimed to be defending democracy on the reserve. It dissolved the traditional government, held elections, and confiscated the wampum belts that testified to past treaties between the Iroquois and other governments. Faced with such a brutal assault on Iroquois ways, General pronounced his last major speech in U.S. territory. In it, he desperately emphasized the continuity of Iroquois loyalty toward Anglo-Americans: "One word more," he pleaded, "so that you will be sure to remember our people. If it had not been for them, you would not be here. If, one hundred and sixty-six winters ago, our warriors had not helped the British at Quebec, Quebec would not have fallen to the British. The French would then have driven your English-speaking forefathers out of this land, bag and baggage. Then it would have been a French-speaking people here today, not you. That part of your history cannot be blotted out by the stealing of our wampum belts in which that is recorded." Shortly thereafter, General died, harassed by the Canadian government and suspected by some of his own people of having attempted to become a dictator or at least of having unduly claimed to represent them all on the international scene.[17]

Levi General's case testifies to the very specific conditions then prevalent in the United States. Iroquois communities on the other side of the international border also struggled to articulate military service and treaty rights. Both the Canadian and the U.S. governments officially defended assimilation, and both objected to the determination of "their" Iroquois to be recognized as allies. Being part of the British Empire could have facilitated the recognition of Iroquois specificity in Canada. It did not. International mobilization resulted in an assimilationist crackdown on traditional institutions. On the U.S. side, however, the insertion in federal dynamics made it possible for Iroquois to claim a certain degree of autonomy from the states and reinforce their relationship with the federal government. In the United States, Iroquois veterans collectively were never part of a concerted assault on tradition. However fragilely, Iroquois were able to claim the rewards of patriotism in a way that made it compatible with the defense of treaty rights. As early as 1921, this was obvious in the controversy surrounding the granting of a bonus to New York Iroquois veterans.[18]

A few months after the war broke out, Cato Sells, speaking as the head of the BIA, had declared: "I believe that the Indians who have gone in the Army and Navy of our country will at the close of the war receive all credit for brave and honorable careers." On November 26 of the same year, Sells informed BIA agents that Indian recruits would benefit from war risk insurance like all their fellow soldiers. From then on, reservation superintendents, BIA school principals, or even Red Cross volunteers ministering to Indian soldiers regularly encouraged their charges to keep up with their dues. The management of the material rewards of military service was promptly domesticated as another way to teach young Indians about businesslike behavior, thrift, and private property. Other rewards were more contested.[19]

This was notably the case in New York state. In April 1921, the state announced it would offer veterans residing within its boundaries

an exceptional reward for their willingness to face the supreme sacrifice in the war. Like other states, it termed it a "bonus"—and explicitly excluded Iroquois from its benefit. The announcement came
at a bad time for Iroquois: How could they claim the bonus from a
state from which they were trying to dissociate themselves? Once
again, Arthur C. Parker acted as a mediator, deftly emphasizing the
heroic record of his fellow Iroquois. Very familiar with Indians' war
experience, which he had advertised in the journal of the Society of
American Indians, Parker attempted to educate the white readers in
New York state on Iroquois patriotism, so as to bridge the gap separating supporters of U.S. citizenship for Indians and defenders of
Indian sovereignty. In Parker's view, denying Iroquois the bonus was
yet another stab at the project of turning Indians into full citizens
of the United States. Just as the federal government deprived them
of voting rights and prevented them from managing their own lands,
the state refused to acknowledge their unique contribution to the
war effort. Since the founding of the SAI, Parker had consistently
defended Indians' position as citizen-soldiers. The denial of the bonus
was another opportunity to make a well-established argument.

Other Iroquois organized to have their own defense of veterans'
rights heard. A statewide committee was created. Iroquois veterans
of the Civil War, the Spanish-American War, and World War I
mobilized. They were not, in the words of a non-Indian journalist
working for the Syracuse *Post-Standard*, "traitors or bolcheviks."
Many had testified in front of Everett's commission, some white,
like Erl A. Bates, others Iroquois, like Chapman Skenandoah, Jesse
Lyons, David R. Hill, or William Rockwell. Many, unlike Parker,
were no supporters of U.S. citizenship for Iroquois and certainly no
supporters of state jurisdiction. The work of the committee left no
archival record and remains little known, but the publicity it gener-
ated was ultimately efficient. For Adjutant General Leslie J. Kincaid,
who presided over the New York Bonus Commission, Iroquois had
proved their loyalty during the war, and all that was needed was to
revert the Commission's original decision to exclude them. By the
end of July, this had been accomplished. The publicization of the
injustice done the Iroquois had attracted the sympathies of many
members of the white public. As far as Minnesota, newspaper readers could, like Clarence A. Anderson in the *Minneapolis News*, re-

gard the bonus question as an instance in which Indians, like African Americans before them, needed to be granted "Lincoln's justice." Having witnessed Indian soldiers' bravery in the trenches himself, Anderson made use of the color-coded symbolism that linked slackers and cowards to yellow and instead emphasized red as the symbol of courage linking Indians to the national flag: Like the colors of the flag, Indians didn't "run" when confronted with the enemy. While it was true that a veteran's reward couldn't be material only, Indians had deserved the bonus—just like their fellow non-Indian veterans. Iroquois managed to save the bonus for their veterans without compromising treaty rights.[20]

The fight had been a close one. It had also made it clear that Indians' ability to claim the rewards of loyalty depended on local conditions. Not all states embraced Indian citizenship and voting rights. As late as 1940, Minnesota, Idaho, Maine, Mississippi, New Mexico, Washington, Arizona, South Dakota, Utah, North Carolina, and Colorado barred Indians from voting on various grounds, with some degree of local variations. In areas of the country where anti-Indian sentiment intersected with Jim Crow discrimination, this reduced the possibility of using citizenship to vote to zero.

The Owl brothers of Eastern Cherokee country provide a good picture of how Indian veterans could be affected by the shortcomings of their newfound rights. In North Carolina, the Cherokee vote had long been a major local political issue. Beginning in 1900, white citizens of Swain and Jackson counties blocked all attempts by Cherokees to register and take part in elections. Denied political representation, several Cherokees resisted the draft in 1917. George Allen Owl was among them. He left for France under protest but when he returned made sure to join the local Legion post to defend his hard-earned rights as a veteran. After the war, Cherokee tribal lands were progressively made available to individuals. On November 6, 1919, after two years' debate, the allotment of tribal lands started. The next year Cherokees tested their new status as landowning citizens and voted in national elections, ensuring the local victory of Republicans. The counties' electoral boards promptly invalidated the Indian vote, however, arguing that, as they were wards of the federal government, Indians couldn't properly be regarded as citizens.

George's brother, David Owl, was a veteran and a Legionnaire like him. He was part of the Cherokee delegation that went to Washington to lobby for a special citizenship act for Cherokees. Passed two days after the Indian Citizenship Act of June 2, 1924, the act specifically granted citizenship to Eastern Cherokees but also placed their lands under federal trust, thus making them untaxable. This proved another opportunity for white North Carolinians to keep denying them the franchise. A new act was passed in 1929 in an attempt to remove this pretext, but to no avail.

The next year Henry Owl, the third Owl veteran and the holder of a master's degree in history from the University of North Carolina, still couldn't vote despite his impressive credentials. Like his brother David, he went to Congress, managed to have another law passed, but also like him, he had to admit failure and leave the reservation. Henry started working as a teacher for the BIA. David went to New York state and, alongside William B. Newell, founded the Society for the Propagation of Indian Welfare, an initiative that ultimately made him the only veteran to receive, in 1932, the Golden Arrow Award of the Indian Council Fire. George was the only one to stay on the reservation and avoided getting involved in the issue of Indians' voting rights.[21]

While Iroquois had attempted to ward off the negative effects of citizenship, for Eastern Cherokees it was the very possibility of voting that remained out of reach. The Republican synthesis did not obtain everywhere. But Indians did not remain silent in the face of discrimination. They soon claimed the rewards of soldier-citizenship in an unexpected area: tradition.

Claiming the Patriotic Right to Tradition

Whether in the form of compensation for land lost and treaty rights ignored or as part of "the bonus," Indian communities did not have to wait very long to receive the material reward of their loyalty, but the fight continued well after the immediate postwar years. For veterans all over the United States, turning the "compensation" promised by the federal government in 1924 into actual monies became an objective that the onset of the Great Depression only made more relevant, especially to Indians living on reservations. In 1931, the federal government authorized veterans to get loans for as much as 50 percent of the amount inscribed on their compensation certificates. Soon, as unemployment became more widespread, this was not enough. Veterans started claiming the entirety of what they continued to call the "bonus." In 1932, anxious to get governmental help, they marched on Washington, D.C., where they set up a makeshift camp of tents. Photographer Theodor Horydczak documented the camp. In one rare snapshot reproduced at the beginning of this chapter, he captured the presence of Native veterans among the Bonus marchers.

The unnamed former soldier whom Horydczak portrayed, sitting on a bench among his comrades, made no mystery of being an Indian: He wore a head roach, a headband, and Indian insignia on his pants and waistcoat. His presence must have struck the Washington-based photographer as particularly picturesque, and it was. But Horydczak's interest matters here for another reason, as it produced one of the few testimonies that Indian veterans, far from erasing their ethnic or racial difference in the citizen-soldier universalism so powerfully defended by the American Legion and other veterans' organizations, also participated in national mobilization for veterans' rights without abdicating their identities.[22]

On reservations, veterans like Sam Kenoi did more and mobilized to get pensions for Indian veterans of previous wars as well. The fight for pensions and the bonus had an intergenerational component to it. Already in March 1917, the white-dominated organization called the Veterans of Indian Wars had pressured Congress into granting pensions to all surviving veterans of wars waged in the West in the nineteenth century. This was a month before the United States declared war on Germany. Requests for pensions by Indian scouts became abundant in the 1920s. In economically depressed reservations, war-related benefits were often the only regular source of income for entire families. Before the New Deal created old-age pensions, military pensions were also the only thing standing between many an elderly Indian man and relief.

This was a new development, and one that had been eagerly awaited by Indian veterans of the Indian wars. As Chief Little Wolf wrote to Joseph K. Dixon in February 1920, "We have kept patient. [. . .] I am anxious to have these Cheyenne scouts get the benefit from their services." While Indian veterans of the World War were never subjected to the same kind of discrimination as their Canadian counterparts, whose pensions were structurally inferior to those of white soldiers, claiming war benefits was a good opportunity to address other wrongs suffered at the hands of the federal bureaucracy and, in so doing, to act as representatives for older generations. Moreover, money received from the federal government, whether through the BIA or the Veterans Bureau, could easily be construed as the same kind of payment that the federal government had promised during treaty negotiations: a material recognition of the debt, inextricably moral and material, that the government had incurred when its representatives signed treaties with Indian nations. Little Chief himself followed up his request for pensions with a claim for material compensation for the Black Hills, which the Cheyenne, like the Sioux and other tribes, regarded as their possession before the advent of whites. Because Indian veterans received compensation just like other ex-soldiers, they were ideally placed to extend the meaning of the moral debt the nation owed them and merge their individual, war-related claims into collective claims rooted in U.S. colonization and assimilationist policies.

This took patriotic claims into uncharted territory. To the already long list of his demands, Little Wolf added a request that the government lift its ban on Indian dancing. He thus connected the benefits that were owed to Indian veterans of all wars with other privileges no non-Indian would have recognized as justified by patriotism. In effect, he proposed using patriotism to uphold not just Indian claims or veterans' benefits but Indian customs as well. This was riskier and decidedly more innovative. But it was far from an idiosyncratic move.[23]

During World War I, the BIA had allowed or tolerated Indian dances as a means to raise funds for the war effort. Many local superintendents tried to end the privilege as soon as the conflict ended. Their efforts met stiff resistance: In reservation communities, the idea that patriotism had gained Indians the right to dance was everywhere present. In some cases, reservation denizens even specifically claimed dances as rewards granted them by the government for good services in wartime. The Sioux "49," for example, during which dancers were invited to choose their partner holding a U.S. flag, was accompanied by a song that transparently proclaimed: "The President, the flag,/gladly take it, he said, so I took it. From that this dance was returned to me."[24]

After the war, when the BIA sent police to interrupt dances, protest came swiftly, couched in patriotic terms. To the government's request that they return to prewar regulations, Indian communities reacted with moral outrage. "We always thought that our world war veteran was to receive everything first," Indian leaders adamantly complained in a letter written from the Standing Rock Reservation. When faced with the BIA agents' claim that Indian dances were immoral, Indian organizers were quick to compare them with white dances, and, turning the moralistic approach of the BIA on its head, declare their mores morally less questionable than those of their white neighbors. Violence even seemed a distinct possibility when BIA employees attempted to enforce official orders to stop what they regarded as objectionable features of the dances.

On January 1, 1920, residents of the Cannonball district of Standing Rock crowded the local dance hall, located on a piece of trust land under the control of the BIA. Organizers made no secret of their intentions: They wanted to dance and collect money to raise a "memorial hall" to Indian soldiers. Arguing that he was a citizen, Basil Two Bear, well known for his association with local Republicans, superbly ignored the orders of Indian policemen that he desist from giving away money. The stepfather to Albert Grass, after whom a neighboring Legion post had been named, Two Bear wanted to honor the local war hero and saw no better way than publicly acknowledging him with a gift of money. He was not alone in standing his ground. The dance had been authorized for Indians over forty years of age only. But when the police tried to prevent young World War I veterans from joining the dance, they felt outnumbered. The four ex-servicemen, all citizens, were keenly aware of their moral rights and ready to uphold them. "Angry in his talk," one of them, John Spotted Bird took hold of a policeman and told him that "the boys give their life to their country and he sees no reason why they should stop them from dancing." The crowd seized the other policemen, and the female relative of a veteran shouted: "Kill them, they are only five!" Although no one was killed, there could have been no clearer proof that communities felt that the war had entitled them to their dances. They banded together around their veterans to defend this right as patriotic.[25]

As the BIA stepped up its campaign against supposedly "immoral" social functions, dance organizers repeated and enlarged their patriotic argument. In Cannonball, residents selected a committee to remind the BIA in writing that it was according to its own instructions that dances had been used to collect funds during the war. Indian dances were morally beyond reproach and Indian fundraising methods exactly comparable to those used by Christian churches. Petitioners had no qualms about branding as unpatriotic the local missionaries of German extraction who had accused them of immorality. "For this reason," they insisted, "we wonder if they making complaint against us for raising all funds to help lick the Germans." Emphasizing yet again that money was raised for a monument to Indian soldiers, petitioners added that it had also been used to fund an organization for war mothers that saw to the welfare of poor veterans. Dancers were not only the exact opposite of the picture of improvidence the BIA painted of them; they were also model patriots. On the other end of the reservation, in the Bullhead district, another petition signed by forty residents, many of them "old Indians," requested that "the ex-service-men be allowed to participate in Indian dancing, because they think that '[the veterans] have that much coming to them for what they did for us.'" Dancing was indeed a patriotic right.[26]

This was not the opinion of BIA agents such as Eugene D. Mossman, who showed nothing but contempt for ceremonies he regarded as "heathen" and "reactionary." Avoiding violent confrontation, Mossman instructed his "boss farmers" to keep instead an accurate account of the number of participants in dances, especially young veterans, so as to address each veteran's attitude individually. "These young men are our hope for the future and they should be an example to the older Indian in every way," he explained in 1923. They had simply done their duty and shouldn't claim special privileges. For Mossman, by all accounts a traditional BIA agent, steeped in the discourse of assimilation, dances accumulated all the vices that he regarded as the bane of veterans' life: return to the "blanket" of old customs, travel to white towns for dancing demonstrations, reckless spending, and debauchery. Worse, Indian communities' insistence that dancing was a patriotic reward testified to the illegitimate nature of Indian patriotism itself. Speaking of the money raised in the war, Mossman ventured that "had it been given outright or raised in any other way, the volume of patriotism would have been wonderfully diminished." Under the mask of patriotism, Indian leaders seized every occasion to attack the Bureau. During dances, Mossman explained to the BIA's central office, "the master of ceremony makes a speech in Indian in which he depicts the German army being destroyed by the valiant Indian soldiers," insisting on his readiness to fight for his people. The conclusion Mossman drew was negative in the extreme. Veterans and other Indians who had been given U.S. citizenship in the preceding years had regressed toward savagery and were simply unworthy of the honor. That an agent was willing to so openly contradict the policy of the Bureau testified to the unsettling potential of patriotism in Indian country. The world Mossman saw growing out of the war was a world that was upside down.[27]

Like many of his colleagues in the BIA, including his closest collaborators and informers, Mossman interpreted the situation as the result of a conspiracy hatched by "old Indians." According to one farmer writing on Standing Rock in 1919, veterans were under pressure from their elders to take up traditions that, without their intervention, would have fallen by the wayside: "The returned soldier boys held back and did not get in the ring when an old man got out and harangued the boys for leaving the old customs until the whole bunch came popping into the ring like a bunch of coyotes." To achieve this result, another farmer analyzed three years later, dance organizers "put young Indians on the committee, but the old ones run the show." The result of this policy was appalling: "the old Indians do their mightiest to have the young Indians or the citizens to take part in the dances. It appears that the young Indians or the citizens now practically dominate the dance and the old people are taking somewhat easy and are seemed to be on the background." By a mix of shaming and honoring, "old Indians" appeared to have effectively enlisted veterans into their fight in defense of tradition. Elders were the ones responsible for derailing the BIA project of turning veterans into model, assimilated U.S. citizens: "They believe in it and think it their natural right to dance because they are Indians and it is their custom and must never be given up."[28]

While tainted by prejudice and intended for police purposes only, the description BIA agents gave of intergenerational dynamics in Indian dances had a kernel of truth. On Standing Rock and in the Plains more generally, "Indian dances" as varied as the Grass Dance, the Victory Dance, the Scout Dance, and others were really opportunities for elders to assert control over young veterans who were potentially rebellious or contemplating assimilation. Among the Sioux during Victory Dance ceremonies, once marked by a black spot it was a veteran's duty to join other dancers. Judging by published reports, veterans' role as organizers was often limited to Armistice Day and Memorial Day. More often than not, they helped with the policing of the dance, the fundraising, and such military features as parades and salutes. Only in the first years after the conflict were they granted prominent but essentially symbolic positions in organizing committees. In 1921, Thomas DeRockbraine and Daniel Yellow Earrings, two veterans from Bullhead who had served in France, were respectively the secretary and the auditor of the Fourth of July Committee. In Kenel, the "Martin Yellow Fat" post of the American Legion was given control of a portion of the Independence Day program. Lewis Crowskin, one of the post's most active members and soon to be its commander, was the committee's vice president, a rare honor for a man of only thirty years of age. But most of the time, these honors were temporary. To compete with older, more established notables, veterans had to go through the same learning processes as other young men. Only by regular interactions with elders and patient training could they hope to master the rules and demonstrate the appropriate behavior associated with the practice of "old dances." In Little Eagle, Benedict Red Eagle, son of a warrior enrolled in the old military society known as Tokala or Little Foxes, was one of these young veterans who listened to more experienced men. As early as 1923, BIA agents criticized his excessive traveling, a telltale sign of his dancing proclivities. A decade later, by 1934, Red Legs was the only veteran on the committee in charge of organizing the inauguration of the Little Eagle monument to Indian soldiers and chiefs—even though he had never left training camp or seen combat. Straddling, like many, the boundary between "tradition" and "modernity," he was equally regarded as a good dancer and singer, a faithful Episcopalian, and an assiduous member of the local farm chapter promoting Indians' agricultural skills. For one highly respected leader in the district, Red Legs was simply "one of the most progressive young men of the reservation, a natural leader of the people, he was extremely well liked." Things were clearly more complex than Mossman and his underlings imagined.[29]

By adhering to the view that returning young men were simply made to toe the line set by older, more influential ones, without any reason of their own for joining dances, Mossman missed the young veterans' political motivations and larger project of emancipation. As they had done in the camps or on the front lines, veterans on reservations took the pen to claim their rights, and in the 1920s they regarded dancing as one of them. The sense of entitlement brought by the war turned practicing the Grass Dance, often regarded as a privilege "allowed by Treaty Law, as a memorial dance" to "old Indians" only (in the words of a 1927 petition), into a legitimate extension of citizen rights. The war, in other words, had ended old-fashioned regulations. Never quite articulating it as part of religious freedom (a move that would have to wait until the following decade to start spreading on reservations), veterans simply regarded danc-ing as both a natural right and a privilege attached to their status as citizen-soldiers.

"Poor us ex-servicemen and citizens we are barred from the dance," Joseph Grey Day wrote from Shields, North Dakota. "I am a young Indian age 24 and I've been in the service during the world's war and I am a patent in fee too. [. . .] Us young Indians we like to take in the dance and have a good time before we die anyway." Such petitions articulated age- and treaty-based privileges, on one hand, and moral and political legitimacy earned by military service on the other. The freedom to do "as I please" and "have a good time" came with veteran status, with the franchise, and with the right to own and sell land. Ensuring that dances took place on "fee patent land" was not simply a common strategy to bypass BIA regulations. It also linked dancers to the powerful ideology of emancipation though citizenship that assimilationists could ill afford to oppose without seeming to contradict themselves. If veterans, who were supposed to be the poster children of assimilation, could use citizen-ship to uphold "backward" customs, was the assimilationist program even viable?[30]

This was a political question many people involved in Indian affairs began to ask after World War I. As early as 1921, the Society of American Indians had considered supporting the candidacy of a veteran to the post of BIA commissioner to implement the reform of the BIA. While this particular idea remained a paper project, veterans soon learned that their fight for freedom didn't have to be limited to confrontation with policemen and boss farmers. Their mobilization, while overshadowed by that of more famous white activists like John Collier (who eventually did become BIA commissioner), soon took on national relevance. As a reward for their loyalty, Indians claimed more than financial compensation or support for their treaty claims: They demanded a major overhaul of Indian policy in the United States.[31]

Yet before we examine in greater detail how this articulation of citizenship, veterans' rights, and tradition played out in the political arena, we need to acknowledge that it was far from a unanimous proposition in Indian country and that the political fight pitted Indians against one another as much as it turned them against non-Indians. Whether on Standing Rock or on other reservations, many disagreed with the politicization of tradition, and they were as eager to use patriotism as their rivals. Assimilationists had long insisted that "tribal relations" prevented Native Americans from taking their rightful place in the U.S. body politic. Accordingly, many Indian boarding school graduates remained strongly opposed to the idea that citizenship and patriotism could be used to defend the right to dance or uphold other communal institutions. Against "radicals" on or off reservations, they sided with the BIA, confident that they were waging the "progressive" fight. Indeed, few veterans would have openly admitted to being unprogressive or "backward."

In parts of Indian country where political life was structured by factionalism, this meant that veterans could be the most aggressive supporters of assimilation as well as bitter enemies of traditional authorities. In 1931, Joseph Filario Tafoya, a Santa Clara Pueblo embroiled in factional politics, openly claimed veteran status to enlist U.S. senators' help against his political enemies. In a letter in line with his wartime correspondence, Tafoya framed his approach to patriotism in "progressive" terms: "First. Introduce myself, Joseph Filario Tafoya, from Santa Clara Pueblo, member and president of progressive party of New Mexico Indians, ex-soldier, overseas man of United States Army, two years soldier in World War, in action—St. Mihiel and Argonne Forest, France—where our buddies lying beneath the sod in sunny France and Belgium, so that people on earth may live in peace."

When he returned from the war, Tafoya explained, "reactionaries" dominated the local council and turned down his application for a tract of land, an indispensable step, in his view, to getting married and starting a family: "A man who loves his people and country, ready to sacrifice his own life [was] treated unfair and unjust." His fight "for the Government of the United States and for the citizens and people and their land" and "Uncle Sam" had been voided of meaning. A representative of the "progressive members that have no land" who, throughout the 1920s, opposed John Collier's fight to preserve Pueblo communal landholdings, Tafoya was especially incensed at the Santa Clara governor's ability to demand community work from the village residents. Tafoya belonged to a group of Pueblos making their living among whites (he worked with tourists at Manitou Springs, in Colorado) and felt that he should not be constrained into working within the village. "Is this just or unjust for a man to work for nothing, and at the end of the season one man has plenty and the other man have nothing?" he asked. Like Iroquois veterans in Canada, he saw only one solution to his predicament: requesting democratic elections. As he wrote, "Let the people elect their governors and the parties to select four or five men in each group to make the rules and regulations to be carrying on the year until next election."[32]

On Standing Rock, there was no more vocal representative of this mindset than Eugene Younghawk. Before the war, Younghawk had worked as an assistant boss farmer in his district of Bullhead. In 1917 and 1918 he had not left the United States, but in training camps he had risen through the ranks, eventually leaving the service as a corporal. After selling part of his estate, he hired out to white farmers in North Dakota and Canada and worked in sawmills and meat packing plants in Rapid City. Back on the reservation in the mid-1920s, well-liked by his white neighbors, Younghawk was often (like other fellow veterans) chosen as an election judge by county officers. In 1926, he became the adjutant of the Bullhead Legion post. Regularly reinstated by his fellow Indian Legionnaires, Young-hawk used his position as post officer to lead the fight against danc-ers in his district. His was a deeply factional approach. Remembered today as an aggressive "politician," he defined himself in his corre-spondence with BIA agents as an enemy of old superstitions. His camp was made up of self-designated "progressives." The local dis-trict council was the most obvious place to wage the battle against "radicals" and "agitators." It was also a stepping-stone to look for allies in other (at first mostly Sioux) reservations. Mobilization for the Black Hills required the holding of assemblies at the level of each reservation but also at the level of the entire Sioux Nation—both meetings being called "general councils." Regularly present in the district council and serving as its secretary in 1930, Younghawk also familiarized himself with the Black Hills claim. Allied to several local Indian leaders and Protestant missionaries, in contact with both the reservation superintendent and South Dakota politicians, he devel-oped his own blend of patriotism, one compatible with the respect of Indian treaties but not with Indian dancing, a practice he regarded as responsible for Indians' poverty and inability to prove themselves worthy of citizenship. The time, however, was not yet ripe for the likes of Younghawk. In the 1920s, defending Indian dances in the name of patriotism was the more popular strategy. It led to more powerful attacks against the Indian Bureau.[33]

Engaging the Indian Bureau in the Name of Patriotism

Veterans' fight for material and symbolic rewards, we have now es-tablished, was not simply about adjusting specific rights and regula-tions or defending the integrity of Indian cultures. Rather, it cut at the heart of the Indians' relationship with the state, the embodiment of which on reservations was none other than the Indian Bureau. After the Great War, reservation communities protesting during and after patriotic celebrations formulated a critique of BIA power that went beyond dances to denounce general abuse at the hand of gov-ernmental agents. Veterans were well placed to take the lead in the movement, and patriotism was a ubiquitous instrument in the de-nunciation. As ever, it is by turning to a local case that this becomes clear. After yet another BIA interruption during an Armistice Day celebration in November 1923, veterans on Standing Rock in particular started a campaign to question the "regime" installed by their superintendent, Eugene D. Mossman. They ended up joining a general fight against the very existence of the Bureau of Indian Affairs. The sequence of events that ensued demonstrates how veteran and non-veteran activisms interacted. It also makes clear how very specific, often personal issues could develop into questions of national import and bring patriotism to bear against the BIA, the agency that had seemed best placed to harness the symbolic power of the flag. And it suggests another narrative for the great Indian revolt against the Bureau in the 1920s, which most historians see as starting in the Southwest in the Pueblo fight to defend their communal lands.

Patriotism played a crucial role in the Indian politics of the time because it could connect rights of various origins to powerful, inter-ethnic symbols and thus transcend racial boundaries. One of the most portentous moves that veteran status allowed was the establishment of direct contact with representatives in Congress at a time when those of them interested in Indian affairs were more prone than ever to question the actions of the Bureau. Getting the support of congressmen to defend "old customs," however, was not easy, for all were still staunch defenders of assimilationism. On Standing Rock in North Dakota, veterans joined their elders in using patriotism to circumvent that stumbling block. In 1923, residents wrote Lynn Frazier, their U.S. senator, who also chaired the Senate committee on Indian Affairs. At first, they only complained that BIA agents had stopped a patriotic celebration. Soon, they denounced another injustice: Mossman had called them "savages" despite all the signs pointing to their "civilization." These were two major arguments to call out the BIA for trampling on its own principle of upholding the civilization of the Indians.

At first, BIA officials in Washington reacted in the usual defensive way. Under pressure from North Dakota representatives, they could not avoid sending an inspector to investigate the conflict. As was the case in similar situations, the latter promptly cleared Mossman of all charges. Native veterans were undeterred. In 1924, David M. Means, the Indian adjutant of the "Albert Grass" Legion post in Fort Yates, renewed the attack on Mossman. This time, he sent a petition to the North Dakota branch of the Legion. The charges he drew up could

not have been more specific to ex-servicemen. Evoking the burial
of Richard Blue Earth in 1921 (the Legion post in Cannonball had
been named after him), David M. Means claimed that Mossman had
seen fit to use the occasion to question veterans' right to employment preference. According to Means, Mossman had even gone further: He had barred a veteran from accessing the local BIA hospital,
had forced the Legion post in Fort Yates to pay for the casket and
the headstone of another returned soldier, and had rounded off his
abuse by insulting Indians collectively. White enemies of Mossman
and friends of Indian veterans, like Alfred B. Welch, were happy to
chime in. Ordering their own investigation, the Legion authorities
in North Dakota concluded that Means was right. They contacted
the BIA head office and had Washington send another inspector to
Standing Rock. In the meantime, Indian veterans themselves contacted Clyde M. Kelly, a representative from Pennsylvania whose
enmity toward the BIA and project to abolish it were well known.

As reservation representatives lined up in Mandan to receive
the presidential certificate of recognition for Indian patriotism in
the war, new accusations emerged: The superintendent had turned
veterans away from their homes and allowed whites to take their
places, and he had started systematically refusing them jobs. Veterans made sure to qualify this behavior as arbitrary and tyrannical,
code words that pointed to Mossman's betrayal of his mission to
turn his wards into full-fledged citizens and give them the respect
such status warranted. Mossman himself seemed happy to oblige. In
lieu of a defense, he painted a hostile, bleak portrayal of the plaintiffs as alcoholics affected with mental retardation, thieves intent on
instrumentalizing the Legion, and braggarts whose days of actual
service were few and far apart—unlike his own son, who had seen
combat in France.[34]

Interpersonal conflicts permeated fights around legitimate uses
of patriotism. But the time was particularly favorable to give such
conflicts a national and ideological relevance. Beginning in 1923,
John Collier, a former social worker, wrote a series of vitriolic articles
denouncing the catastrophic effects of BIA rule in Indian country
and resurrecting the old picture of a corrupt and inefficient Indian
Bureau in need of reform or even abolition. By December 1927,
Collier and other activists, both white and Indian, in favor of a rad-

ical change in federal Indian policy managed to get Congress to appoint a senatorial committee to look into the often desperate living conditions of Native Americans throughout the country. The enormous endeavor lasted more than fifteen years, much longer than the Meriam Report published in 1928, which is considered the only major fact-finding effort of the time. Over tens of thousands of pages, during countless hours of hearings, the senatorial investigators were not confronted by the predicament of unspecified "Indians." Instead, they met with well-identified groups, some reservation-based, other not, and listened to the complaints of individuals who did not all have an equal claim to their attention.

Among them, veterans were a special interest of Lynn Frazier. He systematically asked witnesses whom he believed to be veterans a similar set of questions: "were you in the world war; were you overseas; how long; what important battles were you in; were you gassed over there; what branch of service were you in over there; how many members of your tribe were in the service?" In asking these questions, Frazier helped the witness establish his credentials in front of the rest of the visiting committee. Veterans, for him, had specific rights to health care or to the "bonus." He was otherwise a strict assimilationist. When he elicited (from whites) a figure pointing toward the overrepresentation of Indians in the armed forces, Frazier used it to demonstrate that Indians were patriots who shouldn't be granted collective rights but merely given better service by the federal state. Faced with veterans who claimed veterans' preference and employment, he turned them down. But in his home state, his approach was more nuanced—and more political.[35]

On Standing Rock, the visit of the senatorial committee was eagerly prepared by a veteran hailing from another (partly) Sioux reservation: Fort Peck, a Montana territory over which Mossman had ruled before being transferred to North Dakota. Meade Steele, who had served in the Army since 1913 and reenlisted in the war in November 1917, had returned home and quickly taken up activism. In 1923, he guided William Madison, sent by the dying Society of the American Indians to report on the Fort Peck, Blackfeet, and Flathead reservations. In the following years, Steele traveled to Washington, where he testified in Congress against white cattlemen's exploitation of reservation lands. In the U.S. capital, Steele presented himself as "an Indian overseas soldier of the Second Division and secretary of the tribal council of his tribe on the Fort Peck." He made contact with lawyers involved in the Black Hills claims and joined Madison when the latter testified in favor of the soon-to-be-passed Indian citizenship bill. Steele was versatile and mobile, articulating local concerns and major issues in Indian national politics, careful to always remind his white audience that his patriotism was eminently compatible with defending Indian causes: "I have General Pershing's statement to me which says: 'With a consecrated devotion to duty you have loyally served your country.' Now, I must serve my tribe no matter what kind of hell they make for me."

New, sometimes unexpected allies joined him in the fight. Steele even enlisted the help of Mormon missionaries. In 1926, he threatened BIA agents that he would contact Legion posts around the country if he was not compensated for losses incurred at their hands during the world war. Always on the lookout for allies, he struck an alliance with the Indian Protective Association of Montana, a coalition of tribes struggling against the BIA. The same year he became the secretary of Bonnin's National Congress of the American Indians and helped with the creation of local NCAI groups in Oklahoma and South Dakota. In a bid to "end the tyrannical power of the Indian Bureau over our lives," he opposed HR 7826, a bill that purported to enlarge the power of superintendents. Instead, he helped promote S. 1088, which would have granted tribal governments more legitimacy—a move anticipating developments that would arrive during the New Deal.[36]

In March 1928 in North Dakota, Steele, preparing to take the stand in front of the senatorial committee "from a sense of public duty and patriotic duty," requested a full investigation into Mossman's wrongdoings on both Fort Peck and Standing Rock. As Steele geared up for the visit of the committee, Gertrude Bonnin herself drove to Standing Rock to help residents prepare their testimonies. They added new items to the already long list of charges against Mossman. Through "pernicious political activity," they claimed, the superintendent used his influence to weigh in on the election of county officers on the southern side of the reservation, manipulated the tribal council, and repeatedly abused his administrative prerogatives. When Frazier finally arrived on the reservation, he showed a singular willingness to pay attention to the complaints of Indians in general and veterans in particular.

In line with their fellow reservation denizens but with greater vehemence, veterans produced a consistent picture of abuse—verbal, physical, and symbolic—at the hands of Mossman and his cronies. One even concluded: "And they call this America 'the land of the free and the home of the brave.'" Veterans were steadily supported by leaders of the older generation who, like Thomas Frosted, had also become used to evoking their children's military service (as Frosted himself had done as part of the Black Hills claim). As reservation lands were ravaged by drought and the end of the trust period protecting them from sale was fast approaching, the parents of veterans eagerly reminded the committee that their children had been forced to sell their property upon their return, that their insurance had not been paid after their death, or that they themselves had been harassed by Mossman's team. Grievances added up to a call for ousting the superintendent. By the end of the hearings, Mossman's job was clearly on the line.[37]

More than individual jobs were at stake. Among the protesters, veterans who, like Steele, mixed patriotism with progressive credentials and sympathy for tradition used the senatorial hearing to produce road maps for Indian emancipation. The son of a devoted Catholic, well regarded by boss farmers for having held on to his allotment and achieving financial independence, George Sleeps From Home from Standing Rock claimed only a sixth-grade education but spoke good English. After the war he came back to the reservation and received a fee patent to his allotment but then lost it to taxes. Married in 1922, he had to spend the next six months in the Hot Springs sanatorium, the probable residue of a gas attack in France. In 1924 Sleeps From Home founded and commanded the Kenel Legion post. He was particularly involved in Fourth of July events and Victory Dance ceremonies. Probably active in the Kenel district council, he also became a tribal councilman before 1933, one of only five such veterans on Standing Rock at the time.

Addressing Frazier in the name of his fellow Legionnaires in 1929, Sleeps From Home outlined a comprehensive plan to overhaul BIA activities on the reservation. Boss farmers, Sleeps From Home claimed, should be replaced by tribal members educated in agricultural colleges, with veterans receiving preference in hiring. Trust status should be extended by twenty-five years on the lands of those unable to fend for themselves. But "all able-bodied men having the necessary qualifications to become a self-sustaining citizen [should] be relieved from all jurisdiction from the federal Government after the 25-year trust period expire." As far as fee-patent Indian citizens were concerned, it was necessary that "we have a voice in the expenditures of our money and property." In Sleeps From Home's argument, veterans squared the patriotic circle. They were models for their people on the way to citizenship as well as the good farmers the BIA agents wanted them to be. They were also protective of the weak and the old, as their elders had encouraged them to be. And finally, they took care of themselves and claimed the preference they were owed, but only after having tied it to Indian preference in BIA employment.[38]

The 1929 hearing thus proved an extraordinary opportunity to convert the stigmatization of Indians and veterans into a denunciation of the scandalous record of the Bureau and an affirmation of Indian independence. At every step of the process started in 1923 and grounded in the experience of the war, invocations of patriotism catalyzed anger and focused outsiders' attention. A protest started in defense of dancing on Armistice Day survived multiple denials by the BIA and turned into a major conflict to remove the incumbent superintendent and reform the local workings of the Bureau. Mobilizing allies outside of the reservation was not a novelty in the 1920s. It was the variety of channels and strategies that veterans' status opened up for protest that was unprecedented. As soon as the Legion was brought into the process, Standing Rock's complaints resonated with the predicament of veterans nationwide and signaled out the reservation superintendent's behavior as abnormal or indeed unpatriotic. Framed as a conflict over the meaning of patriotism and the freedom of citizens, the power struggle that opposed Indian "plaintiffs" and BIA "defendants" on the reservation became part of a larger and concerted attack on the Bureau. In a decade, patriotism had effectively been turned into a first-rate political weapon for Indians. While veterans were originally mere foot soldiers in the fight, by 1930 they had managed to make their own voice heard in the collective melee.

On the eve of the Depression, it was still unclear, however, if they would speak with one voice; even less clear whether patriotic rights as diverse as dancing and giving away money; getting housing, jobs, pensions and compensation; pursuing Indian claims; or attacking the local superintendent were compatible goals in the long run. Making claims, often contradictory ones, under the umbrella of patriotism and citizenship had proved efficient against the Bureau. It could also be deeply divisive, as the "Indian New Deal" would demonstrate.

CHAPTER SIX

A Dream of Emancipation

THE "INDIAN NEW DEAL" was a time of intense mobilization, debate, and controversy in Indian country. It was also a time when World War I veterans came out of the shadow of their elders to assume increasingly visible positions of leadership in their respective reservations. As John Collier left his role as oppositional activist to become Franklin D. Roosevelt's commissioner of Indian affairs, tribal politics changed, often dramatically. The voices of veterans were among the loudest to be heard. Not all returned soldiers achieved prominence. On Standing Rock, World War I veterans occupied more than 29 percent of seats on the tribal council between 1933 and 1950. But only six of them, or 4 percent of all Great War Indian soldiers on the reservation, occupied 18 percent of the seats, about the same percentage that veterans represented in the overall male population. At first sight, veterans were often overrepresented in tribal politics. But on closer scrutiny, the picture was more complicated: The veterans reelected most often were the most militant, and many of them adamantly opposed the New Deal, clashed repeatedly with the fiery new chief of Indian affairs in the United States, and made careers out of blaming his reform for the state of Indian affairs. Their rise to power, in other words, closely mirrored the federal government's attempts to reform Indian policy.

Native communities in the 1920s had used patriotic legitimacy to claim multiple and sometimes contradictory rewards for their loyalty during the war. They had requested compensation for treaties, the bonus for their veterans, and sometimes citizenship so that all would be allowed to vote, dance, and escape the "tyranny" of the Indian Bureau. By 1934, however, the Bureau was changing rapidly and with it, its opponents. On many a reservation, "Old Dealers" now led the fight against governmental agents. As many had already done in the 1920s, Old Dealers claimed both treaty rights and citizenship, change on the reservation and revolution at the highest levels of the BIA, tradition and modernity. But because the Indian

previous page: Frank Fiske, *Good Boy Grave, Fort Yates, N.D.*
(© Fiske Collection, 1952-0472, State Historical Society of
North Dakota, Bismarck, North Dakota)

New Deal appeared to postpone the promise of emancipation from government control and called into question established patterns of interaction with the government and between reservation denizens, the Old Dealers became more radical. They requested not just the removal of individual superintendents but also the abolition of the relationship tying reservations to the federal government. While all sides invoked patriotism, it was this active minority that most effectively harnessed it, even enlisting the help of veterans from World War II. As they approached elder status in the 1950s, they had become one of the most influential groups in reservation-based tribal politics. In a move historians have so far ignored, they sowed the seeds of termination.

Saying No to the New Deal

Emphasizing Native veterans' partisanship, not as a timeless phenomenon but as a historical one, requires questioning three received ideas about them. First, veterans did not turn automatically to politics. Second, their political activities cannot be reduced to taking sides for preexisting factions. Third, veterans were not mere intermediaries between reservations and a white world that their military service had sometimes made them more familiar with than their fellow tribal members. Anthropologist Loretta Fowler, describing the Shoshone-Arapaho reservation in Wind River, Wyoming, at the end of the 1970s, insisted that election to the tribal council almost always required veteran status. Speaking of the Cheyenne and Arapaho in Oklahoma, she wrote that World War I veterans often worked as interpreters and that their participation in Armistice Day ceremonies and military-style funerals "impress[ed] spectators with the leaders' success in the white man's army as well as their ability to cope with the pressures of the wider society." Earlier, anthropologists had been eager to emphasize the role of veterans as bridges between existing factions. These are valid observations when replaced in their proper tribal and historical contexts. They cannot, however, help us make sense collectively of the position of veterans in Indian society before World War II.[1]

Nationwide, there is anecdotal evidence that veterans of the

Great War served as interpreters and cultural intermediaries. On Standing Rock, Eugene Younghawk was a salaried interpreter for Corson County in 1925 already, and then years later he filled the same position for a New Deal agency, the Indian Emergency Conservation Work. Edmund Many Deeds, also of Corson County, had the same experience. On Pine Ridge, William Fire Thunder interpreted Lakota and worked for the BIA, as did Thomas White Cow Killer, or, on Cheyenne River, Thomas Hawk Eagle. Interpreting was often accompanied with making cultural knowledge available to outsiders. Jesse Rowlodge, Bill Shakespeare, and Clyde Standing Bull among the Arapaho and Jesse Cornplanter for the Iroquois worked with field researchers, anthropologists, or historians. Thomas Butler Reed, an Aleut, assisted the linguist and anthropologist Edward Sapir. Robert Spott, a Yurok, worked with Alfred Kroeber. Jonas Poweshiek, a Meskwaki, lectured on Indian life in historical societies, as did William Fire Thunder, who assisted Scudder Mekeel in 1931. On Standing Rock, Francis Zahn, Eugene Younghawk, Martin Medicine, and Francis Bullhead also collaborated with academics. Sometimes, as in the case of Jesse Cornplanter and Harold Conklin, an anthropologist and World War II veteran, military service was a commonality between collaborators that facilitated bonding. Sometimes military service made veterans aware of the level of ignorance of Indian customs prevalent in the non-Indian world, with consequences sometimes as problematic as the "scout syndrome" denounced by William Fire Thunder. Clearly, military service facilitated interactions with non-Indians. But how did this translate into political action?[2]

Anecdotal evidence is not enough to generalize about veterans' political use of skills and knowledge acquired in the service. Lest we overemphasize the testimony of veterans themselves in this regard, we can look at the specific question of the influence of the constitution of the American Legion on tribal constitutions written in the 1930s. Jake Kills in Sight, on the Rosebud Reservation, was proud to point out the role he had played in drafting this type of document using his knowledge of the veterans' organization founding text. In his work as a Legionnaire, Kills in Sight familiarized himself with patriotic texts, Robert's Rules of Order, and the various positions as president, vice president, secretary, and so on that were common to

Legion posts and to the parliamentary mode of political organization promoted by the New Deal. Kills in Sight was certainly an expert on patriotic symbols like the flag, was used to talking in public on Armistice Day, and had founded a Legion post and was a member of several of them. Yet it was by no means a foregone conclusion that such skills and knowledge would guarantee his prominence in tribal politics. Upon close examination, the similarities between the Rosebud constitution and that of the Legion are limited to a very specific set of ideas: invocation of God, community, order, freedom and justice, and work for future generations. The central idea of protection of tribal resources, among them land and control over tribal membership, that distinguished Rosebud's 1935 constitution had, on the other hand, nothing to do with Legion tenets. The text may have borne the mark of Kills in Sight's acquaintance with patriotic phraseology, but it was not decisively shaped by it. Moreover, veteran status was a disposition that returned soldiers needed to learn to use, and they did so in different, often discordant ways. This was especially evident in the 1930s.[3]

At first, the new Democratic administration seemed to foster consensus among Native Americans in general and veterans in particular. In fact, during the first two years of the New Deal, divergences between veterans were at a minimum. In 1933 and 1934, under Collier's leadership, the Indian Bureau fine-tuned the Indian Reorganization Act (or Wheeler-Howard Act), the most radical text that the former social worker was able to negotiate with Congress. In the meantime, hopes were high on reservations, and this played in favor of inclusive uses of patriotism. On Standing Rock, in March 1933, Eugene Younghawk, despite having established a reputation as an archenemy of dancers, joined with the very traditional Strong Heart society, which was prominent in dances, to support Senator Lynn Frazier's S. 529 and Representative James H. Sinclair's HR 84. The first bill would have given tribal councils all around the country the legal standing and the ability to manage tribal funds; the second proposed to return to tribal ownership Indian lands appropriated by the federal government but never sold. These were projects in line with Collier's ideas, and on Standing Rock they were popular in general and supported by veterans in particular. Other issues mobilized reservation communities with a high degree of consensus: controlling the leasing of Indian land to whites and the rules governing the intergenerational transmission of land; creating cattle cooperatives; or replacing boss farmers and other BIA agricultural experts with Indian experts or policemen.[4]

Reform was Collier's objective. It was also the goal of local communities on reservations. In the Bullhead district of the Standing Rock Reservation, the boss farmer Martin R. Logerwell was the common enemy of many. Supporting reform and opposing his rule were closely related positions. A World War I veteran himself, Logerwell participated in Legion activity in the neighboring white town of McLaughlin but antagonized Indian Legionnaires in Bullhead. Accordingly, the district's veterans were strongly represented in petitions drawn up to request his removal from the Indian Service. Legionnaires like Willis White Mountain, a close friend of Younghawk's, expressed outrage: "I am an Indian ex-service man with services overseas, which has brought me into contact with all kinds of men, but never in my life have I met a man in a responsible position who was so indifferent to the suffering and wants of those who are under his care, as the present farmer in charge here at Bullhead, S.D., Martin R. Logerwell."

Eugene Younghawk agreed. He even claimed that the BIA agent had insulted the U.S. flag by refusing to stand when it was raised on Memorial Day. Worse, Logerwell was vindictive and prone to use his administrative power to starve his enemies. "In my case," Younghawk wrote,

> simply because I was working through the action of the tribal council and American Legion post to have him removed from his abusive administration, I have been denied all benefits from Logerwell in the way of work and rations. With the help of the American Legion post here, I seeked aid from the County Relief Agent. He helped me out to the extent of four dollars and a half and a little grub. [...] Being an ex-service man, I know I have the privilege of getting work according to preference laws for the Government and the State, but Mr. Logerwell, having all kinds of authority invested in him, he simply ignores all this and I cannot do anything at the present time.

Freshly elected to the tribal council, Younghawk directed his energies toward changing this local regime. Early in 1934, he voted in
favor of Collier's outline for reform, the "Indian Self-Government"
circular. Younghawk had many followers. In May, the entire reservation approved the Indian Reorganization Act (IRA) before its passage in June. In October, voters returned to the polls and validated
the now officially adopted act of Congress by a large majority in a
plebiscite. Standing Rock seemed firmly on Collier's side, as did the
greater part of Indian country.[5]

But then things changed. After adopting the IRA, reservation
communities were requested to adopt tribal constitutions, charters,
and by-laws, one of the main features of the act. This proved especially divisive, and many veterans occupied positions that made it
necessary for them to take a stand. Mobilized as election judges, in
the tribal council, and in various tribal committees, veterans were
in the front line of the efforts to "reorganize" reservation groups. As
important as their political clout were their internal divisions. Some
disagreements, such as that opposing dancers and enemies of dancing,
were not new. They did, however, reach a new level of intensity as
the stakes became higher. Veterans were now competing not for the
approval of the BIA but for leadership in their own communities—
and the power to decide who, really, ruled over them. In a letter
to the IRA's main architect written on American Legion letterhead,
George Sleeps From Home bluntly asked: "What I want to know,
Mr. Collier, is this: could a chartered community be invested with
power to remove or dismiss a government official?" Convinced by
Collier's reassurance that greater power would be granted Indians,
Sleeps From Home joined the commissioner's camp. Younghawk,
on the other hand, remained unconvinced. Finding that the new
administration made too little effort to renounce the paternalism of
its predecessors, he turned to the opposition. Again, he was far from
alone. In November 1935, a majority of Standing Rock voters rejected the proposed, BIA-approved constitution.[6]

Many reservations did the same, but Collier persevered. Interpreting opposition as the product of a misunderstanding or a leftover
from the previous era, he organized his troops to drum up support
and draft new constitutions. Looking to restore Indian groups to
their pre-reservation states, he also attempted to create purportedly

more natural electoral precincts, thus further antagonizing reservation communities. To many, his obstinacy and direct involvement
in reservation politics made a mockery of his promise that BIA med-
dling in tribal affairs was a thing of the past. On Standing Rock,
districts were divided, and old distinctions resurfaced. In December
1935, Francis Bullhead, a veteran and companion of Younghawk's,
suggested that the reservation be split along the state line between
the Dakotas, thus reviving the distinction between the Dakota bands
that settled the northern side and the Lakota bands who lived to the
south. BIA efforts to control this opposition failed. Having formed
a new constitution committee, BIA superintendent Lorenz C. Lippert, Eugene D. Mossman's successor, discovered that most committee members were enemies of the IRA. Some of the most determined of them were also veterans. Petitions and counter-petitions
drafted by what the BIA regarded as "factions" started flowing to
the agency's central offices and the Senate Committee on Indian
Affairs in Washington. In a new referendum organized in April
1938, the constitution and charter were again rejected, as was a new
law and order code proposed by the BIA. A new attempt in October
1939 did not meet with greater success. For Collier and his team,
the verdict was cruel. On Standing Rock, as on two-thirds of the
Indian reservations consulted, voters consistently turned down BIA-
approved constitutions.[7]

Collier's failure has been addressed many times by historians,
but the specific question of the role of veterans among his enemies
has not. Why were veterans at the forefront of the opposition to the
administration? Certainly not because the New Deal refused them
help. By 1940, 97 percent of the Indian population on Standing Rock
depended on governmental aid. Half of the total amount was channeled to reservation communities through the Civilian Conservation
Corps, a relief agency created by the New Deal, the Indian Division
of which (known as CCC-ID) had been placed under the authority
of the BIA. Given its economic importance and its subordination to
the Bureau, the CCC-ID was bound to be the focus of opposition,
but veterans massively benefited from CCC-ID employment. They
were familiar with the military style prevalent in the agency's work
camps. There, ex-soldiers were in demand for the skills they had accumulated in the armed forces, with their sense of hierarchy and

leadership at the top of the list and hygiene finishing right behind. On Standing Rock, veterans represented a fifth of all CCC-ID employees and a third of the low-level management made up primarily of crew foremen. Some even managed to develop their technical abilities. Edmund Many Deeds, with his six months of non-combat service in the U.S. Army Aviation, and Daniel Yellow Earrings were in this case. Allen Little Eagle, a high school dropout, was sent by the CCC-ID to a training school for leaders. Although his superintendent saw him as "too easy going with the men," he also garnered praise on the job. Little Eagle had done "surveying work in the Navy during the war and seems to have retained what he knew exceptionally well." He eventually earned an appreciable $1,020 a year.[8]

High status in CCC-ID camps was grounded on veterans' ability to claim employment preference. Using their slowly earned political capital in their respective communities, politicized veterans managed to have this most special of rights recognized by their fellow reservation residents. On Standing Rock, in 1935, the tribal council requested that positions of foremen in the CCC-ID be reserved for tribal members, especially veterans. In Kenel, George Sleeps From Home and the district council asked for disabled veterans to be given only "light duty" jobs as foremen, timekeepers, and truck drivers. Sometimes, however, they were turned down. When the Cannonball Legion post requested preference for the district's veterans, John Collier himself refused. In line with Franklin D. Roosevelt's refusal to recognize special rights, he preferred to grant jobs based on family income.[9]

In the complex political and economic environment of the Depression, veterans opposed to Collier gained momentum from such slights. Many veterans used the old image of the warrior as defender of his group, and Collier's opponents had an easier time posing as upholders of tradition against paternalistic interlopers. They proved adept at taking over local factions and redirecting their energies. In Bullhead, Eugene Younghawk and Willis White Mountain headed the opposition; on Collier's side, Daniel Yellow Earrings, also a veteran, led IRA supporters with non-veteran James Red Fish. Ex-servicemen able to appeal to their likes demonstrated particularly well the political potential of tools such as petitions. Younghawk, for example, signed more petitions than his rival James Red Fish. More people signed petitions with him, and more were frequent signers of petitions than was the case for Red Fish. Among those frequent co-signers was a small but tightly knit group of Legionnaires. Evidently, this was not the only commonality between them: Kinship or work on the district council provided other, equally relevant ties. Yet it is clear that signing petitions for veterans' rights reinforced and politicized these ties and that they transferred seamlessly into anti-IRA mobilization. Legion membership also allowed Younghawk's faction to reach out to other Legionnaires on the reservation, thus easing the transition from district-based to reservation-based politics. Having learned to master the rhetorical and social exercise of drafting, signing, and having other people sign petitions, Younghawk was well armed to use against the New Deal the very democratization of Indian life it promoted. Several of the petitions he organized reached all-time highs on the reservation, at least in the category of openly political documents (as opposed to the more frequent requests for relief or services or ad hominem attacks against BIA agents). And petitions made it possible to be both on the council and in the opposition, thus expanding Younghawk's ability to do more than merely respond to government initiatives.[10]

Anti-IRA veterans also owed their success to their off-reservation connections, which were based on ideology. While a multiplicity of distinctions helped solidify opposing camps, such as interpersonal and family rivalries, geographical locations, and the categorization of full-bloods and mixed-bloods, veterans channeled them toward specific political positions. The context of the Great Depression created an ideological powder keg that the new commissioner's pushiness only ignited. It allowed opponents, above all the veterans among them, to merge their personal grievances, many of them economic, with more general objections to the New Deal's reform politics. By 1937, Old Dealers led their troops in a frontal assault against the New Deal. Rejecting constitutions was not enough. They also attacked the administration for ending the allotment of Indian land, forbidding the sale of Indian land, and apparently forcing communal property back onto reservation communities. They fell back easily onto a well-worn theme: the betrayal of the meaning of citizenship in Indian country. This was a powerful way to reach out to allies well beyond reservation boundaries.

On June 26 of that year, Younghawk and forty-seven "World War American Indian veterans and ex-service men and scouts" met and signed an "Emancipation Memorial." They addressed their manifesto to the president of the United States, the World War Veterans' Legislation Committee, and Congress. In a solemn preamble, they evoked the Allotment Act of 1906 and the Indian Citizenship Acts of 1919 and 1924. Citing the service of ten thousand Indians during the conflict and the 187 Great War veterans on the reservation, Albert Grass's exemplary sacrifice on the front, as well as the founding of six Legion posts on Standing Rock, they followed with a biting critique of the Indian New Deal. A plan was offered, most notably requesting that the United States

> 1. proclaim ex-service men free from Bureau wardship; 2. create a commission authorizing and directing them as agents of the U.S. government to transfer as soon as practicable to these Indians, ex-service men who have honorable discharge papers, borne on the tribal rolls of their respective tribes, any and all assets, real and personal property belonging to such Indian ex-service men by the government of the United States, such transfers to be evidenced in such a manner as the Commission can prescribe; 3. The Commission shall consist of representatives of the Indian ex-service men, the Secretary of the Interior, one member of the Committee on Indian affairs of the Senate.

The authors of the memorial concluded: "We who have served our country honorably in time of peril and particular those of us if we were good enough to shoulder the gun along with our white comrades why no grant us an emancipation by the enactment of such legislation and proclamation, to the end that the American Indian serviceman may obtain at least fair play and an equal footing with his fellow citizen." As they had learned to do in the 1920s, veterans combined a general criticism of the Bureau with their own specific grievances. As they had done almost ten years before also, they claimed to be the vanguard of progress on reservations and demanded the right to manage their property as they saw fit. As if nothing had changed in Washington, they recycled all the arguments but expanded their reach, first defending the rights of World War I soldiers, then those of all veterans and policemen, then of all Indian citizens, and finally demanding the abolition of the Indian Bureau.[11]

Looking for allies, they created new networks. Standing Rock memorialists, for example, cited Joseph Bruner. In 1923, this Creek businessman had helped found the Society of Oklahoma Indians, with a small cadre of educated individuals hailing from the Central Plains state. Strongly assimilationist, the organization regularly reminded the reader of its magazine of Native Americans' war record. Bruner in particular liked to emphasize the anomaly of Indians' incomplete citizenship. "We are one hundred percent Americans, our boys volunteered as soldiers. Why aren't we one hundred percent American?" Renamed the Indian National Confederacy in 1933, the organization joined others the following year to form the American Indian Federation (AIF), a coalition that soon devoted the bulk of its energy to attacking the Indian New Deal and the IRA. It drew support from U.S. senators in Utah, California, Oklahoma, Arizona, and North and South Dakota as well as from Indian supporters of assimilation and various patriotic organizations.[12]

In the eyes of AIF activists, citizenship was an ideology that did not lend itself to the many uses to which Indians had put it in the 1920s. Bruner and his allies used a much stricter and more militant version of both citizenship and patriotism to attack Collier in the name of Americanism and anticommunism. Bruner in particular used the theme of the overrepresentation of Indians in the war. But no one was more adept at manipulating patriotic pathos than Iroquois activist Alice Lee Jemison. In the pages of *The First American*, the AIF's newspaper, and in congressional hearings, Jemison mentioned the war service of AIF members and made contact with the American Legion and the Veterans of Foreign Wars to boost the patriotic assault on the Indian New Dealers. Speaking not just as an activist and representative of Indians nationwide but as a woman, she described Indians as a derelict population abandoned by the BIA and betrayed in spite of their heroism:

> I speak for the great army of valiant Indians who plead only
> for the opportunity to be recognized as human beings with
> the same rights and privileges as other Americans. I speak

for those fathers and mothers who earnestly desire the same education for their children that other American children receive and not the experimental program of the Commissioner. I speak for those who have lost their homes and property under this act. I speak for the hollow-eyed, silent children. I speak for the aged Indians, thin and wasted with starvation. I speak for the Gold Star mothers and World War veterans, shivering today in thin canvas tents and lowly hovels where the temperature is 30° below zero. [. . .] I speak for all Indians who have suffered under this Wheeler-Howard bill.

Anxious to have veterans tell of their plight themselves, the AIF managed to get several of them to testify in person in front of congressional committees investigating the effects of the IRA.[13]

The fragile alliances Collier had managed to create in Congress to pass the IRA began to crumble. In 1937, as they were drawing up their "Emancipation memorial," Eugene Younghawk and other Standing Rock veterans were not isolated in the fight against the Indian Bureau. The cause had become national. A reader of the *Congressional Record* and regular correspondent with senators and congresspersons in Washington, Younghawk was among the veterans who regularly testified in front of the Senate Committee on Indian Affairs. In February 1937, four months before sending out the memorial, Younghawk and his colleague Francis Bullhead wrote Oklahoma senator Elmer Thomas, the committee's chairman. They specifically recommended abolishing the IRA and the CCC-ID. They also declared in favor of state jurisdiction, describing their willingness to see the federal government turn over to them its control over schools and relief involving Indians. By March, Lynn Frazier and Burton K. Wheeler, former allies of Colliers, launched a full-scale attack on the IRA. Their Indian allies organized. Younghawk, in particular, participated in the foundation of the Black Hills Treaty Council in September 1937 and acted as its secretary on Standing Rock. Bringing the question of Indian claims into the debate on the IRA, the pan-Sioux organization immediately joined the AIF. A new synthesis linking citizenship, Indian rights, and patriotism was afoot.[14]

This started Younghawk's decade-long war against Collier's communism, the BIA's wasting of "taxpayer's money," the "tyrannical" Bureau agents, and the violation of treaty rights and citizenship acts beginning with the Dawes Act of 1887. The attraction of his discourse allowed him to get allies off the reservation. His close veteran friend Willis White Mountain mobilized the Non-Partisan League in North Dakota to fund his trip to Washington and contacted the VFW when he got there. On the north side of Standing Rock, a chapter of the National American Indian Voters' Association made good use of patriotism in its anti-IRA activism. In 1938, its representatives, Josephine Kelly and Mary Many Wounds, a veteran's wife, demanded the bonus for veterans and pensions for all Indians, better schools, and the abolition of the BIA. As in the case of Jemison, with whom they were connected, it was not accidental that women were among the most vocal against the Bureau. As homemakers and mothers, they were especially well placed to question shortcomings in relief and the perceived injustice toward veterans, sons, husbands, and "boys." As Kelly told the senators:

> When the United States called them [our boys] to arms they went, without one word about the treaties that they had signed. We were not supposed to fight white people any more. But they went just the same. Some of those World War veterans are out there living like tramps. War mothers are living in tents. It is a disgrace to the United States of America. We were the first American citizens, the only Americans in the country. We want to be turned loose from the Indian bureau.

In the late 1920s, hostility had remained almost exclusively directed toward local agents of the BIA. It was now part of a full-blown attack on its very existence in which veterans were both prominent and central actors, connecting as they did many parts of a multifaceted fight. In what could appear as the ultimate sign that veterans had turned the IRA against itself, in 1940 Younghawk himself became Standing Rock's tribal chairman.[15]

Collier's administration contended that these activists were mere agitators or the representatives of factional minorities. This was disingenuous. As the case of Standing Rock demonstrates (examples could have been drawn from other Lakota reservations or from the Iroquois), the New Deal's enemies were able to use political connections and reservation-based organizations to mobilize nationwide networks linking local communities to the Senate halls. These Old Dealers used an ideology that many in Indian country could feel comfortable with, arguing for full citizenship but insisting that it not be made an excuse for ignoring treaty rights. The specific mix of tradition and change they advocated was not Collier's, even if it had taken shape in the 1920s in the shadow of his activism. It was, however, extremely relevant for populations that had symbolically invested in patriotism since World War I.[16]

Saying No to the State

The movement only grew in the 1940s, when it received a massive boost in the context of the war against Japan and Nazi Germany. Writing in 1944, Dakota anthropologist Ella Deloria, who grew up on Standing Rock, explained to a non-Native readership how World War II rekindled the patriotic relationship between the federal government and Indians. "It was right that Uncle Sam should help the Indian," Deloria wrote in *Speaking of Indians,* speaking of U.S. Indian policy before the war and outlining the viewpoint of the Sioux. "It was Uncle Sam's duty to show himself a man in that way. They [the Sioux] could not return the compliment now, maybe never. But if ever a time came when they could, they would not be found wanting. Nor were they, for a time *did* come." Showcasing Indian military skills, she expressed hopes that would not have been out of place twenty years earlier when the World War I generation prepared to don the uniform: "The war has indeed wrought an overnight change in the outlook, horizon, and even the habits of the Indian people— a change that might not have come about for many years yet." In 1944, in words reminiscent of earlier commentators in 1917, Deloria claimed that Indians soldiers would

> come back with perspective. [. . .] They have fought and suffered for their country. They are Americans, and they will want to be treated as such. They will want to be able to talk the common language of America, and I don't mean just

literally, but figuratively as well. That is to say, they will
want to participate in the larger thought and life of the land
and not be given special work scaled down to their abilities,
as if those abilities were static, or to their needs, as if those
needs must always be limited to tribal life. Tribal life is only
a phase in human development anyway. The next step, for
every people is national life.[17]

Deloria voiced the thoughts of many. At almost every level,
World War II elicited intellectual and social responses that had already arisen in 1917 and 1918 when discussing the place of Indians
in the country. Imagining military service as part of a debt-based
relationship between Indians and the federal government; hoping
for expanded horizons and greater familiarity with the "non-Indian
world"; dreaming that Indians would finally be citizens like the
others: Those prospects were not new. Even claims for Indian Day
celebration were renewed. As they already had in 1917, non-Indians
also wondered how to draft Indians, whether or not they should
segregate them, whether they would be loyal. Such repetitions had
much to do with their ignorance of history and of their Indian fellow citizens' rights and duties. Not all repetition, however, could be
blamed on ignorance. Supporters of Indian citizenship actively emphasized that since 1917 little appeared to have changed. Indians were
still second-class citizens despite their willingness to defend their
own country. World War II only magnified the scandal that enemies
of the New Deal had tried to use against Collier and his team.

Before World War II, the combative commissioner of Indian
affairs had not had much trouble calling the American Indian Federation's credentials into question. Denouncing Bruner's ties to foreign
and extremist groups, Collier effectively turned patriotism against
the Creek businessman—for a while. The political realignment
brought about by U.S. involvement in World War II undermined
his ability to do so. Standing now firmly on the side of democracy,
Indian patriots could not easily be regarded as mere radicals anymore. As it had done twenty years earlier but on a more massive
scale, the war unmoored thousands of Indians from the tutelage of
the BIA. Around twenty-five thousand Indians became soldiers, and
hundreds of thousands of them left reservations to work for the war

industry in the cities. By 1942, the BIA had lost to the war not only a good part of its clientele but also much of its staff. It also lost one of its most potent levers in the fight against poverty on reservations when, the same year, the CCC-ID was phased out.[18]

For assimilationists, the context was ideal. Having failed to force the cancellation of the IRA in 1937 and 1938, they returned to the fight in 1943 with new ammunition. On June 10, 1943, the Senate's investigative committee created in 1927 at the request of, among others, Collier published a report of its activities that not only called for the cancellation of the IRA but also advocated the end of the Bureau of Indian Affairs. U.S. congressmen returned to the old formulation of "the Indian problem" and the need to supply a prompt solution. The approach they pursued was familiar: Following the lead of Representative Francis H. Case of South Dakota, they recommended full citizenship for Indian soldiers of both world wars; the creation of an Indian claims commission that would once and for all settle the troubling issue of treaty rights; and the end of federal rule in Indian country in favor of state jurisdiction. The concerted attack on the New Deal turned into a project to end the relationship between Indians and the United States. By the beginning of the 1950s, it was known as "termination."[19]

Understanding how the attack developed requires looking at the impact of World War II on the World War I generation. The Great Depression had largely hampered veterans' mobility. World War II made it possible to leave reservations once more but also confronted veterans anew with the fact that government regulations, not just poverty, had limited their prospects. As they took on the role of guardians of the patriotic temple for young generations, helping to take young men to recruiting stations or raising new service flags next to Old Glory, they also experimented with off-reservation life. Willis White Mountain, Eugene Younghawk's friend, found no easier way to leave than reenlisting in the Army. Using training acquired under rehabilitation provisions after World War I, he became an aircraft mechanic and an auto mechanic and was later a patrolman at an Army depot. The opportunity to break loose from reservation strictures loomed large on his horizon. Writing in 1943 to Francis H. Case from the town of Springle in the Black Hills, he asked the South Dakota representative for help in selling his land on Standing Rock.

Forced to go back in 1946, he applied for off-reservation positions as a mechanic or a Veterans Administration employee. In 1947, he left again for the interdenominational Cook Christian Training School in Phoenix, Arizona. There he studied to become a minister using his GI Bill benefits. Back again in 1952, he managed to send his children to school in Rapid City but kept dreaming of a clean break with the reservation, a territory he did not hesitate to describe as under the domination of a corrupt tribal council—this despite his own involvement in local politics, which lasted until his death on the reservation in 1968. Having reactivated hopes for change initiated by World War I, the second global conflict of the century reproduced the frustration that had started so many a veteran's activist career in the interwar years.[20]

As early as 1945, ex-soldiers of the Great War started organizing and reorganizing veterans' posts to lead the new generation in addressing this frustration. The new war expanded the activities of the posts. The sheer number of returning veterans made it possible to start new posts even when old ones already existed. This promoted competition in veterans' activities but also helped to homogenize posts racially where, before the new war, Indians had had to cohabitate with whites. The move was especially in evidence in Sioux or Iroquois country and in Oklahoma. Although some in Pueblo country rejected the new posts, they multiplied in the postwar years and continued to grow with the return of Korean War veterans. As after World War I, strong collaboration with women's organizations such as the War Mothers and the Legion Auxiliary allowed for the involvement of women in veteran welfare, and the organization of ceremonies for departing, returning, or furloughed soldiers. As soon as war industry workers and veterans from war in Europe and the Pacific came back to reservations, Legion posts resumed their activities.

Adding the surnames of new heroes to the name of the post was often the first move toward the material and symbolic reintegration of the young generation. Sitting as they did on the tribal committees planning for the return of young veterans, World War I soldiers also defended their right to a bonus or to preferential access to tribal programs. Another symbolic strategy to turn young veterans into allies involved selecting them for Legion positions of leadership. In Bullhead, on Standing Rock, Clayton Brownotter thus became the old World War I post's first commander after World War II. To a strong military record, he added equally strong oratorical skills that made him an ideal recruit for the post and launched his political career. In 1955 already, he was a councilman of the tribe and in 1959 its chairman. Such meteoric rises, however, were exceptional. In Bullhead, World War I veterans still dominated the Legion post in 1956. Conversely, when the young generation founded its own posts, they made sure to enlist the help of their elders. On the Flandreau Reservation, the new Gordon-Weston post of the Veterans of Foreign Wars selected Alexander Wakeman as its commander in 1945. This made political sense: The World War I veteran had also been the tribe's chairman since 1941 and had occupied that position until 1948. Continuity and respect between the generations was emphasized, and interactions between them turned World War I veterans, by then mature men, into elders. Evidently this did not always go without conflict. Jesse Rowlodge, an Arapaho veteran from Oklahoma, had struggled during the interwar period to have his elders recognize him as a valid tribal representative. But after World War II, he showed no disposition to make things easier for the younger generation. Denouncing their alcoholism, he also emphasized that veteran status, in and of itself, was not enough to become a leader.[21]

Rowlodge had good reasons to fear the political ambitions of the young generation. In 1945, however, their aspirations were remarkably similar to those of their elders. Speaking a few months before his early demise in training camp, Joe Allen Littlecrow, from Bullhead, made declarations that seemed inspired by the district's Legionnaires most involved against the Indian New Deal: "When the war with the Japs is ended, Joe says he will join the Barney Brought post no 82 at Bullhead and wants to take an active part in its work and keep the Indian boys as an organization for their welfare. Joe hopes that the government will see the light of day when the war is over and grant full citizenship to the Indian boys who have offered their services and life if necessary, to the country they love." This was the language of emancipation that World War I veterans had long promoted.[22]

National organizations both old and new competed for the new generation's attention, but it was anti-IRA leaders who stood to gain the most from their return. In a major departure from the post–World War I era, all stood poised to welcome and embrace veterans. In 1944, Indian leaders supported by Collier's administration created the National Congress of the American Indians. They actively prepared to recruit returning soldiers. In 1943, a year after accepting World War II soldiers into its ranks, the American Legion requested full citizenship rights for those among them who happened to be Indian as well as for all Indians who had had enough education to satisfy voting requirements in their respective states. In the years following the end of the war, delegates from western states repeated the demand at the organization's annual national conventions. The spread of anticommunism helped frame the restrictions weighing down on reservation Indians as unpatriotic and un-American. The defense of individual freedom now encompassed the right to drink, for which Indian soldiers and their representatives had fought throughout the war. Prohibition had ended in 1933 everywhere but on reservations. Speaking at a meeting chaired by South Dakota U.S. representative Karl Mundt, Josephine Kelly called prohibition for Indians a disgrace "especially now that our boys are taking part in the war and doing the same thing as their white brothers." After World War I, veterans considered drinking a privilege but had met with suspicion from Indians and non-Indians for doing so. In a striking reversal, prohibition now stood as the epitome of Indian "slavery," and the right to drink was widely regarded as a quintessential civil right.[23]

In Congress, the war brought new allies for Indian enemies of the New Deal. Most of them were Republicans. Old-guard progressives like Wheeler and Frazier were joined in North Dakota by William Langer, Gerald P. Nye, Usher L. Burdick, and Charles Robertson and in South Dakota by Karl Mundt, Chan Gurney, William Bulow, E. Y. Berry, and Francis H. Case. Case, himself a veteran of World War I, developed a cordial relationship with Standing Rock veterans— a much better relationship than he had with white settlers on the reservation. Like Berry and Langer, he had been adopted by a reservation elder. Nye, Burdick, and Robertson themselves were highly regarded as friends of the tribe, especially by opponents of the IRA.

Berry's ties to Standing Rock veterans were especially strong. He had spent his childhood in the white town of McLaughlin, in the middle of the reservation, and had been a county judge and a regular participant in Memorial Day and Armistice Day ceremonies. A state senator from 1939 to 1943 and a U.S. representative from 1950 to 1971, he brought to the job a conviction that Americanism and patriotism needed to guide the fashioning of Indian policy. This architect of termination was especially eager to promote full citizenship for Indians and end tribal relations. He was also a firm believer in courting the Indian vote on reservations, where he counted many friends.[24]

Strong support for Indian citizenship at the national level rapidly translated into successful fights for voting rights locally. World War I veterans were especially prominent in the struggle of the Eastern Cherokees for the franchise. In the 1930s, the fight for the franchise had halted, but the IRA had politicized Cherokees in North Carolina just as it had Indians elsewhere. By 1945, some of the most politically active leaders on the reservation had good anti-IRA credentials. Fred Bauer, in particular, was a Cherokee veteran who had fought Collier alongside Alice Lee Jemison, opposing liberal reform in the schools. Angered by the end of the flag salute in the evening, he had also questioned the BIA superintendent's patriotism when the latter refused to fund the activities of the post of the Veterans of Foreign Wars that he and other Eastern Cherokee veterans like George Owl started on the reservation. Bauer's appeal was notable, and he managed to be elected as tribal vice chairman alongside his cousin Jarrett Blythe, one of Collier's supporters. In 1939, the reservation's veterans reorganized under the American Legion. In 1940, as would-be recruits registered for the draft, veterans attempted to take advantage of the patriotic atmosphere and be registered on electoral rolls. They failed. In 1945, as 321 Cherokees came back from the armed forces, pro-franchise activists changed their strategy. They now had the backing of superintendent Joe Jennings, himself a World War I veteran and an ex-member of the semi-Indian Legion post on the Pine Ridge Sioux Reservation. Jennings teamed up with the Eastern Cherokee Legion post to survey the needs of returning soldiers. He organized an on-the-farm agricultural training program that reached 213 Indian and 189 white veterans and enlisted the help of the Legion in putting together an annual show to draw tourists onto the reservation. By the end of 1945, a six-member committee, half made up of World War I veterans, had been organized: In May 1946, its members organized a new campaign to register Eastern Cherokee voters in Swain and Jackson counties. Failing again to force the hand of white election officers, they turned for assistance to the white post in neighboring Bryson City and hired as a lawyer a Democratic candidate for a seat in the State Senate. The Legion's district officers also lent a hand to the new campaign. In the November elections, the Legion took voters to the polls. At last, county authorities relented. A year before the President's Committee on Civil Rights found little justification for the remaining restrictions on Indian vote and two years before World War II veterans conquered the vote for their communities in Arizona and New Mexico, it was in North Carolina that an intergenerational alliance and a temporary truce between enemies and supporters of the New Deal scored the first major success in the fight for Indian civil rights.[25]

The attraction of the anti-IRA camp, however, was palpable. On Standing Rock, George Sleeps From Home, for a long time a supporter of Collier's program, switched sides during the war, in which two of his sons were fighting. In January 1943, he contacted Francis H. Case and explained his motivation for joining the fight against the Indian Bureau: "We must back up our boys who are fighting. We do not know what for. It certainly cannot be for freedom as we are denied certain things other class of citizens enjoyed. We want to at least vote as Americans as to who shall be our superintendent if this so-called guardianship must continue." Sleeps From Home had not signed the "Emancipation Memorial" in 1937. In 1943, the text was discussed again on the reservation, and he began to reconsider his position. Sitting on the tribal committee in charge of veterans' welfare, Sleeps From Home paid special attention to veterans' rights to housing, education, and loans. Not losing sight of the wrongs suffered by members of his generation and remembering in particular the lands lost to taxes after World War I, he was involved in the Black Hills Claim and supported the creation of an Indian claims commission to settle all treaty-related controversies. This did not contradict his determination to see veterans freed from the strictures of BIA

control. Writing to Case in December 1944, he requested emancipation from the Bureau just like anti-IRA activists, his former rivals:

> We are not a free people by any means. There are hundreds
> of Indians that will become self-sustaining citizens if given
> the opportunity. Here are many Indians who farm for the
> white farmers all summer and then live in tent all winter.
> There is something radically wrong. It is time for a change.
> Sometime we wonder what we are fighting for. It is also time
> for the U.S. government to wash its hands. To live up to its
> treaties with the Indians and pay us for all the lands and
> property taken away from us without compensation. Other-
> wise Uncle Sam cannot seat at the peace table with a clean
> conscience.

To help the war effort, Sleeps favored "a drastic reduction in this
gigantic Indian Bureau." In 1946 and 1947, he campaigned for Case's
bill HR 1113. Like its first (HR 5115, June 23, 1944), second (HR
3681, July 5, 1945) and third versions (HR 3710, July 6, 1945), HR
1113 purported to "emancipate" U.S. Indians in general or, more
modestly, to mandate the "removal of restrictions on property of Indians who served in the armed forces." In the spring of 1946, Sleeps
From Home accompanied Younghawk to Chicago, the (temporary)
new seat of the BIA headquarters, to support the plan. As Younghawk put it: "If Abraham Lincoln freed the negroes, why not some
president free the original Americans?"[26]

This was far from a complete reversal for Sleeps From Home.
In his letters to Case and his testimony in Congress, he articulated
the same principles he had defended more than fifteen years earlier
in front of the investigative Senate Committee. But he also made
them more radical. In 1929, he had emphasized the need to protect the lands of the old and the uneducated. He was now willing to
see the old who were poor but "land-rich" be emancipated the same
as the young, so that they could sell their land and survive. Prompted
by the belief that the sacrifice of "the boys" could again have been in
vain and aware that many of them were encountering difficulties in
taking advantage of the GI Bill of Rights on the reservation, Sleeps

From Home now denounced "the old system" of BIA law and regulations. Even more radically, he welcomed state jurisdiction, so that Indians would finally have the same rights as whites. This validated a strategy that had been pursued by Younghawk and his allies since 1935: Opposing John Collier's attempt to set the pace of assimilation, they requested immediate emancipation from the Bureau and made full use of patriotic legitimacy to achieve this goal. Having become elders for the young generation, World War I veterans easily garnered support for this project on Standing Rock. In a new round of petitions, they collected the signatures of World War II veterans and of the surviving "old warriors" in their communities. They seemed on the verge of becoming a major force behind the passing of a termination law.[27]

Case's bill did not pass in 1947, but veterans remained committed. In the postwar years, the concerns of ex-servicemen of all generations were pressing. As lands under trust could not be used as guarantee, veterans of World War II were unable to claim their right to business loans on the reservation. Collier had left his position as commissioner of Indian affairs in 1945, but the legacy of the Indian New Deal kept weighing on veterans' special rights. Cash-strapped and committed to a cattle program initiated in 1935, Standing Rock's tribal council could not cushion the blow: Tribal monies were directed toward the general economic development of the tribe and could not be used to ensure that veterans receive a loan or get an education. World War I veterans kept pushing for change and found the tribal council responsive to their stance, whether they were demanding their rights or emphasizing leaving the BIA's orbit. Younghawk, in particular, recommended that the Veterans Administration open up a school and offer vocational education for veterans on the reservation. In 1948, under Josephine Kelly's leadership, councilmen voted in favor of extending the state's jurisdiction over the reservation. In 1950, uncertain as to the status of the 1947 bill, Sleeps From Home wrote Case that he still supported his effort at emancipating Indians: "We on the Standing Rock reservation are much in favor of your bill. [. . .] It is true we should be treated as individuals and not as tribes. There are hundreds, yes, thousands who are capable of managing their own affairs and should be but under state control." The new commissioner of Indian affairs, Dillon S. Myers, seemed willing to work in the right direction: In 1951, he made it possible, for veterans in particular, to turn trust land into fee-patent land. Many Indians, both on and off reservation, took advantage of this opportunity to guarantee a loan, buy a home, or simply attend to their daily needs.[28]

In 1953, Congress passed House Concurrent Resolution 108 and PL 280, the acts that historians have termed the termination laws proper. The onset of the Cold War and the growing tension in Korea legitimized renewed attacks on the architecture of the Indian New Deal. Identified with communism, Collier's defense of collective life on the reservation was now completely out of fashion. Reservations were recast as prisoner-of-war camps or even concentration camps, BIA control as the same kind of discrimination that Indians and African Americans were suffering at the polling booths at the hands of white segregationists. Consequently, HCR 108 and PL 280 planned for the end of the trust relationship between reservation Indians and the federal government, the demise of tribal governmental entities, and the takeover of the states. Emancipation was to happen progressively, however. Only the tribes that were the most advanced on the road to what was still called "civilization" would be "freed." Standing Rock was not among them. There, throughout the 1950s, veterans of World War I continued to press their senators and representatives to help them get full control of their lands from the BIA. In public, however, their voices became more tenuous. While several of them continued their political careers well into the 1960s, it was not possible to identify a generational take in their public interventions anymore.

This was a measure of their success and of their failure. They had managed to make Native veterans' rights a foremost political concern for Indians and non-Indians alike, and new generations took over their role. They had also gotten compromised in a movement that in the 1960s would come to be perceived as the most reactionary and anti-Indian movement in the twentieth century. Even if Standing Rock Reservation had not been targeted as prime material for termination, it still reeled under assimilationist pressure. Culturally and economically crucial lands were flooded under the waters of the massive Oahe Dam in 1958. In 1959, Standing Rock and other Lakota reservations had to fend off South Dakota's attempt to take over control of their law and order. "Emancipation" didn't seem compatible with special Indian rights anymore. True, some veterans, like Hobart Keith from Pine Ridge, would later take part in the struggle for sovereignty at Wounded Knee. But these were isolated experiences. Termination laws had in effect terminated the collective voice of the World War I generation.[29]

Conclusion

I F THE PREVIOUS PAGES HAVE SUCCEEDED in convincing the reader that Indian patriotism is indeed a historical phenomenon, connected to the ebb and flow of war, embedded in political struggles for freedom or protection, and created by the individual and collective actions of Indian people themselves, this book will have achieved its purpose. Instead of taking it for granted that all Indians were patriots by nature or, on the contrary, that no Indian could reasonably be expected to claim the status of a U.S. patriot, I have documented the concrete, varied positions that Native Americans, whether veterans or not, took between 1917 and the onset of the termination movement.

A complex picture has emerged. Obviously, World War I made it possible to claim U.S. patriotism on an unprecedented scale. Whether one looks at the number of Indian veterans, their level of political organization, or the sustained mobilization of patriotic arguments on the local and national scene by Indians on or off reservations, there can be no doubt that something changed in 1917. Change, however, needed people to happen. It was not enough that Indians joined the armed forces without a major rebellion and demonstrated their loyalty on the battlefields of France. Their loyalty had to be noted, publicized, celebrated, and memorialized by them and by others. It had to be interpreted.

At first, non-Indian contemporaries imagined that they were witnessing the "return of the repressed" after the most violent years of assimilation: Savage virtues were showing under a veneer of civilization, and Indians were reclaiming their "warrior traditions." This thinking is still very much with us, and it has prevented us from understanding the conscious efforts it took Indians to give social and political relevance to these traditions in a world that, once the war was over, did not care much for them anymore. After the war ended, nativistic and racialist thinking prompted white promoters of patriotism, especially on and around reservations, to consciously devise a picture of Indians as super-patriots whose innate attachment to their land had been successfully appropriated by the freedom-loving, democracy-promoting United States. Celebrating Indian patriots made it possible for them to imagine a happy ending to the Indian wars and confirm that the Indians' destiny was assimilation. In this framework, Indian loyalty, manifested in World War I and repeated in patriotic celebrations all year round, proved that the colonization of the country, especially west of the Mississippi River, was now accepted even by those who had suffered the most from it. Furthermore, Indian combativeness signaled that the impending demise of the Indian race itself, which had so long been anticipated, was now a thing of the past. Indians were back in history and firmly on the side of their conquerors. The frontier was finally closed. History textbooks could be revised accordingly.

Many Indians embraced these analyses, if not all the racial representations that underlay them, because they offered opportunities they could ill afford to pass up. Some of these opportunities carried only symbolic rewards—then as now, symbols carried great weight. Celebrating Indian soldiers' bravery in the war was good for self-respect. It opened the door—ever so slowly—to speaking of other brave Indians whose heroic deeds had been performed not for but against the United States. Once Indian soldiers came home, it became possible for their families to claim the U.S. flag as an Indian symbol and in the process, to publicly celebrate ethnic, tribal identities. Other opportunities promised more material rewards. In a time when the nation fought over the need to compensate its veterans financially, educating non-Indians about the Indian contribution to the war effort ensured that Native veterans would not be passed over and, perhaps more importantly, that their loyalty could help Indian communities settle old claims, rooted in treaties. In the end, the distinction between symbolic and material benefits didn't matter much: Regardless of what the question at issue was, invoking patriotism commanded non-Indians' attention and almost systematically gave Indians more room for maneuver in their dealings with non-Indians. As soon as the war ended, Indians on or off reservations tried to imagine ways to make the most of their new legitimizing and emboldening identity trait as patriots.[1]

Reconstructing the logic of patriotic claims allows us to move beyond sterile debates focused on elucidating whether or not Indians were *truly* patriots. Patriotism (particularly in the sense of acknowledging American superiority) may or may not have been located in Indians' hearts and minds at any one time. But after World War I, patriotism was certainly addressed in a series of widespread social practices on Indian reservations that made it a crucial part of Indians' public identities as individuals, communities, and peoples. Telling stories about the past, digging graves for dead soldiers, building monuments, dancing, and claiming rights became tightly connected in Indians' collective attempts to reap the rewards of loyalty. From within the limits of a race-based patriotism, Indians actively redefined their relationship with a nation that had colonized them and that continued to deprive them of their land and most of the other resources they could have used to sustain a distinct way of life. In this process of redefinition, Indians themselves revised history.

This story was the result of a collective endeavor. For many Native Americans, it was also a personal struggle. Throughout the book, we have encountered the cases of tribal leaders and veterans from many Native groups and their specific efforts to have non-Indians make good on the promises of patriotism. Their cases demonstrate how some individuals developed "careers" as patriots, how they worked on individual and personal emotions and memories marked by their experience of the war and shaped them to give them political relevance. It became evident that this came at a personal cost and that not all were equally able to do so. To bring these points home, it is worth returning one last time to an individual case.

Jonas Poweshiek is a good example of the veteran-revisionist. Born in 1894 to a Meskwaki (Fox) family identified as "progressive," he left for the war in 1917. Five years after his return, Poweshiek became a janitor at the Historical Society in Des Moines, Iowa. He was knowledgeable about Meskwaki history and soon became a consultant, a lecturer in the schools, and later a full-fledged researcher who collaborated with anthropologist Edgar R. Harlan. Writing his autobiography for Harlan in 1936, Poweshiek narrated how he had volunteered in 1917. Loyalty, he explained, made sense in his personal and family history. He had joined the fight just as his father had sided with the United States and become a policeman. His enrollment had taken place after years of traveling from one off-reservation school to the next, a series of peregrinations that led him finally to Oklahoma, far from the family home: "While I was in Oklahoma I went to Tulsa and enlisted in the Army June 2, 1917, and I was shipped along with the other boys to Ft. Sill, Oklahoma, where we were sworn in on June 5. It was quite an experience for me and I wanted to go across so bad. It was more of a trip and to see how it was to be in the war that I was anxious to go." His letters in 1917 had been more enthusiastic—and evidenced a more collective experience. At the time he had written: "We are all anxious to go across the pond and ready to meet Fritz."

In 1945, during the last days of World War II, with his son Richard still away in the armed forces, Poweshiek took up his pen again and fashioned himself into a historian.

> Back in World War I, the Sac and Fox Indians of Tama [Iowa] were exempted from any war service on account of non-citizenship and being wards of the government, which was true of many other Indian tribes of the United States. But the Indians loved their homeland so much that they didn't take advantage of being exempted; they wanted to fight for their country, so they volunteered to the extent of 85 per cent, a contribution as large as any of the races in proportion to their number. They invariably performed the duty required of them. Having proved and earned their right to be citizens of their own country, in 1924 their president automatically made all Indians in the United States citizens which gave them the right to vote.

The Meskwaki historian then proceeded to list, in piecemeal fashion, facts characteristic of "Uncle Sam's greatest fighting men"—

Indians. He compared World War I soldiers and their forefathers' struggle against white aggressors, evoked their war cries and their fighting skills, and listed numerous individual Indian heroes and every single Meskwaki in the conflict, complete with their rank, length of service, status as draftee or volunteer, citations, and medals. After a brief description of Indian war tactics, he then proceeded to give ethnographic information on Iowa's tribes, insisting on their desire not to "lose sight of their customs" and concluding on Indians' contribution to U.S. history.

War was a good opportunity to remind whites that Indians were still around and still different; patriotism was a good school for those willing to learn new ways to articulate Indian grievances. For Poweshiek as for many Indian veterans, patriotism reinforced the conviction that Indians were on the right side of history. They kept demonstrating it by enlisting in disproportionately high numbers. Whites had been forced to acknowledge the fact. Indian soldiers' service in the war had gained them the franchise. Propagated by whites and Indians alike, these beliefs solidified a sense of racial pride and moral righteousness that could serve to counteract the deleterious effects of non-Indians' paternalism or contempt.

The fight was not without its ups and downs. In 1954, Sol Tax, a University of Chicago anthropologist working with the Meskwaki, met Poweshiek at the Iowa State Fair. The World War I veteran handed him "a rudely composed article (in his handwriting)" attacking whites as corrupters of the Indians and listing, once more, the contributions of Indians to the making of America before telling of his intention to give his work to visitors of the state's museum. Though still combative, Poweshiek adamantly warned Tax that Indian ways were fast disappearing. Under the influence of Mormonism, he even predicted a future where "the whole world [would] have one language, one religion."[2] His frustration was palpable. Participation in two world wars had changed little in Indians' ability to retain their traditions. But it had undeniably taught Poweshiek a way to make sense of his place as an Indian living in the United States.

Not all Indians were similarly able to make sense of patriotism to their advantage. Tellingly, we have encountered few cases where reservation political life was divided along a clear-cut patriots/anti-patriots line. Promoters of patriotism of all ethnicities used it to mandate unity and even unanimity, foreclosing direct protest and opposition. Partly because publicly claiming a status as "hostile" was still immensely counterproductive less than half a century after the end of the Indian Wars, outright rejection of patriotism was almost nonexistent. At the very least, alliance with the United States and a treaty-based relationship was acknowledged, leading to claims of patriotism. In the process, patriotism reinforced existing hierarchies in Native societies and created new ones. Not all claimed U.S. patriotism. Some couldn't, some wouldn't. Some went to patriotic celebrations looking forward only to the pleasure of eating, drinking, dancing, singing, renewing old acquaintances, and making new ones. They consented to patriotic rites but were not the best positioned to reap all the symbolic rewards attached to them. Leaders and would-be leaders, "politicians" and "agitators," people with a reasonably good command of English were those who stood to make the most varied uses of patriotism. They used it to reinforce their positions and bolster their demands. They made sense of it in the context of local and family histories, as we have seen in the case of the Crows or in the discussion of Sam Kenoi's or Jonas Poweshiek's itineraries. In certain groups, such as the Santa Clara Pueblos, veterans like Joseph Filario Tafoya could be suspected of being irretrievably on the side of an alien modernity; in others, they easily donned the garb of tradition. Local situations opened up different pathways. Everywhere, however, this required effort and selected individuals who could see the potential benefits of patriotism better than others and were more willing to use it.

These positions were not predicated on the past only. New events challenged them. On many a reservation the advent of the Indian New Deal, in particular, led to a level of polarization and ideology that made patriotism the quasi-proprietary weapon of the Old Dealers—the opponents of John Collier's policy to revitalize collective life on Indian reservations. The New Dealers could and did claim patriotism, but they couldn't, like their rivals, harness the most powerful resources that patriotism had to offer: the image of the forgotten veteran (and forgotten war mothers), the help of the American Legion and the Veterans of Foreign Wars, the claim to represent old-fashioned Americanism against revolutionary leftism, and above all, an orthodox understanding of the meaning of citizenship as rooted in private property and freedom from government control. Between 1917 and the early 1950s, the voices of those who made use of these associations were the loudest. In the years following World War II especially, they seemed to be on the verge of getting what they wanted: a world where Indians on and off reservations would not be under the tutelage of the BIA anymore. They led the assault against the federal agency and denounced the Indian Reorganization Act as the ultimate attempt to deprive Indians of their hard-earned rights of citizenship.

Because their actions were ultimately bound up with termination, which cost thousands tribal membership and the loss of Indian lands, and because termination became the most reviled shift in Indian policy in the twentieth century, the actions of these activists have been forgotten. With them, original ways of claiming and demonstrating patriotism apparently fell into oblivion. Or did they? We have become used to considering the period following the passing of termination laws as one of increasing Indian (anti-U.S.) nationalism, a time during which the U.S. flags in Indian communities were often turned upside down in a sign of protest and defiance. Undeniably, Red Power activism born in the cities after the relocation programs of the 1950s changed the style of Indian presence on the political scene. Locally, nationally, and internationally, Indians were associated with the militant activism of the American Indian Movement (AIM), which conjured up images of the Indian Wars—indeed, which consciously played on them. Described as tribalistic or nationalistic, this movement claimed full sovereignty over Indian lands, not full citizenship for veterans and for the Indians most advanced on the road to "civilization." Its leaders denounced colonialism and forcefully rejected assimilation. Differences with their grandparents were apparent in walk, talk, and dress. World War I veterans had appropriated U.S. nationalism in claiming their indigenous status as the first inhabitants of the land. But they had never threatened to rise up in arms against whites. To many, Native or not, the change was so brutal that it was as if Indians had not spoken in their own voice before that time.

Yet differences of style should not lead us to overstate the break between generations. World War I veterans' understanding of patriotism didn't disappear. Embedded in powwows, veterans' organizations, burial ceremonies, and memories, it remained a part of local landscapes. New generations constructed new interpretations of the U.S. flag or military service. The Sioux National Anthem, also called the Sioux Flag Song, was composed on Pine Ridge in 1954, at the house of James E. Emery. Five years later, Emery designed a flag for the Oglala Sioux Tribe. His interpretation of the symbols was purely Lakota, but the design carried the stars, colors, and stripes of the military service flag. Emery's flag didn't become the tribal emblem, but the U.S. flag remained part of local life on Pine Ridge. From 1961 to 1969, when anthropologist Robert E. Daniels did fieldwork on the reservation, it was still ubiquitous at veterans' funerals. Even as the ongoing war in Vietnam elicited discontent, caring for the war dead still implied displaying the symbols of U.S. patriotism and mobilizing the "Sam White Bear" post of the American Legion, chartered after World War I. In 1973, the casket of one of the two victims of the Wounded Knee siege, Buddy Lamont, a Vietnam veteran, was duly wrapped in both the U.S. flag and the AIM flag. The young activists of the 1970s didn't renounce their grandfathers' strategy of appropriating patriotism and its symbols, even if they developed new uses for them. Like their elders, they saw patriotism as a tool that could be turned against those they regarded as the enemies of Indians' collective identities. Like them, they always emphasized their status as "First Americans" and fought against what they saw as the baneful effects of the New Deal. Few World War I veterans were, like Hobart Keith, in a position to join the struggle that pitted AIM activists against the Pine Ridge tribal government in 1973. They could nonetheless easily understand what was at stake. Thirty-five years earlier, questioning the legitimacy of IRA-organized tribal governments had been at the center of the activities of the Old Dealers.[3]

This is not to say that new understandings of the relationship between the United States and Indian groups did not develop. The most important innovation of nationalistic Indian movements in the 1970s—the blending of religion and politics in projects to systematically revitalize Indian cultures—articulated old claims for lands, treaty rights, the right to choose one's leaders, and a desire to break away from the federal government in a way that would have been all but unimaginable two generations earlier. U.S. patriotism in Indian country was problematized as new activists broke the ultimate taboo of the World War I generation: demanding independence from the United States. This most radical claim was only ever made by a tiny minority of them. The sense that there was something wrong in serving in the U.S. military was more widespread, however. To re-assure themselves that they were not betraying their cause, Indian recruits in the U.S. armed forces insisted that they did it as members of their own tribes and that they enrolled to emulate their brothers, uncles, fathers, and grandfathers—not to show loyalty to the American government. In this too, however, they solidified a tradition of making service in the military compatible with one's identity as an Indian and the descendant of colonized people. In funerals and powwows, they reaffirmed the links connecting local, district-based communities, reservation communities, a wider ethnic and racial identity, and, if only to contest their supremacy, the U.S. govern-ment and people as a whole. Essentially, they drew on a tradition that had coalesced during and after World War I. In Indian country, the event itself never became as important as wars fought alongside or against the United States prior to the twentieth century. It was even overshadowed by later wars. But embedded in rituals and habits cre-ated after it ended, it has remained a vital, if rarely acknowledged, part of collective memory.

It is perhaps worthwhile to insist, as a final note, that these phe-nomena were not uniquely Native American. Undoubtedly, Ameri-can Indian veterans' itineraries through World War I were specific, as was their reinsertion in their respective groups. Contrary to many colonized people, they did not rebel against the draft. They served within white units instead of being incorporated within the existing racially segregated regiments. Upon their return from Europe (many colonial soldiers served in colonial territories), they seem generally to have been feted with a degree of unanimity that was not common in the rest of the colonial world and that, even within the United States, starkly differentiated them from African American veterans. These differences were informed by the fact that they posed no se-curity concern for the United States (the fear of revolts was, on the other hand, a major source of anxiety for European colonizers). They

overlap with but are not identical to other differences often held decisive by proponents of the theory of "settler colonialism": Indians'
relative numbers vis-à-vis the overall non-indigenous population or
their location within a nation-state rather than in an overseas territory. Much more decisive in their compliance and symbolic integration among non-Indian veterans, however, was the fact that the
country they lived in was the United States. Clearly it made a difference in the history of Native American veterans that they served
under a flag that was becoming, as they themselves matured, that of
the world's hegemon and that they could lay claim to it as the original owners of the territory. The complex mix of colonialism and
anti-colonialism that informed America's rise to world power contributed not a little to the specific connection of Native American
patriotism to American nationalism and to the ability of Native Americans to articulate seemingly contradictory claims for equality and
distinction, tradition and modernity, local and national identities.[4]

Even within that framework, the difference between the historical trajectories of Native American and other veterans coming from
colonized areas seems to have been of degree rather than of nature.
Indeed, when looked at from the perspective of reservations, the
true colonial territories for Indians, the difference with African and
Asian colonies seems far less obvious, whether one chooses to look
at the question of the relative number of soldiers, compliance with
the draft, or political mobilization. After all, Indians were confronted
with the same pressure to enlist or register for the draft as West
African French troops or the (East) Indian soldiers of the British
Raj; were equally invited to display, in a racially based manner, their
patriotism and mobilize their virile virtues for the sake of the mother
country and the defense of allies like France and Belgium; were similarly confronted with alien ways in camps and on the front lines and
paid a heavy price to the war effort; and upon their return, were the
objects of monitoring by their colonizers, just like their counterparts in Africa or Asia. Native American veterans' political assertion
labored under the same structural constraints as recruits from Ni-
geria or Kenya: Military compliance theoretically entailed rights,
but confirming, let alone bringing these rights to bear on, their daily
lives in a colonial environment that still abided by racial distinctions

was far from a foregone conclusion. In most, if not all, colonial territories, it required pushing back the limits rather than attempting to break through walls. Whether in the United States or elsewhere, World War I colonial veterans were, on the whole, no revolutionaries—even when, as was often the case with Native Americans, they were not shy about claiming what they were owed. While they lived in territories that went through dramatically different trajectories, some gaining independence while others were granted only self-determination, the political behavior of colonized veterans seems to have been remarkably similar around the world.[5]

Because no systematic comparison of World War I colonial veterans exists, that is admittedly an impressionistic conclusion.[6] It provides, however, food for thought for at least two distinct historical inquiries. One is the U.S. empire's divergence from European colonial empires. Quite clearly, this divergence, even when it brought about differences so symbolic as having colonized people serve in the same units as white Americans, had ambiguous consequences in the marginalized colonial territories that were Indian reservations. Veterans of the world war experienced this firsthand. Symbolically, service in the same units reinforced the claim of blood brotherhood —and the distinction between Indians and African Americans in this regard undoubtedly played a role in solidifying the claim. But patriotism also reinforced existing distinctions between white inhabitants of reservations and Native Americans, as memory of common service was mobilized in patriotic ceremonies that celebrated loyalty and the end of interracial conflicts—just like they did in other colonial territories.

Nowhere was there, in other words, an easy way out of the colonial situation. Increasingly, in the interwar period and in the 1940s and 1950s, unrestricted citizenship was imagined as just that wonder cure. In the United States or in the European colonies, the efficacy of the remedy was equally doubtful to many colonized people. In the end, Native American veterans' possibly higher symbolic status compared with other colonial soldiers derived not from their service alongside whites but from their position as the first inhabitants of the country, a country in which the difference between metropolis and colonies had become invisible and in which they could be regarded as both predecessors and contemporaries, a proud heritage and a shameful debt. Comparisons between Indians, Hawaiians, Puerto Ricans, Filipinos, Samoans, and other peoples who were under direct American control between the 1920s and 1950s, in the Americas and elsewhere, would undoubtedly further our understanding of Native American specificity in this regard.[7]

Comparing Native American veterans with other veterans hailing from colonized territories is also an invitation not to isolate Indians as "indigenous" people by essence distinct from all others. The current strength of the indigenous movement worldwide, and its origins, among other places, in North America, should not make us forget that the distinction between indigenous and other colonized peoples is first and foremost a matter of political pragmatism and that, since World War I at least, North American Indians have had strong incentives to develop precisely this aspect of their political collective identity for local, national, and international audiences. What are today considered indigenous peoples are groups that were not able or willing to claim their independence and join in the wave of decolonization that brought the end of the better part of European colonial empires between the 1940s and the 1970s. This doesn't mean that they were isolated from the ebb and flow of colonialism or that they were insensitive to the similarity of their situation with that of colonized peoples who eventually achieved independence. The current trend in calling for decolonizing methodologies in addressing Indian history and problems in particular is a testimony to this enduring fact: Since the 1960s, anti-colonialism has played a notable role in Indian politics and, even toned down and adapted to a changing world order or to local political scenes, has been an important factor in the birth of the indigenous movement itself.[8] International contacts and alliances between activists partly explain this phenomenon. But as the case of Native American veterans demonstrates, other factors need to be taken into account. Similarities between far-flung territories living in colonial circumstances could also appear despite vastly different social configurations. In many locales, the politics of commemoration, the family- and community-based dynamics of memory that allowed war monuments and ceremonies to be appropriated by local societies made World War I a symbol of broken promises, an opportunity to talk about local heroes, past and present, and to adjust the relationship between colonizer and colonized. The comparable local appropriations of a world event ensured that participation in common wars led not just to similar political discourses but also to analogous social phenomena. This gave claims of fraternity between colonized people an emotional component the impact of which is still felt today.[9]

Notes

Abbreviations

NARA-CHI	National Archives and Records Administration, Chicago, Illinois
NARA-DEN	National Archives and Records Administration, Denver, Colorado
NARA-DC	National Archives and Records Administration, Washington, D.C.
NARA-KC	National Archives and Records Administration, Kansas City, Missouri
CCF	Central Classified Files
DCF	Decimal Correspondence File
DCAIOH	Duke Collection of American Indian Oral History, Western History Collections, University of Oklahoma, Norman, Oklahoma
GPO	U.S. Government Printing Office, Washington, D.C.
SHSND	State Historical Society of North Dakota, Bismarck, North Dakota
SRA	Standing Rock Agency
WD	Wanamaker Documentation, William Hammond Mathers Museum, Indiana University, Bloomington, Indiana
WPA	Works Progress Administration
BIA	Bureau of Indian Affairs, a.k.a. Indian Office, Indian Service, Office of Indian Affairs

Introduction

Epigraph: C. L. Hall, "The Next Forty Years: The Indian in the World," *The Word Carrier* 16, no. 1 (January–February 1918): 1.

1. On the integration of Native Americans in white units, see Michael L.

Tate, "From Scout to Doughboy: The National Debate over Integrating American Indians into the Military, 1891–1918," *Western Historical Quarterly* 17, no. 4 (1986): 417–37.

2. On the war experience for Native Americans, see Susan Applegate Krouse, *North American Indians in the Great War* (Lincoln: University of Nebraska Press, 2007); Thomas A. Britten, *American Indians in World War I: At Home and at War* (Albuquerque: University of New Mexico Press, 1997); and "The Creek Draft Rebellion of 1918: Wartime Hysteria and Indian Baiting in WWI Oklahoma," *Chronicles of Oklahoma* 79 (Summer 2001): 200–215. See also Lonnie J. White, "Indian Soldiers of the 36th Division," *Military History of Texas and the Southwest* 15 (1979): 8–14; Louis Coleman, "Oklahoma's 'Greatest' Hero? A Review of the Military Record of Joseph Oklahombi," *Chronicles of Oklahoma* 80, no. 2 (Summer 2002): 201–15; Bonnie Lynn-Sherow and Bruce Susannah Ural, "'How Cola' from Camp Funston: American Indians and the Great War," *Kansas History: A Journal of the Central Plains* 24 (2001): 84–97; Russel Lawrence Barsh, "American Indians in the Great War," *Ethnohistory* 38, no. 3 (1991): 276–303; John R. Finger, "Conscription, Citizenship, and 'Civilization': World War I and the Eastern Band of Cherokee," *North Carolina Historical Review* 53, no. 3 (July 1986): 537–66; Frederick Hale, "Going on the Great White Father's Warpath: Reactions to World War I on the White Earth Reservation," *European Review of Native American Studies* 11, no. 1 (1997): 43–50; Paul T. Murray, "Who Is an Indian? Who Is a Negro? Virginia Indians in the World War II Draft," *Virginia Magazine of History and Biography* 95, no. 2 (April 1987): 215–31; Erik M. Zissu, "Conscription, Sovereignty, and Land: American Indian Resistance During World War I," *Pacific Historical Review* 64, no. 4 (1995): 537–66; David L. Wood, "Goshute-Shoshone Draft Resistance, 1917–18," *Utah Historical Quarterly* 49, no. 2 (Spring 1981): 173–88; Richard N. Ellis, "Indians at Ibapah in Revolt: The Goshutes, the Draft, and the Indian Bureau, 1917–1919," *Nevada Historical Society Quarterly* 19 (Fall 1976): 163–69; Morris W. Foster, *Being Comanche: A Social History of an American Indian Community* (Tucson: University of Arizona Press, 1991), 125–49.

3. On patriotism, see Michael Billig, *Banal Nationalism* (Thousand Oaks, Calif.: Sage, 1995); John Bodnar, *Remaking America: Public Memory, Commemoration, and Patriotism in the Twentieth Century* (Princeton, N.J.: Princeton University Press, 1993); Merle Curti, *The Roots of American Loyalty* (New York: Columbia University Press, 1946); Gary Gerstle, *American Crucible: Race and Nation in the Twentieth Century* (Princeton, N.J.: Princeton University Press, 2001); Michael Kazin and Joseph A. McCartin, eds., *Americanism: New Perspectives on the History of an Ideal* (Chapel Hill: University of North Carolina Press, 2007); John R. Gillis, ed., *Commemorations: The Politics of National Identity* (Princeton, N.J.: Princeton University Press, 1994); Hans Kohn, *American Nationalism: An*

Interpretive Essay (New York: Macmillan, 1957); Stephen Nathanson, *Patriotism, Morality, and Peace* (New York: Rowman and Littlefield, 1993); Cecilia E. O'Leary, *To Die For: The Paradox of American Patriotism* (Princeton, N.J.: Princeton University Press, 2010); Richard Rorty, *Achieving Our Country: Leftist Thought in Twentieth-Century America* (Cambridge: Harvard University Press, 1999; John H. Schaar, "The Case for Patriotism," *American Review* 17 (May 1973): 59–99; Paul M. Sniderman, *A Question of Loyalty* (Berkeley: University of California Press, 1981); and Maurizio Viroli, *For Love of Country: An Essay on Patriotism and Nationalism* (Oxford: Oxford University Press, 1995). A notable exception to the low levels of interest of Indian patriotism per se is Paul C. Rosier, *Serving Their Country: American Indian Politics and Patriotism in the Twentieth Century* (Cambridge: Harvard University Press, 2009). See also Christian W. McMillen, *Making Indian Law: The Hualapai Land Case and the Birth of Ethnohistory* (New Haven: Yale University Press, 2007); Clyde Ellis, Luke E. Lassiter, and Gary H. Dunham, *Powwow* (Lincoln: University of Nebraska Press, 2005), 21–27; John William Troutman, "'Indian Blues': American Indians and the Politics of Music, 1890–1935" (Ph.D. diss., Austin, University of Texas, 2004, mimeograph).

4. For an example of the emphasis on continuity between pre-reservation and reservation-era experiences of war, see William C. Meadows, *Kiowa, Apache, and Comanche Military Societies: Enduring Veterans, 1800 to the Present* (Austin: University of Texas Press, 1999).

5. For a recent example of the vibrant historical literature on African American veterans, see Christine Knauer, *Let Us Fight as Free Men: Black Soldiers and Civil Rights* (Philadelphia: University of Pennsylvania Press, 2014).

6. For examples of the long tradition of representing traumatized Indian veterans, see the movies made about Ira Hayes: Delbert Mann's 1961 *The Outsider*, with Tony Curtis in the lead role, and the more recent Clint Eastwood opus, *Flags of Our Fathers* (2006); see also John Woo's take on the Navajo code talker experience in *Windtalkers* (2002). On the impact of the Vietnam War on our perception of veterans in general, see Eric T. Dean, "The Myth of the Troubled and Scorned Vietnam Veteran," *Journal of American Studies* 26, no. 1 (April 1992): 59–74; on Indian veterans, see Tom Holm, "The National Survey of Vietnam Era American Indian Veterans: A Preliminary Reconnaissance," *Wicazo Sa Review* 1, no. 1 (1985): 36–37; and N. Scott Momaday, *House Made of Dawn* (New York: Harper & Row, 1968) and Leslie Marmon Silko, *Ceremony* (New York: Viking, 1977). On the role of the U.S. armed forces in writing a celebratory history of Indian participation in twentieth-century wars, see the United States Department of Defense (Roger Bucholz, William Fields, Ursula P. Roach), *20th Century Warriors: Native American Participation in the United States Military* (prepared for the U.S. Department of Defense by CEHP Inc., Washington, D.C., 1996).

7. For an analysis of Indian patriotism that avoids these pitfalls while remaining focused on the Cold War, see Rosier, *Serving Their Country.*

8. On the risks involved in taking identities as a given, see especially Rogers Brubaker, *Ethnicity Without Groups* (Cambridge: Harvard University Press, 2006).

9. On the new emphasis on reciprocity between state and veterans, see especially Theda Skocpol, *Protecting Soldiers and Mothers: The Political Origins of Social Policy in the United States* (Cambridge: Belknap Press of Harvard University).

Chapter One. Back in History?

1. O'Leary, *To Die For;* Chad L. Williams, "Vanguards of the New Negro: African American Veterans and Post–World War I Racial Militancy," *Journal of African American History* 92, no. 3 (Summer 2007): 347–70; Steven A. Reich, "Soldiers of Democracy: Black Texans and the Fight for Citizenship, 1917–1921," *Journal of American History* 82 (March 1996): 1478–1504; Felix James, "Robert Russa Moton and the Whispering Gallery After World War I," *Journal of Negro History* 62 (July 1977): 235–42; Martin Anthony Summers, *Manliness and Its Discontents: The Black Middle Class and the Transformation of Masculinity, 1900–1930* (Chapel Hill: University of North Carolina Press, 2004): 66–110.

2. See Jonathan Zimmerman, "'Each "Race" Could Have Its Heroes Sung': Ethnicity and the History Wars in the 1920s," *Journal of American History* 87, no. 1 (June 2000): 92–111. On nativism in the 1920s, see John Higham, *Strangers in the Land: Patterns of American Nativism, 1860–1925* (New York: Atheneum, 1963), 204–12; Nancy Gentile Ford, *Americans All! Foreign-Born Soldiers in World War I* (College Station: Texas A&M University Press, 2001), 25; Gary Gerstle, "Liberty, Coercion, and the Making of Americans," *Journal of American History* 84, no. 2 (September 1997): 552–53; and Mae M. Ngai, *Impossible Subjects: Illegal Aliens and the Making of Modern America* (Princeton, N.J.: Princeton University Press), 2004.

3. See Brian W. Dippie, *The Vanishing American: White Attitudes and U.S. Indian Policy* (Middletown, Conn.: Wesleyan University Press, 1982), 218–20; on William (Buffalo Bill) Cody's framing of Indians as "original Americans" and owners of the land, see Colin G. Calloway, Gerd Gemünden, and Susanne Zantop, eds., *Germans and Indians: Fantasies, Encounters, Projections* (Lincoln: University of Nebraska Press, 2002), 108.

4. George B. Seitz, *The Vanishing American,* Famous Players-Lasky Corporation, 1925, 110 minutes; Angela Aleiss, "Hollywood Addresses Indian Reform: *The Vanishing American,*" *Studies in Visual Communication* 10, no. 4 (Fall 1984): 53–60.

5. Ferris Greenslet to Joseph K. Dixon, 1 September 1923, Boston, WW-12, Wanamaker Documentation; Russel Lawrence Barsh, "An American

Heart of Darkness: The 1913 Expedition for American Indian Citizenship," *Great Plains Quarterly* 13, no. 2 (Spring 1993): 110; Krouse, *North American Indians in the Great War*, 179–98; Joseph K. Dixon to Cox, 9 June 1924, WW-11, Wanamaker Documentation.

6. See the outline of *From Tepees to Trenches* in WW-13, Wanamaker Documentation. On Dixon's general writing strategy, see his conference at Bellevue Stratford's Rotary Club on 24 March 1920; see also Joseph K. Dixon, "The Indian in the World War and War on the Indians," 24 March 1920, WW-72.

7. Hugh Lenox Scott, *Some Memories of a Soldier* (New York: The Century Company, 1928): 564.

8. Helen Hunt Jackson, *A Century of Dishonor* (New York: Harper & Brothers, 1881). On Wise, see Virginia Military Institute Archives, "A Guide to the Jennings C. Wise Papers, 1910–1960," available at http://ead.lib .virginia.edu/vivaxtf/view?docId=vmi/vilxvoo038.xml; McMillen, *Making Indian Law*, 102; and Jennings C. Wise, *The Red Man in the New World Drama: A Politico-Legal Study with a Pageantry of American Indian History* (New York: Macmillan, 1971 [1931]), 327, 328, 332.

9. John Joseph Mathews, *Sundown* (Norman: University of Oklahoma Press, 1998 [1934]), 208–10, 260, 297, 311; John Joseph Mathews, *The Osages: Children of the Middle Waters* (Norman: University of Oklahoma Press, 1961); and Garrick A. Bailey, "John Joseph Mathews, Osage, 1894–1979," in *American Indian Intellectuals of the Nineteenth and Early Twentieth Centuries*, ed. Margot Liberty (Norman: University of Oklahoma Press, 2002 [1978]), 232–44.

10. See Margaret Mead, *The Changing Culture of an Indian Tribe* (New York: Columbia University Press, 1932).

11. See Arnold Krupat, *Native American Autobiography: An Anthology* (Madison: University of Wisconsin Press, 1994); and Charles Alexander Eastman, *Indian Heroes and Great Chieftains* (Boston: Little, Brown, 1918). For more biographical details about Walter Campbell, see the preface by Raymond J. DeMallie in Stanley Vestal, *Sitting Bull: Champion of the Sioux* (Norman: University of Oklahoma, 1989 [1932]), xiii–xx; the passage quoted is on page 315.

12. H. Scudder Mekeel, "The Economy of a Modern Teton Dakota Community," *Yale University Publications in Anthropology*, vol. 6 (New Haven: Yale University Press, 1936), 5–6; H. Scudder Mekeel, *A Modern American Indian Community in the Light of Its Past: A Study in Culture Change* (Ph.D. diss., Yale University, 1932); and "Field Notes Summer of 1931 and 1932: White Clay District, Pine Ridge Reservation, South Dakota," 25, Mekeel Papers, National Anthropological Archives, Suitland, Maryland.

13. See Gordon Macgregor et al., *Warriors Without Weapons: A Study of the Society and Personality Development of the Pine Ridge Sioux* (Chicago: University of Chicago Press, 1946).

14. John Adair and Evon Z. Vogt, "Navaho and Zuni Veterans: A Study of Contrasting Modes of Culture Change," *American Anthropologist* 51, no. 4 (October–December 1949): 547–61; E. Z. Vogt, *Navaho Veterans: A Study of Changing Values* (Cambridge, Mass.: The Museum, 1951); Beverly H. Hackenberg, "Social Mobility in a Tribal Society: The Case of Papago Indian Veterans," *Human Organization* 31, no. 2 (Summer 1972): 201–9; J. R. Fox, "Veterans and Factions in Pueblo Society," *Man* 61 (October 1961): 173–76; Alan R. Beals and Bernard J. Siegel, *Divisiveness and Social Conflict: An Anthropological Approach* (Stanford, Calif.: Stanford University Press, 1966); Keats Begay and Broderick H. Johnson, *Navajos and World War II* (Tsaile, Ariz.: Navajo Community College Press, 1977). For rare (and late) biographies of Native American veterans, see James McCarthy, *A Papago Traveler: The Memories of James McCarthy* (Tucson: University of Arizona Press, 1985); and Joe Starita, *The Dull Knifes of Pine Ridge: A Lakota Odyssey* (New York: Putnam, 1995).

15. Leo Srole, "The Winnebago and the Modern War," Annual Meeting of the American Anthropological Association, Philadelphia, 27–31 December 1940, Warren Hunting Smith Library, Hobart and William Smith Colleges, Geneva, New York, esp. 1, 3, 4; "Leo Srole Papers, 1933–1993: A Finding Aid," Hobart and William Smith Colleges Archives and Special Collections website, available at https://library.hws.edu/archives/findingaids/findingaid.cfm?name=srole; and David L. Browman and Stephen Williams, *Anthropology at Harvard: A Biographical History, 1790–1940* (Cambridge, Mass.: Peabody, 2013), 448. See also Nancy Oestreich Lurie, "Winnebago Veterans and the Warrior Tradition," *Ho-Chunk Wo-Lduk* (Early November 1994): 3–4.

16. On the official history of the war, see United States, Department of the Army, Office of Military History, *United States Army in the World War, 1917–1919*, 18 vols. (Washington, D.C.: GPO, 1948).

17. For the various assessments of the number of Indian soldiers, see "A Brief Sketch of the Record of the American Negro and Indian in the Great War," March 1919, Boston, 9; "The Indian's War Activities," Commissioner's report, n.d., in "Records Relating to Indians in World War I and World War II, 1920–1945," box 1, entry 998E, CCF 1907–1939, RG 75, NARA-DC; Department of the Interior, OIA, "The American Indian in the World War," Bulletin 15 (1927), 4; and *The Tomahawk*, the newspaper of the White Earth reservation, which mentioned eighteen thousand Indian soldiers, "most of them scouts" in its 29 March 1919 edition (*The Tomahawk*, White Earth, Minnesota).

18. "National Catholic War Council," *The Indian Sentinel* 1, no. 11 (1918–19): 48.

19. For a correspondent requesting a list of South Dakota Indian soldiers, see W. A. Morris to P. H. Moller, 22 October 1919, "War," box 125, Crow Creek Agency, RG 75, NARA-KC. For a state's certificate of recognition

to an Indian soldier, see Memorial to Charley Spear, "He Died to Make Men Free," Records of Indians in World War I, box 14, Potawatomi Agency, RG 75, NARA-KC. On the Liberty Memorial in Kansas City, see C. R. Whitlock to Bazil Flannigan, 28 April 1926, file 610, box 72, Pierre Indian School, RG 75, NARA-KC.

20. On Haskell, see Kim Warren, "'All Indian Trails Lead to Lawrence, October 27 to 30, 1926'": American Identity and the Dedication of Haskell Institute's Football Stadium," *Kansas History* 30, no. 1 (Spring 2007): 2–19. For an example of a BIA textbook, see United States, Department of the Interior, OIA, *Course of Study for Indian Schools* (Washington, D.C.: GPO, 1922), 71. For an invitation to consult Indian elders to teach the history of Indian wars, see *The* [Phoenix, Ariz.] *Native American*, 5 April 1919, 1–3.

21. Amelia F. Harris, "Interview with Colonel Victor M. Locke, Choctaw Indian," University of Oklahoma Libraries Western History Collections, *Indian-Pioneer Papers*, vol. 55, interview no. 9003, available at https://digital.libraries.ou.edu/WHC/pioneer/; Jessie Chisholm, "Interview with Bill Chisholm," vol. 17, not numbered; Johnson H. Hampton, "Interview with Ben Cartarby," vol. 16, Interview no. 7469.

22. On the WPA and Indian reservations, see A. W. von Struve, "Two WPA Projects of Historical Interest," *Southwestern Historical Quarterly Online* 42, no. 2 (October 1938): 117–21, available at http://texashistory.unt.edu/ark:/67531/metapth101107/m1/131, accessed 15 May 2016; Herbert S. Lewis and L. Gordon McLester, *Oneida Lives: Long-Lost Voices of the Wisconsin Oneidas* (Lincoln: University of Nebraska Press, 2005), esp. xxxii–xxxvii; Mindy J. Morgan, "Constructions and Contestations of the Authoritative Voice: Native American Communities and the Federal Writers' Project, 1935–1941," *American Indian Quarterly* 29, no. 1 (2005): 56–83. On Matthew Rivers, see Andrew S. Gross, "The American Guide Series: Patriotism as Brand-Name Identification," *Arizona Quarterly: A Journal of American Literature, Culture, and Theory* 62, no. 1 (2006): 94. On Standing Rock, see *The WPA Guide to South Dakota: The Federal Writers' Project Guide to 1930s South Dakota*, introduction by John E. Miller (St. Paul: Minnesota Historical Society Press, 2006), 204.

23. On the WPA and Grave Registration in South Dakota: South Dakota Graves Registration Project, "Field Data," Shannon, Todd, and Mellette counties, Manuscripts, South Dakota Historical Society.

24. George Buckland, Anadarko, 17 April 1920, WW-3, Wanamaker Documentation; Mrs. Joseph Brown to Joseph Dixon, 1 June 1920, La Creek, South Dakota; Sam Charger to Joseph K. Dixon, 2 February 1920, La Plant, South Dakota, emphasis in original.

25. On race-specific commemorative days, see Matthew Dennis, *Red, White, and Blue Letter Days: An American Calendar* (Ithaca, N.Y.: Cornell University Press, 2002), 144. On Indian Citizenship Day, see Jon L. Brudvig,

"Francis Kennedy, Indian Day, 1898, Industry," in *First Person Accounts as Written by American Indian Students at Hampton Institute, 1878–1923*, available at www.twofrog.com/hamptonstories3.html; and David Wallace Adams, *Education for Extinction: American Indians and the Boarding School Experience, 1875–1928* (Lawrence: University Press of Kansas, 1995), 186–90. On urban Indians' ethnic pride, see Brookings Institution, *The Problem of Indian Administration: Report of a Survey Made at the Request of Honorable Hubert Work, Secretary of the Interior, and Submitted to Him, February 21, 1928* (Baltimore: Johns Hopkins Press, 1928), 678, 705, 727. The participation of boy scouts is mentioned in Congress, Senate, Committee on Indian Affairs, *Report 84 to Accompany S. 309*, Calendar 88, 78th Cong., 1st sess., 5 March 1943, 12, in "S. 309," box 2, Indian Affairs Investigating Subcommittee, RG 46, NARA-DC. See also Hertzberg, *Search for an American Indian Identity*, 83. On Indian Day, see Michelle Wick Patterson, "'Real' Indian Songs: The Society of American Indians and the Use of Native American Culture as a Means of Reform," *American Indian Quarterly* 26, no. 1 (2002): 44–66, esp. 53. For Parker's point of view on Indian Day, see "Editorial Comment" and "Indians with the Allies," *The American Indian Magazine* (January–March 1917): 5–7.

26. For the BIA's take on Indian Day, see circular 1115, 2 May 1916, file 31196-1922, entry 44, Cheyenne River Agency, CCF 1907–1939, RG 75, NARA-DC, and circular 1300, 26 April 1917, file "600. Military Activities," box 177, Crow Creek Agency, RG 75, NARA-KC. For the reaction of the Society of American Indians, see "Reasons Why Indians Should Join the Regular Army," *The American Indian Magazine*, Washington, D.C. (January–March 1917): 141–42; Frederick E. Hoxie, *Talking Back to Civilization: Indian Voices from the Progressive Era* (Boston: Bedford-St. Martins, 2001), 125–38.

27. "Chicago American Indian Day 1920," *The Indian Leader* (8 October 1920): 1. On Gillispie, see Robert Gillispie to CIA, 20 January 1920, box 6673-20, entry 44, Pine Ridge Agency, CCF, RG 75, NARA-DC; Commissioner E. B. Merritt to superintendent Munro, 3 May 1922, file "31196 Cheyenne River, 1922, 044," box 5, entry 44, Cheyenne River Agency, RG 75, NARA-DC; Charles H. Burke, "The President has referred to me for answer," n.d. [late 1920s], box 38574-1944, General Services, CCF 1940–57, RG 75, NARA-DC. On Madison, see Hazel W. Hertzberg, *The Search for an American Indian Identity: Modern Pan-Indian Movements* (Syracuse, N.Y.: Syracuse University Press, 1971), 198; Jeffery R. Hanson, "Ethnicity and the Looking Glass: The Dialectics of National Indian Identity," *American Indian Quarterly* 21, no. 2 (1997): 199. On the Indian Fellowship League, see David Beck, "Developing a Voice: The Evolution of Self-Determination in an Urban Indian Community," *Wicazo Sa Review* 17, no. 2 (Fall 2002): 125–26.

28. See "Visit Jackson in Interest of an 'Indian Day,'" *Citizen Patriot*, Jackson,

19 June 1923; "Wants Memorial Day for Indians," *The Evening Star*, Washington, D.C., 26 December 1924. See also Brookings Institution, *The Problem of Indian Administration*, 722–23; "Indians Olan Curtis Rally," *Los Angeles Times*, 28 September 1928, 9.

29. David Beck, "Developing a Voice," 126–27; "Memorial and Recommendations of the Grand Council Fire of American Indians," *Congressional Record*, vol. 69, part 8 (11 May 1928): 8369.

30. For Lane's endorsement of bill HR 5007, see Congress, House, 66th Cong., 1st sess., *Report to Accompany HR 5007*, report no. 140, 21 July 1919, 2, in "HR 5007," box 112, Committee on Indian Affairs Accompanying Papers RG 233, NARA-DC; on Dowanee, see "Suggests the Name of "Amerinds" for Indians of America," *Niagara Falls Gazette*, 30 December 1920, 9.

31. "War-Whoops Echo at Powwow Here," *New York Times*, 30 September 1935, 19; "50 Indians Dance in Tribal Day Here," *New York Times*, 28 September 1936, 21; Essie E. Lee, *Nurturing Success: Successful Women of Color and Their Daughters* (Westport, Conn.: Praeger, 2000), 235.

32. "S. 1240," "S. 169," box 31, 77th Congress, "S. 1240," 79th Congress, box 97; "S. 309," box 11, 80th Congress, Papers Relating to Specific Bills and Resolutions, RG 46, NARA-DC; and "American Indian Day," box 2, Committee on Interior and Insular Affairs, Indian Affairs Investigating Subcommittee, RG 46, NARA-DC; for Ford's quote, see "Ford Proclaims Indian Day," *Montana Standard*, 22 September, 1946, clipping in "S. 1240." Pan American Union, *Final Act of the Second Inter-American Indian Conference held in Cuzco, Peru, June 24–July 4, 1949* (Washington, D.C.: Division of Conferences and Organizations, Dept. of International Law and Organization, Pan American Union, 1949), 24.

Chapter Two. The Names of Local Heroes

1. Antoine Prost, "Les Monuments Aux Morts. Culte Républicain? Culte Civique? Culte Patriotique?" in *Les lieux de mémoire*, vol. 1, ed. Pierre Nora (Paris: Gallimard, 1984), 199 (translation mine).

2. McDuffee's diary is at the Minnesota Historical Society (Acc #1990.506).

3. For an official history ignoring the Indian contribution, see Joseph Mills Hanson, *South Dakota in the World War, 1917–1919*, South Dakota State Historical Society, Pierre, South Dakota, 1940. On Oklahoma Choctaws, see Louis Coleman, "Oklahoma's 'Greatest' Hero? A Review of the Military Record of Joseph Oklahombi," *Chronicles of Oklahoma* 80, no. 2 (Summer 2002): 215; and Thomas Grillot, "'Cette terre est mienne à présent': Les Indiens, la Grande Guerre, et la France (1917–1918)," in *Un continent en partage: Cinq siècles de rencontres entre Amérindiens and Français*, ed. Gilles Havard and Mickaël Augeron (Paris: Les Indes savantes, 2013), 415–24. For an example of local history, see William H.

Mason, *Snohomish County in the War: The Part Played in the Great War by the Soldiers, Sailors, Marines, and Patriotic Civilians of Snohomish County, Washington, USA* (Everett, Wash.: Mason Publishing Company, 1920), 141–42, 196–98, 411. On the monument recognizing the Winnebagos, see *The Indian's Friend*, March 1924; "Winnebago Indians," Historical Marker Database, available at www.hmdb.org/marker.asp?marker=17748, accessed September 2016; "Honor Paid to Indian Heroes," *The Tomahawk*, 1 May 1924, 1.

4. On the death of Barney Brought, see interview with Melvin Shoots The Enemy, 28 June 2009, Fort Yates, North Dakota [interviews with only the date and a place are by the author]. For a similar story of German poisoners, see Martha Royce Blaine, *Some Things Are Not Forgotten: A Pawnee Family Remembers* (Lincoln: University of Nebraska Press, 1997), 146. On rural immigrant communities in the nineteenth century, see Jon Gjerde, *The Minds of the West: Ethnocultural Evolution in the Rural Middle West, 1830–1917* (Chapel Hill: University of North Carolina Press, 1997), 225–50; Clyde Ellis, "'There Is No Doubt . . . The Dances Should Be Curtailed': Indian Dances and Federal Policy on the Southern Plains, 1880–1930," *Pacific Historical Review* 70, no. 4 (November 2001): 543–69. On the Lakota petition, see "Sioux County Indians Demand Loyalty from Our Foster Sons," *Sioux County Pioneer*, Sioux County, 6 February 1919, 1; and "Catholic Bishop Defends Our Foreign Born Slope Citizens," *Sioux County Pioneer*, 20 February 1919, 1.

5. Anderson W. Cash to Joseph K. Dixon, 10 October 1921, WW-01, Wanamaker Documentation; Hertzberg, *The Search for an American Indian Identity*, 232; Nancy Shoemaker, "Urban Indians and Ethnic Choices: American Indian Organizations in Minneapolis, 1920–1950," *Western Historical Quarterly* 19, no. 4 (1988): 431–47; and Roger L. Nichols, *The American Indian: Past and Present* (New York: McGraw-Hill, 1992), 127; Jane Pejsa, *The Life of Emily Peake: One Dedicated Ojibwe* (Minneapolis: Nodin Press, 2003).

6. "Good War Record of Lee Rainbow," *The Native American*, 20 September 1919, 11.

7. On Sam Swaskegame, see "Big 'Cry' Comemorated [*sic*] Sam Swaskegame Death," *Mohave County Miner*, 1 July 1921, 7; see also McMillen, *Making Indian Law*, 202n21. On Solis, see "Impressive Ceremonies at Soldier's Grave," *The Native American*, Phoenix, 5 November 1921.

8. For more on Joe White Hand Bear's funeral as the biggest in the history of the Bullhead district of the Standing Rock reservation, see "Bullhead Soldier Dead," *Sioux County Pioneer*, 20 March 1919.

9. On a VFW post named after an Indian soldier of the Spanish-American War, see Frank F. Finney, "William Pollock: Pawnee Indian, Artist, and Rough Rider," *Chronicles of Oklahoma* 33, no. 4 (1955): 509–11. For an example of the systematic involvement of the American Legion in the

burial of Indian veterans, see A. S. [initials], commander of the Abner Dahlberg post no. 7 in Rhinelander, to Mrs. William Mattigosh, 9 October 1926, file 175, "Murder of William Mattigosh," box 11, General Correspondence File, Great Lakes Agency, RG 75, NARA-CHI.

10. See the "Arthur Frazier" post in South Dakota, the "Ponca" post in Oklahoma, the "Ira Spring" post in New York, the "Chief Peo" post in Oregon, or the "James L. Trimble" post in Mississippi. "Class Post—Indians," Correspondence Files—Administration and Organization, American Legion Library, American Legion Headquarters, Indianapolis.

11. Orvil Ogle and Roland F. Thompson, *History of the Sam White Bear Post No. 251 of the American Legion, Pine Ridge, South Dakota: Tent Anniversary, 1930–1940* (Pine Ridge, S.D., 1940) (American Legion Library, Indianapolis, Ind.). On the 5 percent of Indian dead (as opposed to 1 percent in the American Expeditionary Force at large), see Russel Lawrence Barsh, "American Indians in the Great War," 278.

12. "Speech of Plenty Coups at Grave of Unknown Soldier, National Cemetery, Arlington, Virginia, November 11, 1921," in "Card file relating to Indians in World War I, 1916–1920," box 19, entry 997B, CCF 1907–1939, RG 75, NARA-DC. On Indian delegations to the Tomb of the Unknown Soldier during World War II, see "Wreaths from Pine Ridge on Unknown Soldier's Tomb," *Daily Republic*, 26 November 1943, in "Dr 125," Correspondence and related papers exchanged between Francis Case and individual Indians in South Dakota, Francis H. Case Papers, Dakota Wesleyan University, Mitchell, South Dakota.

13. On Stone, see E. B. Meritt to Calvin H. Asbury, 18 November 1924, file 110155, entry 125, CCF 1907–1939, Crow Agency RG 75, NARA-DC. On Plenty Coups, see National Park Service, United States Department of the Interior, "National Historic Landmark Nomination: Chief Plenty Coups (Alek-Chea-Ahoosh) Home/Chief Plenty Coups State Park," National Park website, available at http://pdfhost.focus.nps.gov/docs/NHLS/Text/70000354.pdf, accessed 3 August 2009; Plenty Coups to Foch, 13 December 1922, box 98760-22 137, Crow, entry 44, CCF 1907–1939, RG 75, NARA-DC.

14. Pete Taylor, Kaw nation, Language resources, "Monument Dedication Speech, Council Grove, KS, August 1925," available at www.kawnation.com/WebKanza/LangResources/LangTexts/text26.xml; R. Alton Lee, *The Bizarre Careers of John R. Brinkley* (Lexington: University Press of Kentucky, 2002), 119.

15. On Nishu, see McLean County Historical Society, *McLean County Heritage* (McLean, N.D., 1978), 435; on the later history of the Old Scouts cemetery, see Evangeline Mongram and Rhoda Star, interview with the author, 14 July 2009, White Shield, North Dakota.

16. Joseph Takes The Shield Sr. to Cato Sells, 24 January 1921, box 85599, entry 125, SRA, RG 75, NARA-KC, "Touching Tribute Paid by Indian

Soldiers to Dead Comrade," *The Indian Sentinel* 3, no. 4 (1923): 162; "Indians Pay Tribute to Comrade," *The Indian Sentinel* 4, no. 1 (1924): 11; "American Legion Post at Wakpala Keeps the Faith," *McLaughlin Messenger*, 29 May 1936, 1; "Indians Buried at Arlington Cemetery Honored by D.C. Group," *Indian Record*, November 1970, 12.

17. Cato Sells to Colonel Clarence S. Ridley, 26 April 1921; "Memorandum," 12 December 1920, box 33664, entry 44, General Services, RG 75, NARA-KC; Charles H. Burke to James A. Wehn, 23 December 1921, file 98851, entry 44, General Services, RG 75, NARA-KC.

18. On the debates on the Osage monument, see J. George Wright to Charles H. Burke, 30 April 1926; "Proceedings of the Osage Tribal Council," 6 April 1925, 13, 15, 17, 21, box 23420, entry 44, Osage, CCF 1907–1939, RG 75, NARA-DC. On useful monuments, see Steven Trout, "Forgotten Reminders: Kansas World War I Memorials," *Kansas History: A Journal of the Central Plains* 20 (2006): 206–7; for similar considerations on the Rosebud reservation, see James L. Glasscock to Commissioner of Indian Affairs, 10 February 1921, file 12978, entry 44, Rosebud Agency, CCF 1907–1939, RG 75, NARA-DC; Charles H. Burke, CIA, to John A. Buntin, 3 May 1921, and Vance Moore to Royal C. Johnson, 2 March 1921, file 1040857-1920. On the failure of the Osage project, see Charles Moore to Charles H. Burke, 18 June 1926; Tribal council resolution no. 51, 25 October 1929; J. George Wright to C. J. Rhoads, 28 October 1929; C. J. Rhoads to J. George Wright, 21 November 1929, all in file 23420, entry 44, Osage, CCF 1907–1939, RG 75, NARA-DC.

19. See "Capt. Ben Locke, Noted Indian Soldier, Passes Away," *The* [Tulsa, Oklahoma] *American Indian*, January 1928, 6; file 61587-1925, entry 44, Five Tribes, CCF 1907–1939, RG 75, NARA-DC; and "The E. M. Viquesney Doughboy Database," available at http://doughboysearcher.tripod.com/id105.html, accessed 6 August 2016.

20. "Movement Begun for Sioux Memorial Hall," *Sioux County Pioneer*, 6 February 1919, 1; "Standing Rock Memorial Hall May Be Built in Spring," *Sioux County Pioneer*, 1 January 1920, 1; "Reservation's Memorial Hall Project Revived," *Sioux County Pioneer*, 29 January 1920; Guy H. Houchen to James B. Kitch, 2 June 1919, "044 Standing Rock Memorial Celebration 1932–1934," box 152, SRA, RG 75, NARA-KC; E. D. Mossman to CIA, 27 September 1924, file 73235-1924, entry 44, SRA, CCF 1907–1939, RG 75, NARA-DC; E. D. Mossman to P. B. Garberg, file "600.1, Removal of Sitting Bull, Gall, and Rain in the Face," box 287, SRA, RG 75, NARA-KC; E. D. Mossman to CIA, 27 September 1924, file 73235-1924; and Traveling Auditor to Commissioner of Indian Affairs, 25 March 1925, file 228421, RG 60, NARA-DC. On the monument erected in 1932, see "044 Standing Rock Memorial Celebration 1932–1934," box 152, SRA, RG 75, NARA-KC. On the connections

between the memory of Sitting Bull and the commemoration of World War I heroes, see Thomas Grillot, "Sitting Bull's Second Grave Colonial Metamorphoses in Twentieth-Century America," *Annales. HSS* 68, no. 1 (January–March 2013): 135–68.

21. Cf. Walter F. Dickens to Commissioner of Indian Affairs, 27 November 1931, and "Tribal Council Resolution," 9 October 1929, in "Cheyenne River Indian Memorial," Indian Materials, William Williamson Papers, University of South Dakota, Vermillion, South Dakota.

22. Inauguration speeches can be found in file 61658, Cheyenne River, entry 44, CCF 1907–1939, RG 75, NARA-DC (for fundraising efforts especially, see Walter F. Dickens to CIA, 2 September 1931); see also file "410 Indians in World War I," box 68, Cheyenne River, RG 75, NARA-KC. On veterans as mere tokens of patriotism, Luke Gilbert to William Williamson, 15 November 1929, and William Williamson to Charles J. Rhoads, CIA, 15 March 1932, in "Cheyenne River Indian Memorial," Indian Materials, Williamson Papers, University of South Dakota, Vermillion, South Dakota.

23. On the marginalization of World War I in American memory, see Trout, "Forgotten Reminders"; and James M. Mayo, "War Memorials as Political Memory," *Geographical Review* 78, no. 1 (January 1988): 62–75.

24. *Thucydides in English; Chiefly from the translation of Hobbes of Malmesbury* (London: Bohn, 1830), 31.

Chapter Three. Patriotic Gifts

1. For mentions of the Great War in winter counts, see N. A. Higginbotham, "The Wind-Roan Bear Winter Count," *Plains Anthropologist* 91 (February 1981): 36; Byron Olson, "The Eagle Heart Winter Count," Standing Rock Sioux Tribe Historical Preservation Office, n.d.; SHSND, "John Ears' Winter Count," available at www.history.nd.gov/textbook/unit3_1_john_no_ears.html; Linea Sundstrom, "History in Pictures: Father Buechel and the Lakota Winter Counts," 2006, 46–47, available at http://groups.creighton.edu/sfmission/museum/exhibits/wintercounts/buechel_winter_counts.pdf.

2. On the Takes The Shield celebration, see "Big Celebration Is Unique Affair," clipping from *Mobridge Tribune*, c. 15 August 1924; and Forest F. Bliss to Eugene D. Mossman, 9 August 1924, Eugene Bearking to Eugene D. Mossman, 11 August 1924, file 85599, Standing Rock, entry 125, CCF 1907–1939, NARA-DC.

3. On Lakota terminology, see Ben Black Bear and Ron D. Theisz, *Songs and Dances of the Lakota* (Aberdeen, S.D.: North Plains Press, 1984 [1976]), 48; and "best," "chief," "dominant," "extraordinary," and "honor" in John P. Williamson, *An English-Dakota Dictionary: Wasicun Ka Dakota Ieska Wowapi* (New York: American Tract Society, 1902), 17, 31, 53, 62, 84.

4. For testimony emphasizing the "decadent" state of warriors' societies, see Paul Long Bull, in Ella Deloria, "Dakota Ethnography," box 3, "Yankton and Teton ethnographic notes," p. 10, available at http://zia.aisri.indiana .edu/deloria_archive/browse.php?action=viewpage&id=607. For a mention of the Strong Heart Society as a charity on Standing Rock, see "Little Eagle Celebrated Two Days," *Sioux County Pioneer*, 21 June 1935. On their limited recruiting efforts, see Alfred B. Welch, "Sioux White Horse Riders Society ("Help the Poor" Society), December 10, 1923," *Oral History of the Dakota Tribes 1800's–1945*, available at www.welchdakotapapers .com/2011/08/white-horse-riders-society-help-the-poor-society-twin -buttes-nd-dec-10-1923/; Stanley Vestal, *Sitting Bull: Champion of the Sioux*, foreword by Raymond J. DeMallie, 59–60. On Legion posts as cultural substitutes, see William C. Meadows, *Kiowa, Apache, and Comanche Military Societies*, 396; and John William Troutman, *"Indian Blues": American Indians and the Politics of Music, 1890–1935* (Ph.D. diss., University of Texas, 2004), 15.

5. On giving and the Sun Dance, see Aaron McGaffey Beede, "The Dakota Indian Victory Dance," *North Dakota Historical Quarterly* 9 (April 1942): 167–78; and "The Dakota Indian Victory-Dance" [hereafter Beede 1]; "Sioux Indian Victory-Dance, November 20, 1918" [hereafter Beede 2], box 3, Aaron McGaffey Beede-Ralph McGaffey Beede Papers, Elwyn box Robinson Department of Special Collections Chester Fritz Library, University of North Dakota, Grand Forks, ND; and file 185/37/13, box 37, Orin G. Libby Collection, SHSND. On Sun Dance vows, see Beede 1, p. 12.

6. On the Sons of the Legion, see John J. Backus to C. R. Whitlock, 30 April 1937, file "690 Military Activities. Children program," Rosebud Agency, RG 75, NARA-KC; and John Tiger, box 380, Family Survey 1935, SRA, RG 75, NARA-KC. On the Auxiliary and War Mothers on Standing Rock, see Alfred B. Welch, *Indian Celebrations*, ed. Everett Cox (Standing Rock Tribal Historical Preservation Office, 1941, mimeograph), 22; Clyde Ellis, "'Truly Dancing Their Own Way': Modern Revival and Diffusion of the Gourd Dance," *American Indian Quarterly* 14, no. 1 (Winter 1990): 19–33; "Armistice Day Program at Porcupine," *Sioux County Pioneer*, 17 November 1927, 4; "Two Shield Round Hall Is Gathering Place for Celebration of Armistice," 14 November 1930, 1; "Armistice Day Observed at Two Shield," 18 November 1932, 1; "Armistice Day," 17 November 1933, 1. See also Robert Anderson, "The Northern Cheyenne War Mothers," *Anthropological Quarterly* 29, no. 3 (July 1956): 82–90.

7. On bands and baseball teams, see T. J. McCoy to E. A. Hutchinson, 29 March 1920, file 209, "Indian dances and celebrations," box 4, Wind River Agency, RG 75, NARA-DEN; on Legionnaires during the Fourth of July, see A. B. Welch, "Sioux Celebration at Cannon Ball, July 3–4,

1922," *Oral History of the Dakota Tribes 1800's–1945*, available at www
.welchdakotapapers.com/2011/08/cannon-ball-july-3-4-1922-community
-celebration-and-sham-world-war-i-battles-with-germans/.

8. On class posts, see William Pencak, *For God and Country: The American
Legion, 1919–1941* (Boston: Northeastern University Press, 1989), 68–69;
on the Crow post, see Superintendent to L. McLean, 14 December 1922,
"War Matters, 1930–1925," box 34, entry 156, Crow Agency, RG 75,
NARA-DEN; on the absence of Indian Legion leaders at the state level,
see interview with Maxine White Bull, Elaine Saint-John, Alma Little
Bear, Isabel Crow Feather, 9 July 2008, Kenel, South Dakota; on Catholic societies and ethnic pride, see Mark Thiel, "Catholic Sodalities Among
the Sioux, 1882–1910," *U.S. Catholic Historian* 16, no. 2 (Spring 1998):
56–77.

9. On funeral rituals after the Civil War, see Matthew Dennis, *Red, White,
and Blue Letter Days*, 224. On the GAR in Indian country, see Theda
Perdue, *Nations Remembered: An Oral History of the Five Civilized Tribes,
1865–1907* (Westport, Conn.: Greenwood Press, 1980), 70. On a post
created to bury Legionnaires according to Legion ritual, see post 308
(Cheyenne River), in Dorothy A. Hunt, *Between Prairie and Sky* (Eagle
Butte, S.D.: Bonnie Miller, 2003), 69.

10. E. Bearking to E. D. Mossman, 11 August 1924, file 85599, entry 125,
SRA, CCF 1907–1939, RG 75, NARA-DC; and Blaine, *Some Things Are
Not Forgotten*, 146. For photos of veterans, see George Looking Back, box
380, Family Survey 1935, SRA, RG 75, NARA-KC; James Henri How-
ard and Peter Le Claire, *The Ponca Tribe* (Washington, D.C.: GPO, 1965),
140; and Welch, *Indian Celebrations*, 97; Little Eagle Day School, *Little
Eagle Community History and Development* (Little Eagle, S.D., 1975), 9–14.
On the negative role of gossiping in local societies, see YMCA et al. Pe-
tition, 13 April 1937, file "Ankle, Henry," box 190, DCF, 1906–1959, SRA,
RG 75, NARA-KC, and Henry Ankle, box 380, Family Survey 1935,
SRA, RG 75, NARA-KC.

11. Ella Others's Story (Reminiscences), "Ponca History Material," M-45,
47, DCAIOH.

12. On the American Legion's recruiting efforts in Wakpala and Bullhead,
see Hessie Parker to E. D. Mossman, 20 July 1933, file "610.0 American
Legion 1933–1934," box 288, DCF, 1906–1959, SRA, RG 75, NARA-KC;
interview with Marvin Bertsch, 17 July 2008, McIntosh, South Dakota.

13. On white posts' finances on Standing Rock, see "April 6 1926, Proceedings," *Corson County Commissioner Proceedings*, 1, 446. On "begging" techniques that were used for fundraising, see Frances Densmore, *Teton Sioux
Music*, BAE Bulletin no. 61 (Washington, D.C.: GPO, 1918), 481–84. On
dues, see "Legion," *Sioux County Pioneer*, 25 September 1919, 1; and letter to Walter F. Dickens, 11 May 1932, file "610 Indians in World War,"
box 68, Cheyenne River Agency, RG 75, NARA-KC. On Indian posts'

finances, see Hessie Parker to E. D. Mossman, 20 July 1933; "Saturday, November 11, Will Be Forget-Me-Not Day—Legion Dance Here," *Sioux County Pioneer*, 9 November 1934, 1; "Porcupine and Shields Meetings," *Sioux County Pioneer*, 4 November 1932, 1; interview with Melvin Shoots The Enemy, 9 July 2009, Fort Yates, North Dakota; Germaine Eagle Iron Thunder, South Dakota, 3 July 2009; interview of Andrew DeRockbraine by Steve Plummer, MS 833, 26 June 1972, 3; and Welch, *Indian Celebrations*, 107. For a winter count mentioning a war monument, see N. A. Higginbotham, "The Wind-Roan Bear Winter Count," 36. On the Kenel post's record, Arthur Van Vlissingen Jr., "Chief George Goes on the Peacepath," *The American Legion Weekly* 7, no. 33 (14 August 1925): 6–7, 19–21.

14. On the good leader paying his members' dues, interview with Cecilia Brownotter, 23 July 2008, Rock Creek, South Dakota. On the leader's status as a burden among whites and Indians, interview with Owen Gullickson, 6 August 2008, Cannonball, North Dakota; and interview with Antone American Horse, 27 July 2008, Kenel, South Dakota. Legion positions, it is to be noted, have received translations in Indian languages. In Lakota, a commander is an *akicita itancan*, leader of soldiers-veterans, *itancan* being a title given only to the foremost camp authorities. Interview with Melvin Shoots The Enemy, 9 July 2009, Fort Yates, North Dakota. On leaders and *itancan*, see Catherine Price, "Lakota and Euroamericans: Contrasted Concepts of 'Chieftainship' and Decision-Making Authority," *Ethnohistory* 41, no. 3 (Summer 1994): 449–50.

15. On the Great War and the preservation of warriors' songs and rituals, see Robert Higheagle, "Twenty-Five Songs Made by Sitting Bull, with Translations," 9, Campbell Collection, Western History Collections, University of Oklahoma, Norman, Oklahoma; on Memorial Day songs, see R. D. Theisz, "Acclamations and Accolades: Honor Songs in Lakota Society," *Kansas Quarterly* 13, no. 2 (Spring 1981): 27–43; on Poncas, see Alanson Skinner, "Ponca Society and Dances," *Anthropological Papers of the American Museum of Natural History* 11 (1915): 777–801; Jonathan Holmes, "Ponca Hethuska Society," available at www.powwows.com /2012/07/31/ponca-handhuska-society/; and Meadows, *Kiowa, Apache, and Comanche Military Societies*, 142, 161–70; on the 1929 ceremony in Bullhead, see "Armistice Day Fittingly Observed at Bullhead," *Corson County News*, 15 November 1929, 1. In a February 1930 letter, Eugene Younghawk emphasizes the role of shame in the donation-making process and goes so far as to invoke witchcraft. E. Younghawk to E. D. Mossman, 13 February 1930, file "73, Indian Dances, 2/2."

16. On certain families' special connection to a Legion post, see interview with Loretta Meredith, 12 July 2009, White Shields, North Dakota. On turnover in officers' positions, see O. Ogle and R. F. Thompson, *History of the Sam White Bear Post*, 16; Frank B. Fiske, *History of Albert Grass Post*

No. 173, Fort Yates, North Dakota, American Legion Library, Indianapolis, Indiana, 1937; and Loretta Fowler, *Arapahoe Politics, 1851–1978: Symbols in Crises of Authority* (Lincoln: University of Nebraska Press, 1982), 262. On Agnes One Elk, see interview with Germaine Eagle Iron Thunder, 23 July 2008, Rock Creek, South Dakota.

17. On Armistice Day, see "Harding Says War Was for Our Rights," *New York Times*, 12 November 1920; M. Dennis, *Red, White, and Blue Letter Days*, 230, 231, 235; Warren G. Harding, *Our Common Country: Mutual Good Will in America* (Columbia: University of Missouri Press, 2003), 118. On Memorial Day, see David W. Blight, *Race and Reunion: The Civil War in American Memory* (Cambridge: Belknap Press of Harvard University Press, 2001), 64–97.

18. M. Dennis, *Red, White, and Blue Letter Days*, 233–34. For examples of Memorial Day and Armistice Day among the Sioux, see "Many Attend Memorial Day Exercises," *Sioux County Pioneer*, 31 May 1923, 1; "Memorial Day Program in Park," *Todd County News*, 4 June 1925, 1; "Rosebud Boarding School," *Todd County News*, 16 November 1922, 1; "Saint Francis," 17 November 1921, 1; "Armistice Day Fittingly Observed at Bullhead," *Corson County News*, 15 November 1929, 1; "Armistice Day Fittingly Observed," 15 November 1935, 1.

19. On ethnic boundaries, see Fredrik Barth, ed., *Ethnic Groups and Boundaries: The Social Organization of Culture Difference* (Long Grove, Ill.: Waveland Press, 1998 [1969]), 9–38. On reciprocal visits between Indian and white Legion posts, see "Armistice Day Fittingly Observed," *Corson County News*, 15 November 1935, 1.

20. On white exodus in the 1930s, see Catherine McNicol Stock, *Main Street in Crisis: The Great Depression and the Old Middle Class on the Northern Plains* (Chapel Hill: University of North Carolina Press, 1992), 39; Timothy J. Kloberdanz, "In the Land of *Inyan Woslata*: Plains Indian Influences on Reservation Whites," *Great Plains Quarterly* 7, no. 2 (Spring 1987): 69–82, 72. Two individuals in particular seem to have played a crucial role in the successive creation of posts on Standing Rock: Thomas Crow Necklace (a charter member in Fort Yates in 1920, Bullhead in 1924, and Little Eagle in 1926), and Frank B. Fiske, a U.S. soldier's son and founder of the local newspaper, the *Sioux County Pioneer*, which reported regularly on Legion activities. On white Legion posts as sources of information and places of socialization for Indians, see Mary Austin, "A'Wa Tseighe Comes Home from the War," *The Nation*, 6 April 1927, 367–68; and Russel Lawrence Barsh, "War and the Reconfiguring of American Indian Society," *Journal of American Studies* 35, no. 3 (December 2001): 391.

21. On white help during Indian ceremonies, see "Armistice Day Held Here Sat.," *Sioux County Pioneer*, 16 November 1933, 1. On the demand for Indian dancers in white towns, see Ellis, "'There Is No Doubt,'" 550–54,

and "'We Don't Want Your Rations, We Want This Dance': The Chang-
ing Use of Song and Dance on the Southern Plains," *Western Historical
Quarterly* 30, no. 2 (1999): 138–39; Michael G. Kammen, *Mystic Chords of
Memory: The Transformation of Tradition in American Culture* (New York:
Vintage Books, 1993 [1991]), 401. On Indian ceremonies sponsored by
historical societies, see C. Ellis, "'We Don't Want Your Rations,'" 133;
and Jonathan L. Buffalo, "Green Corn Dance to Annual Powwow: A
History of the Annual Meskwaki Powwow," Iowa City, Buffalo Papers,
Special Collections, State Historical Society of Iowa, December 1979.
On the Fourth of July as a time for inter-community visiting, see "Indian
Celebration July 1–2–3," *Mellette County News*, 17 June 1920, 1.

22. "Armistice Day," *The Tomahawk*, 25 May 1922, 22 October and 5 November 1925; "Armistice Day at 2 P.M.," *Corson County News*, 8 November 1925.

23. Transcript of interview with Joseph Wheeler, 10, T-288, 24 June 1968,
DCAIOH.

24. "Two Shields," *Sioux County Pioneer*, 17 November 1927, 1; Statement of
Thomas Frosted, 6 June 1928, "Sen. 83AF9 SRA," box 109, Committee
on Interior and Insular Affairs, ND, RG 46, NARA-DC; "Judge Berry
Makes Inspiring Memorial Day Address Here," *Corson County News*, 5
June 1924, 1.

25. A. B. Welch, *Indian Celebrations*, 61–62; on sham battles in Indian country,
see W. C. Meadows, *Kiowa, Apache, and Comanche Military Societies*, 73.

26. On German helmets in homes, see "Rouillard, Cyril," Little Eagle District, in South Dakota Emergency Relief Administration, "Survey of Indian Reservations, 1935," Arlington, University Publications of America,
1975. On helmets as rewards sent to Indian schools for participation in
liberty bond drives, see J. D. Huff, Santa Fe Indian school superintendent, to CIA, 10 May 1926, entry 610, "Military Activities: Indians in the
World War," Southern Pueblos, RG 75, NARA-DEN. On the dangers of
sham battles, see "Indian Is Wounded During Sham Battle: Sam Foster
Shot in Skirmish at Little Eagle Armistice Celebration," *Mellette County
News*, 12 November 1926. On the sham battle at Little Eagle in 1946, see
James Henri Howard, "The Dakota Victory Dance in World War II,"
North Dakota History 18 (1951): 31–40.

27. "Memorial Day," *Sioux County Pioneer*, 3 June 1926; "Todd County Record in the Great War," *Todd County Tribune*, Todd County, 9 June 1921;
"Advance Man Celebrat'd Armistice Day with Sioux Indians," *The Beach*
[N.D.] *Advance*, 19 November 1931, 1, 4, available at www.welchdakota
papers.com/2011/08/welch-speaks-at-armistice-day-celebration-cannon
-ball-nov-11-1931/.

28. On patriotism as an ethnic trait, see "By the American Legion Press
Association," 1929 (?), "Class Post—Indians," Correspondence Files—
Administration and Organization, American Legion Library, American

Legion Headquarters, Indianapolis; and North Dakota, *A Guide to the Northern Prairie State* (Fargo, N.D.: Knight Printing Company, 1938), 317; see also A. B. Welch, "Burial (Decoration Day, 1921)," *Oral History of the Dakota Tribes 1800's–1945*, available at www.welchdakotapapers.com /2011/10/life-on-the-plains-adoption-thru-cooking/. On patriotic decorations on Standing Rock, see "The Acts of Indians on Memorial Day," *The Indian's Friend*, May 1922, 1; for descriptions of a "sea" of U.S. flags, see A. B. Welch, *Indian Celebrations*, 10, 37, 56–57, 111; T. J. Kloberdanz, "In the Land of *Inyan Woslata*," 78–80; and May E. Hinton, *South of the Cannon Ball: A History of Sioux, the War Bonnet County* (Grand Forks, N.D.: Washburn Printing Center, 1984), 145.

29. On the adoption of missionaries, see Ross Alexander Enochs, *The Jesuit Mission to the Lakota Sioux: Pastoral Theology and Ministry, 1886–1945* (Kansas City, Kans.: Sheed and Ward, 1996), 144–45; and James R. Walker, *Lakota Belief and Ritual*, ed. Raymond J. DeMallie and Elaine A. Jahner (Lincoln: University of Nebraska Press, 1980), 193–240. On the adoption of Legionnaires, see Al Jones to Fred C. Painton, 25 January 1926, and Harry S. Ruth to Russel G. Creviston, 30 September 1924, "Class Post—Indians," Correspondence Files—Administration and Organization, American Legion Library, American Legion Headquarters, Indianapolis. On Foch's adoption, see A. B. Welch, *Indian Celebrations*, 44–51.

30. On Mayhemotah, see interview of Jennie Medicine Elk by Suzanne Brandt, 19, T-83, 11 July 1967, DCAIOH. On DeRockbraine and Howard, see interview with Cecilia Brownotter, 23 July 2008, Rock Creek, South Dakota. On George Big Owl, see "The Holy Road, Ralph G. Big Owl Walking Bull," *Lakota Country Times*, April 2008, available at www .lakotacountrytimes.com/common/pastarchives/1302.html. On the bestowing of chiefs' names, see James L. Glascock (a captain during World War I and an inspector of Indian primary schools), "American Legion Celebration Big Success," *Todd County Tribune*, 26 January 1921, 1; on Carruth, commander of the North Dakota Legion, being given the name of "Blue Earth" by the post of the same name, see Welch, *Indian Celebrations*, 125.

31. On mockery against "for show" adoptions, see Mark Diedrich, *Mni Wakan Oyate (Spirit Lake Nation): A History of the Sisituwan, Wahpandon, Pabaksa, and Other Dakota That Settled at Spirit Lake, North Dakota* (Fort Totten, N.D.: Cankdeska Cikana Community College Publishing, 2007), 172.

32. On Indian bands and orchestras, see "Red Tomahawk," *Sioux County Pioneer*, 29 December 1929; Frank B. Fiske, *History of Albert Grass Post No. 173*, Fort Yates, North Dakota, American Legion Library, American Legion Headquarters, Indianapolis, Indiana, 1937, 33, and Hinton, *South of the Cannon Ball*, 79. On the Standing Rock band in Franklin D. Roosevelt's inaugural parade, see "Roosevelt to Assume Leadership Today," *Pitts-*

burgh Post-Gazette, 4 March 1933, 5; "Sioux to Visit Capitol," *Fergus Daily Journal,* Fergus Falls, Minnesota, 25 January 1934; "Indian to Stage Entertainment," *The Ellesburgh Capital,* 4 September 1931, Ellensburg, Washington; and J. W. Troutman, *"Indian Blues,"* 152. On drill squads, see Bullhead Day School, *History of the Bullhead Day School and Community* (Bullhead, S.D.: Bullhead Day School, 1975), 36.

33.   On the Sioux dog dance, see Reginald Laubin and Gladys Laubin, *Indian Dances of North America: Their Importance to Indian Life* (Norman: University of Oklahoma Press, 1977), 450–51.

34.   On powwows as rituals, see Foster, *Being Comanche,* 127. On solemnity during Memorial Day celebrations, see Welch, *Indian Celebrations,* 25. On powwows among Ho-chunk, Kiowa, and Ponca, see Ellis, Lassiter, and Dunham, *Powwow,* 63; Meadows, *Kiowa, Apache, and Comanche Military Societies,* 140; "Tribute and Honor Ponca Indian American Legion Post #38," 121st Annual Ponca Powwow, 28–31 August 1997.

35.   On Crow Ghost's flag, see A. B. Welch's interview with Crow Ghost, 29 September 1915, *Oral History of the Dakota Tribes,* available at www.welch dakotapapers.com/2011/10/indian-histories-from-cadotte-to-drags -wolf-30-individuals/; www.welchdakotapapers.com/2011/10/indian-his tories-from-hairy-chin-to-kills-prandty-enemy-22-individuals/; and www .welchdakotapapers.com/2011/11/mythology/. On the use of flags and military honors in Sioux burials in the nineteenth century, see David I. Bushnell Jr., *Burials of the Algonquian, Siouan, and Caddoan Tribes West of the Mississippi* (Washington, D.C.: GPO, 1927), 32–35, 38; and Casler, "Fur Traders as Undertakers," 7–8. On the flag as a symbol of obedience, see "Notes from a Native Pastor's Sermon," *Word Carrier* (January– February 1917), 2; on the violent conflict started by the erection of a flagpole in Lakota country, see Jeffrey Ostler, *The Plains Sioux and U.S. Colonialism from Lewis and Clark to Wounded Knee* (Cambridge: Cambridge University Press, 2004), 54–55.

36.   The close connection between hostile appropriation and imitation has generally been ignored by historians (for example Douglas A. Schmittou and Michael H. Logan, "Fluidity of Meaning: Flag Imagery in Plains Indian Art," *American Indian Quarterly,* 26, no. 4 (2002): 559–604. On the flag in Lakota art, see Richard A. Pohrt, "The American Indian and the American Flag," and "Observations on the Flag Motif in Indian Art," in *Lakota Art Is an American Art: Readings in Traditional and Contemporary Sioux Art,* vol. 2, ed. Ron D. Theisz (Spearfish, S.D.: Black Hills State College, Center for Indian Studies, 1981), 154–68, 169–244; William K. Powers, "The American Flag in Lakota Art: An Ecology of Signs," *Whispering Wind* 28, no. 2 (1996): 4–15. On Red Fish's flag, see A. B. Welch, "Gifts of Tobacco Pouches by Red Fish, Crow Ghost, Fool Bear, July 6th, 1915," *Oral History of the Dakota Tribes 1800's–1945,* available at www .welchdakotapapers.com/2011/10/life-on-the-plains-fighting-the-enemy

-thru-hunting/ and "Red Fish, Yantonaise Sioux Chief," available at www
.welchdakotapapers.com/2012/04/red-fish/; "Seven Fires Council Flag,
June 1915," A. B. Welch, *Shields*, ed. Everett Cox (Mandan, N.D.: Standing Rock Tribal Historical Preservation Office, 1941), 28. On Joseph K.
Dixon's expedition, see "Rodman Wanamaker Expedition of 1913," 468–
77, roll 30, James McLaughlin Papers, SHSND; Richard Lindstrom,
"'Not from the Land Side, But from the Flag Side': Native American
Responses to the Wanamaker Expedition of 1913," *Journal of Social History* 30, no. 1 (Fall 1996): 209–27; and R. L. Barsh, "An American Heart
of Darkness: The 1913 Expedition for American Indian Citizenship,"
Great Plains Quarterly 13, no. 2 (Spring 1993): 91–115. For an interpretation of the U.S. eagle as the eagle "taking care of the [Lakota] nation," see
Inez Hilger, "The Narrative of Oscar One Bull," *Mid-America: An Historical Review* 28, no. 3 (July 1946): 152.

37. "The Indian and the Present Crisis," *The Indian Leader*, 25 January 1918,
14.

38. Frances Bellamy, "A Brief Synopsis of the Story of the Origin of the
Pledge Taken from the Detailed Narrative by Frances Bellamy, Author
of the Pledge," *Congressional Record*, 91st Cong. (1945), 5510–11. On the
link between family and flag among non-Indians, see Stuart McConnell,
"Reading the Flag: A Reconsideration of the Patriotic Cults of the 1890s,"
in *Bonds of Affection*, ed. Bodnar, 113.

39. Beede 1, p. 4. For interpretations of the color red, see Nancy Shoemaker,
"How Indians Got to Be Red," *American Historical Review* 102, no. 3 (June
1997): 625–44.

40. Beede 1, pp. 5n10, 16–17. A *wowapandokeca* is a sign or a miracle, according to Eugene Buechel and Paul Manhart, *Lakota Dictionary: Lakota-
English/English-Lakota* (Lincoln: University of Nebraska Press, 2002),
397. On *okiheya*, see "Subordinate" and "Subordinately," in J. P. Williamson, *An English-Dakota Dictionary*, 234.

41. Beede 1, p. 5n10, and Thomas Frosted, Edward Afraid of Hawk and Albert Heart, to CIA, 1 February 1919, file 28217–18, box 4, entry 44, SRA,
CCF 1907–1939, RG 75, NARA-DC. On Heaven and Earth in Lakota
religion, see J. R. Walker, *Lakota Myth* (Lincoln: University of Nebraska
Press, 2006), 9–10, 28, 206–20; on the use of red flags during Sun Dance
ceremonies, see Raymond J. DeMallie and Douglas R. Parks, *Sioux Indian Religion: Tradition and Innovation* (Norman: University of Oklahoma
Press, 1987), 70.

42. On patriotism in churches, see the photograph "Interior of our Lady of
Lourdes Church with patriotic decoration, 1929," Bureau of Catholic
Indian Missions, Marquette University, Milwaukee, Wisconsin; Sarah
Emilia Olden, *The People of Tipi Sapa (the Dakotas): Tipi Sapa Mitaoyate Kin*
(New York: Museum of the American Indian, Heye Foundation, 1918),
xxiii; and "The Spirit of Patriotism at the Mission Meetings," *The Word*

Carrier, October–December 1918, 1. On yells as salutes to the flag, see "A New Flag Pole," *The Word Carrier*, November–December 1919, 21; on the flag as a living entity, see *United States Code*, title 4, § 8, "Respect for Flag."

43.   For admonitions against participants, see "Fort Yates: Decoration Day," *Sioux County Pioneer*, 7 June 1928, 1. On the flag as an element of clothing, see Mary Patterson Lord to John Barton Payne, Secretary of the Interior, 5 October 1920, file 109123-17-063, SRA, CCF; and Patrick Coleman, "A Rare Find: The Treaty of Washington, 1858," *Minnesota History* 59, no. 5 (Spring 2005): 197–99. On the role of schools, see "Armistice Day Program," *Todd County Tribune*, 16 November 1922, 1. On the Takes The Shield family's visit to Washington, see "Department of the Interior, Memorandum for the press," 28 May 1924, and Charles H. Burke to Mr. and Mrs. Takes The Shield, 29 May 1924, file 85599, Standing Rock, entry 125, CCF 1907–1939, NARA-DC. On stars in the flag, see "Everywhere Is to Be Seen the Service Flag," *The Carlisle Arrow and Red Man*, 2 November 1917, 4. On *Tʼuŋkášila*, see Beede 1, p. 16, and Black Bear and Theisz, *Songs and Dances of the Lakota*, 21. On uses of the flag outside of Sioux country, see (for the Pueblos) C. E. Paris to CIA, 14 November 1924, file "610 Military Activities, Indians in the World War, 1923–1926," box 59, General Correspondence File, 1912–1938, Pueblo Agency, RG 75, NARA-DEN; (for the Osages) Fred Lookout, Principal Chief, 9 November 1925 resolution, file 23420, entry 44, CCF 1907–1939, RG 75, NARA-DC; (for the Crows) "Minutes of Ceremony . . . ," 21 February 1925, 10, file "156 War Matters, 1920–1925," and "Indian Writes to Coolidge," *New York Times*, 24 July 1927, 9. On Flag songs, see Henry Murphy, "History of Henry Has Holy (Henry Owns Medicine)," 3, MS 20063, SHSND; and Black Bear and Theisz, *Songs and Dances of the Lakota*, 32, 61.

Chapter Four. Bad Boys, Forgotten Heroes

1.   Circular 1300, 26 April 1917, file "600. Military Activities," box 177, Crow Creek Agency, RG 75, NARA-KC.

2.   Matthew S. Goldberg and John T. Warner, "Military Experience, Civilian Experience, and the Earnings of Veterans," *Journal of Human Resources* 22, no. 1 (Winter 1987): 78; Joseph J. Gurnoe, "Hampton Normal and Agricultural Institutes American Indian Students, 1878–1923," in *First Person Accounts*, ed. Jon L. Brudvig, 1994–96, available at www.two frog.com/hamptonmale2.txt; William Schenandoah, box HA, entry 977B, RG 75, NARA-DC. A database compiling information on Indian veterans collected by Lieut. Eddy was generously offered me by Dr. Russel Lawrence Barsh. It can be accessed at http://anneloetraphy.free.fr/thomas grillot/eddy1919.xlsx.

3. Stephen Youngdeer to Carlisle director, 20 February 1913, file 1327, box 1222, RG 75, NARA-DC.

4. For an example of the attitude of school principals in Chilocco, Oklahoma, see Edgar A. Allen to H. B. Peairs, 20 April 1917, file "Registrations, 1917–1918," box 18, Haskell Institute, Subject Correspondence File, 1904–1941, RG 75, NARA-KC. Scott Gelber, "A 'Hard-Boiled Order': The Reeducation of Disabled WWI Veterans in New York City," *Journal of Social History* 39, no. 1 (2005): 161–80. On the situation in Canada, see James Dempsey, "Problems of Western Canadian Indian War Veterans After World War I," *Native Studies Review* 5, no. 2 (1989): 1–18.

5. "Chester C. Beaulieu Writes from France," *The Tomahawk*, White Earth, Minnesota, 8 May 1919; McMillen, *Making Indian Law*, 22; Herbert S. Lewis and L. Gordon McLester, *Oneida Lives: Long-Lost Voices of the Wisconsin Oneidas* (Lincoln: University of Nebraska Press, 2005), 195–96; Evangeline Thurber, "Rehabilitation of World War I Veterans in District No. 12," *Pacific Historical Review* 15, no. 1 (1946): 69; Ralph E. Stolz to Chief of Rehabilitation Division, 5 December 1922, 28, box 176, District Files 1918–1925, Rehabilitation Division, RG 15, NARA-CHI; Sevalier [*sic*], Walter, box HA, entry 977B, RG 75, NARA-DC.

6. On Eagle Feather, see Harry W. Jones to Mae Ricketts, 19 June 1919; Claude C. Covey to Federal Board for Vocational Education, 26 June 1919; "Soldier Boys Correspondence," box A-435, Rosebud Agency, Subject Correspondence, 1910–1925, RG 75, NARA-KC. On the model Cheyenne soldier, see "The American Indian in the World War," *Office of Indian Affairs Bulletin*, no. 15 (1922): 2. On Little Chief, see Krouse, *North American Indians in the Great War*, 124. On Tafoya, see Joseph F. Tafoya to Indian Office, 29 May 1918, box 46010-18; and Joseph F. Tafoya to Indian Office, 1 August 1918, box 68820, General Services, CCF 1907–1939, RG 75, NARA-DC; Krouse, *North American Indians*, 122.

7. Guy H. Houchen to E. D. Mossman, 25 September 1930, file "127, Indians Competent, Roll of Honor," box 183, SRA, DCF, 1906–1959, RG 75, NARA-KC.

8. On Crows, see "Minutes of Ceremony," 21 February 1925, file "156 War Matters, 1920–1925," box 34, Numerical Correspondence File, 1914–1927, Crow Agency, RG 75, NARA-DEN; on Ojibway, see John S. R. Hammitt to Commissioner of Indian Affairs, 6 May 1926, file "Indians in World War I," box 6, DCF 1917–1935, Lac du Flambeau Agency, RG 75, NARA-CHI; on Pueblos, Farmer to C. E. Faris, 12 July 1924, file "610, Military Activities, Indians in World War, 1923–1926," box 108, Southern Pueblos Agency, General Correspondence File, 1911–1935, RG 75, NARA-DEN; on Standing Rock, see Family Information Survey, 1922–1923, box Oversize (OS) 36, Standing Rock Agency, RG 75, NARA-KC. On Red Eagle, personal email to the author, 25 June 2007. On New York, see "New York Indian Colony Now Has Its Own Club," *New York Times*,

6 February 1927, p. X15. On Fire Thunder, see H. Scudder Mekeel, "Field Notes Summer of 1931 and 1932. White Clay District, Pine Ridge Reservation, South Dakota," 25, Mekeel Papers, National Anthropological Archives, Suitland, Maryland.

9. Interview with Oscar White Weasel by Steve Plummer, no. 698, 16 June 1971, American Indian Research Program, South Dakota Oral History Center, Institute of American Indian Studies, University of South Dakota, Vermillion, South Dakota; Paul Bald Eagle, box 2, entry 977B, RG 75, NARA-DC.

10. On returning students, see Adams, *Education for Extinction*, 278; and Wilbert H. Ahern, "An Experiment Aborted: Returned Indian Students in the Indian School Service, 1881–1908," *Ethnohistory* 44, no. 2 (Spring 1997): 263–304.

11. On dancing controversies, see Jacqueline Shea Murphy, *The People Have Never Stopped Dancing: Native American Modern Dance Histories* (Minneapolis: University of Minnesota Press, 2007), 81–110; Margaret D. Jacobs, "Making Savages of Us All: White Women, Pueblo Indians, and the Controversy over Indian Dances in the 1920s," in *American Nations: Encounters in Indian Country, 1850 to the Present*, ed. Frederick E. Hoxie (New York: Routledge, 2001), 172–98; and Ellis, "'There Is No Doubt,'" 543–69. On national holidays on reservations, see Francis Paul Prucha, *The Great Father: The United States Government and the American Indians* (Lincoln: University of Nebraska Press, 1995), 339. For a contemporary diagnosis of the prewar decline of traditional dances, see A. DeRockbraine to C. C. Covey, 14 August 1915, file "Standing Rock Fair, 1915," box 153, DCF, 1906–1959, SRA, RG 75, NARA-KC.

12. On patriotic celebrations as a substitute for traditional Indian dancing, see Ellis, "'There Is No Doubt,'" 563; On dancing regulations, see E. D. Mossman to farmers, 18 May 1922, box 42204-1922, entry 44, SRA, CCF 1907–1939, RG 75, NARA-DC; Asa Littlecrow, Acting farmer, Cannonball substation, to Superintendent James B. Kitch, 14 January 1920, file "73, Indian Dances 1/2," box 174, DCF, 1906–1959, SRA, RG 75, NARA-KC; and John William Troutman, *"Indian Blues": American Indians and the Politics of Music, 1890–1935* (Ph.D. diss., University of Texas, 2004), 74. On the supplement to circular 1665, see Jacobs, "Making Savages of Us All."

13. On special honors for Sioux veterans, see Joe Starita, *The Dull Knifes of Pine Ridge: A Lakota Odyssey* (New York: Putnam, 1995), 38; Alfred B. Welch, *Indian Celebrations*, 62 and 89; "Parmelee Indians Celebrated November 11," *Todd County Tribune*, 19 November 1925; "Unique Program Held at Two Shields Hall by Indians in Armistice Day," *Sioux County Pioneer*, 13 November 1931; interview with Adele Little Dog, 23 June 2008, Little Eagle, South Dakota. On Sioux dances, see Black Bear and Theisz, *Songs and Dances of the Lakota*, 45, 49, 51, 53, and 87.

14. On Sioux winter counts, see Byron Olson, "The Eagle Heart Winter Count," Standing Rock Sioux Tribe Historical Preservation Office, n.d.; and Linea Sundstrom, "History in Pictures: Father Buechel and the Lakota Winter Counts," 2006, 45–47, available at http://groups.creighton .edu/sfmission/museum/exhibits/wintercounts/buechel_winter_counts .pdf; Thomas J. Malone, "On the Warpath Again," *American Legion Monthly* (April 1935): 62.

15. On policemen, see William Thomas Hagan, *Indian Police and Judges: Experiments in Acculturation and Control* (Lincoln: University of Nebraska Press, 1980); and Mark R. Ellis, "Reservation Akicitas: The Pine Ridge Indian Police, 1879–1885," *South Dakota History* 29, no. 3 (Fall 1999): 185–210; on *akicitas*, see Eugene Buechel and Paul Manhart, *Lakota Dictionary: Lakota-English/English-Lakota* (Lincoln: University of Nebraska Press, 2002), 13; and Fort Laramie Treaty, 29 April 1868, available at http://puffin.creighton.edu/lakota/1868_la.html, accessed 19 July 2010. On warriors as "defenders" of their people, see Vestal, *Sitting Bull: Champion of the Sioux*, 102. On the war in Europe seen from reservations, see M. Dwire to P. T. Lonergan, 23 April 1917, file "610 Military Activities, Indians in World War," box 59, General Correspondence File 1912–1938, Northern Pueblos Agency, RG 75, NARA-DEN.

16. On military service for Indians before the reservation era, see Thomas W. Dunlay, *Wolves for the Blue Soldiers: Indian Scouts and Auxiliaries with the United States Army, 1860–1890* (Lincoln: University of Nebraska Press, 1982), 109–26. On Kenoi, see "Sam Kenoi's Autobiography," 1938, 486, 615, box 6, box 36, Subseries B, Series I, Morris Edward Opler Papers, Division of Rare and Manuscript Collections, Cornell University Library, Ithaca, New York; Morris E. Opler, "A Chiricahua Apache Account of the Geronimo Campaign of 1886, Narrated by Samuel E. Kenoi," *New Mexico Historical Review* 13, no. 4 (October 1938): 382.

17. Welch, *Indian Celebrations*, 20–21.

18. See, however, Alfred B. Welch, *Chief John Grass*, ed. Everett Cox (Mandan, N.D., on file at the Standing Rock Tribal Historical Preservation Office, 1941), 84–85.

19. On the telling of war deeds, see Theresa D. O'Nell, "'Coming Home' Among Northern Plains Vietnam Veterans: Psychological Transformations in Pragmatic Perspective," *Ethos* 27, no. 4 (1999): 441–65. On old warriors' contempt for 1917–18 veterans' war deeds, see S. Vestal, *Sitting Bull*, 59–60.

20. On Christian churches' ambivalence toward the exercise of patriotic violence, see *The Word Carrier* (the organ of South Dakota's Episcopalians), specifically "The Next Forty Years—The Indian in the World" (January–February 1918), 2, and "The Good Coming Out of the War" (May–June 1918), 11.

21. On pensions, see Jennifer D. Keene, *Doughboys, the Great War, and the*

Remaking of America (Baltimore: Johns Hopkins University Press, 2001), 176; on Takes The Shield, see Charles E. Mulhearn to Commissioner of Indian Affairs, 6 May 1924, and Eugene D. Mossman to Commissioner of Indian Affairs, 15 April 1924, box 85599, entry 125, SRA, CCF 1907–1939, RG 75, NARA-DC; on Bullhead, see Augustine Pleets to Usher L. Burdick, 15 January 1935, box 58508-1918, entry 725, SRA, CCF 1907–1939, RG 75, NARA-DC; "Frank, Son of Lt. Bullhead May Secure Tidy Sum as Compensation," *Sioux County Pioneer,* 7 April 1933, 1, 4; on Shoots Near, see Jacob Shoots Near's file, Veterans Personal Records, Veteran Service Officer's file, Corson County, McLaughlin, South Dakota.

22.   For a traditionalist's account of veterans' struggle with alcoholism, see Frank Fools Crow, Thomas E. Mails, and Dallas Chief Eagle, *Fools Crow* (Lincoln: University of Nebraska Press, 1990), 9, 146–47, 153; on Lac du Flambeau veterans, see John S. R. Hammittee to Commissioner of Indian Affairs, 18 May 1926, file "Indians in World War I," box 6, DCF 1917–1935, Lac du Flambeau Agency, RG 75, ANCI. On Bad River, see Senate, Subcommittee of the Committee on Indian Affairs, *Senate Survey of Conditions of the Indians in the United States* [hereafter *Senate Survey*] 5, GPO, Washington, D.C., 1930, 1959–1960. On Standing Rock, see Asa Littlecrow, Acting farmer, Cannonball substation, to Superintendent Kitch, 14 January 1920, file "73, Indian Dances 1/2"; E. D. Mossman to C. W. Grace, 6 March 1931, "Individuals, Requesting Information," box 174, Standing Rock Agency, DCF 1906–1959, RG 75, NARA-KC. On incest and the world war, see Ella Deloria, "Dakota Ethnography," box 3, "Additional Notes on the Teton-Dakota," 1, available at http://zia.aisri .indiana.edu/deloria_archive/browse.php. For a World War I veteran's denunciation of alcoholism in the Vietnam War generation, see interview of Jesse Rowlodge by Julia A. Jordan, M-4, 12 December 1967, 3 and T-239, 16 April 1968, 1, DCAIOH.

23.   On alcohol consumption, see Andrew Beechtree's testimony in H. S. Lewis and L. G. McLester, *Oneida Lives,* 187; and interview of Oscar White Weasel by Steve Plummer, no. 698, 16 June 1971, 31, American Indian Research Program, South Dakota Oral History Center, Institute of American Indian Studies, University of South Dakota, Vermillion, South Dakota. On alcohol in the trenches, see Alan Doon, "War According to Custom," 10, Native American manuscripts, Western History Collections, University of Oklahoma, Norman, Oklahoma. On the YMCA and other reformist groups' efforts at controlling alcohol consumption and the spread of venereal diseases, see Allan M. Brandt, *No Magic Bullet: A Social History of Venereal Disease in the United States Since 1880* (New York: Oxford University Press, 1985), 96–121. On the stereotype about Indians and alcohol, see Robert J. Miller and Maril Hazlett, "'The Drunken Indian': Myth Distilled into Reality Through Federal Indian Alcohol Policy," *Arizona State Law Journal* 28, no. 1 (1996): 223–98. On

Indian soldiers' sexuality, see "Sam Kenoi's Autobiography," 485–500, box 6, box 36, Subseries B, Series I, Morris Edward Opler Papers, Division of Rare and Manuscript Collections, Cornell University Library, Ithaca, New York; "Romance of a Doughboy with Maiden in Sunny France," *The American Indian* (August 1928): 10–12; Asa Littlecrow, Acting farmer, Cannonball substation, to Superintendent Kitch, 14 January 1920, file "73, Indian Dances 1/2," box 174, DCF, 1906–1959, SRA, RG 75, NARA-KC.

24. On American Legion bars, see R. L. Barsh, "War and the Reconfiguring of American Indian Society," *Journal of American Studies* 35, no. 3 (December 2001): 391; and Mary Austin, "A'Wa Tseighe Comes Home from the War," *The Nation*, 6 April 1927, 368. On alcohol consumption during wars, see John Adair, "The Navajo and Pueblo Veteran: A Force for Culture Change," *American Indian Quarterly* 4, no. 1 (1947): 5–11; and John Adair and Evon Z. Vogt, "Navaho and Zuni Veterans: A Study of Contrasting Modes of Culture Change," *American Anthropologist* 51, no. 4 (October–December 1949): 550. On Longmarsh, see *Senate Survey*, 5, 1930, 2134–35.

25. On the Spanish flu in Indian country, see Britten, *American Indians in World War I*, 194; on Cornplanter, see William N. Fenton, "Jesse Cornplanter, Seneca, 1889–1957," in *American Indian Intellectuals of the Nineteenth and Early Twentieth Centuries*, ed. Margot Liberty (Norman: University of Oklahoma Press, 2002 [1978]), 210–11; "Autobiography," in *Democrat and Chronicle*, Rochester, 16 November 1936, 1; and "Indian Chief Returns from France to Find Kin Claimed by Death," *Post Standard*, 20 July 1919, 14.

26. The number of Standing Rock veterans who were citizens is based on Family Information Survey, 1922–1923, box Oversize (OS) 36, SRA, RG 75, NARA-KC. For Sleeps From Home's quote, see Georges Sleeps From Home to Francis H. Case, 9 June 1943, Correspondence and related papers exchanged between Francis Case and individual Indians in South Dakota, Francis H. Case Papers, Dakota Wesleyan University, Mitchell. On Hickman and Oklahoma, see "Deposition of Witnesses," 2, file "81202," entry 125, Chilocco Indian School, CCF 1907–1939, RG 75, NARA-DC; and Cato Sells to Grant Foreman, 24 January 1918, box 53685-18, General Services, CCF 1907–1939, RG 75, NARA-DC.

27. On Native veterans reenlisting, see Krouse, *North American Indians*, 41, 130; Cato Sells to Evan W. Estep, 21 March 1921, box 20763, entry 125, San Juan School, CCF 1907–1939, RG 75, NARA-DC, and file 108678, General Services, CCF 1907–1939, RG 75, NARA-DC; "Sam Kenoi's Autobiography," 498; James McCarthy, *A Papago Traveler: The Memories of James McCarthy* (Tucson: University of Arizona Press, 1985), 98. On Hawley, see his file and Alvin Hawley to Lilie McCoy, 21 August 1918, 3 January, 5 April, and 25 April 1919; and Lilie McCoy to Alvin Hawley,

21 April 1917, in box 8, entry 977B, RG 75, NARA-DC; and *Official National Guard Register,* 1923, GPO, Washington, D.C., 1925, 183. On Dagenett, see Adams, *Education for Extinction,* 294–95. On Gurney, see *Senate Survey,* 37, 1940, 21921. On veterans as policemen, see "One Feather, Henry," box 204, DCF 1906–1959, SRA, RG 75, NARA-KC. On the relative attractiveness of police work on the La Pointe Reservation in Wisconsin, see John Basina's case in *Senate Survey,* 5, 1930, 1952.

28.   On camp life, see R. D. Hall to Cato Sells, 20 February 1918, box 18126-18, entry 125, General Services, Central Classified Correspondence, 1907–1939, RG 75, NARA-DC; Assistant Commissioner to John W. Clark, n.d., box 16936-18, General Services, CCF 1907–1939, RG 75, NARA-DC; O. W. Severence to Cato Sells, 11 February 1918, box 12360-18, CCF 1907–1939, RG 75, NARA-DC; G. Lee Phelps to Cato Sells, 23 February 1918, box 7161-18, CCF 1907–1939, RG 75, NARA-DC; and Lynn-Sherow and Ural, "'How Cola' from Camp Funston," 92–95. For the individuals cited, see Ernest Red Feather to Commissioner of Indian Affairs, 20 October 1918, box 85480, entry 125, General Services, CCF 1907–1939, RG 75, NARA-DC; and Todd Harden Smith to Cato Sells, 20 August 1918, box 63949, entry 125, Rosebud Agency, General Services, CCF 1907–1939, RG 75, NARA-DC. For an example of a petition, see Henry Peneaux to Dear Sir, 29 November 1917; Millie Peneaux to C. C. Covey, 27 May 1918; C. C. Covey to James L. Howray, 24 November 1917, "Soldier Boys Correspondence," box A-435, Rosebud Agency, Subject Correspondence, 1910–1925, RG 75, NARA-KC. On Indian pupils' "loyalty" toward their boarding schools, see interview of Bob Duncan by B. D. Timmons, T-49-1, 6 May 1967, 10, DCAIOH.

29.   Krouse, *North American Indians,* 28–29, 93; Peter O. Barnaby to Theodore Sharp [Dear Superintendent], 7 November 1917, 26 November 1917; Peter O. Barnaby to Cato Sells, 17 February 1918; and E. B. Merritt to Peter O. Barnaby, 27 March 1918, box 77686-17, entry 125, Flathead Agency, General Services, CCF 1907–1939, RG 75, NARA-DC; Charles Cedartree, box 3; Bret Risingbear, box 14; and John Skeeper, box 14, entry 977B, RG 75, NARA-DC.

30.   The quotations in this paragraph are taken from Peter Tarbell, "Soldiers' Letters," *The Carlisle Arrow,* 26 April 1918, 3; Barsh, "American Indians in the Great War," 283; James G. Raymond to C. C. Covey, 30 November 1918, "Soldier Boys Correspondence," box A-435, Rosebud Agency, Subject Correspondence, 1910–1925, RG 75, NARA-KC; interview of Moses Trudell by Herbert Hoover, 11 August 1970, 15, Interview 0545, Doris Duke Indian Oral History Collection, Vermillion, South Dakota; Krouse, *North American Indians,* 49, 63–64; Frances Densmore, "The Songs of Indian Soldiers During the World War," *Musical Quarterly* 20, no. 4 (1934): 422; Emory A. Marks to C. J. Crandall, 24 September 1924,

file "610, Military Activities, Indians in the World War," box 20, Southern Pueblos Agency, General Correspondence File, 1911–1935, RG 75,
NARA-DEN; R. L. Barsh, "War and the Reconfiguring," 395–96; Melvin Randolph Gilmore, *Prairie Smoke: A Collection of Lore of the Prairies*
(Bismarck, N.D., 1922 [1921]), 40; "Europeans, not Indians, Cruel; Original Americans in Advance of 'Discoverers,' Speaker Says," *Niagara Falls
Gazette*, 1 March 1932, 3 (see also and William B. Newell, "Indian Contributions to Modern Civilization," *36th Annual Archaeological Report,
1928*, appendix to the report of the Minister of Education (Toronto:
King's Printer, 1928), 18–26.

31. On the "scout syndrome," see Tom Holm, *Strong Hearts, Wounded Souls:
Native American Veterans of the Vietnam War* (Austin: University of Texas
Press, 1996), 89–90; and H. Scudder Mekeel, "Field Notes Summer of
1931 and 1932. White Clay District, Pine Ridge Reservation, South Da-
kota," 21, Mekeel Papers, National Anthropological Archives, Suitland,
Maryland; William Carlow to Commissioner of Indian Affairs, 14 June
1919, box 90569, entry 125, New York Agency, CCF 1907–1939, RG 75,
NARA-DC. On slackers, see F. Densmore, "The Songs of Indian Sol-
diers," 423. On Wheelock, see H. S. Lewis and L. G. McLester, *Oneida
Lives*, 186–87. On Tecumseh, see Troutman, *"Indian Blues,"* 232–33.

32. On Coffey, see Roy G. Coffey to Superintendent [Dear Sir], 24 May
1919, file "600, Military Activities, World War I," box 656, Pine Ridge
Agency, General records Main Decimal Files, RG 75, NARA-KC. For
the claims of Crow veterans, see James P. Ryder to Commissioner of Indian Affairs, 25 June 1924, file 13400-1920, box 9, entry 53, Crow Agency,
CCF 1907–1939, RG 75, NARA-DC; Charles H. Burke to Claude J.
Harris, 6 January 1923, "Veteran Welfare—A–Z—Indians," Correspondence Files—Administration and Organization, American Legion Library,
American Legion Headquarters, Indianapolis, Indiana.

33. On Red Bean, see John Red Bean, "Major James McLaughlin, Inspector
Interior Department, Wash. DC, Standing Rock allotments," reel 9, microfilm, James McLauglin Papers, SHSND; J. Red Bean, "List of Indians
in the World War," Wanamaker Documentation; Krouse, *North American Indians*, 102, 152; J. Red Bean to Commissioner of Indian Affairs, 3
June 1919, Cato Sells to J. Red Bean, 13 August 1919, James B. Kitch to
Commissioner of Indian Affairs, 6 February 1920, box 67136-1919, box
7, entry 53, SRA, CCF 1907–1939, RG 75, NARA-DC.

34. See "Iroquois Ceased His Hunting To Become Farmer," *Syracuse Journal*,
7 December 1910, 6; W. N. Fenton, "Jesse Cornplanter," 209; "Indian
Chief Returns from France to Find Kin Claimed by Death," *Post Standard*, 20 July 1919, 14; Jesse Cornplanter to Joseph Keppler, 8 December
1925, box C8.4, box 1, Correspondence, Joseph Keppler Jr. Iroquois
Papers 1882–1944, Division of Rare and Manuscript Collections, Cor-

nell University Library, Ithaca, New York; and J. Cornplanter to J. Keppler, 8 December 1925; 13 January 1926; 1 March 1930; 23 April 1926; n.d. (before 22 August 1928); and 22 August 1928.

35. J. Cornplanter to J. Keppler, 23 April 1926; 22 August 1928; 2 December 1928; 11 February 1930; 13 January 1930; 30 July 1930; 9 December 1932; 11 November 1933; 8 January 1934; 11 February 1930; 19 December 1931, C8.4, box 1, Correspondence, Joseph Keppler Jr. Iroquois Papers 1882–1944, Division of Rare and Manuscript Collections, Cornell University Library, Ithaca, New York; W. N. Fenton, "Jesse Cornplanter," 201, 211. On the role of disabled veterans in veterans' organizations, see also David A. Gerber, ed., *Disabled Veterans in History* (Ann Arbor: University of Michigan Press, 2000), 27; and Antoine Prost, *Les Anciens Combattants et La Société Française, 1914–1939*, vol. 2 (Paris: Presses de Sciences Po, 1977), 150. See also J. J. Cornplanter and Namée Henricks, *Legends of the Longhouse* (Philadelphia: J. B. Lippincott, 1938).

36. Martin Medicine, box 380, Family Survey 1935, SRA, RG 75, NARA-KC. On Thomas Bad Cob, see "Pine Ridge, Case reports, September 1930," *Senate Survey*, vol. 26, 1932, 14326–28.

37. For calls to help Indian veterans, see Edith H. Eddy to Commander of the American Legion, 25 February 1925; and John H. McQuigg to E. H. Eddy, 10 March 1926, "Rehabilitation—A–Z—Indians," Correspondence —Subject Files, American Legion Library, American Legion Headquarters, Indianapolis. On the Veterans Bureau in Indian country, see "Visit Indian Veterans," *McLaughlin Messenger*, 16 November 1923; C. D. Hibbard to Superintendent of Crow reservation, 14 November 1923, "156—War Matters," box 34, Crow Indian Agency, Numerical Correspondence File, 1914–1927, RG 75, NARA-DEN; and D. Gordon to R. R. Gibson, 14 November 1923, file "610 Military Activities Indians in the World War, 1923–1926," box 108, Southern Pueblos Agency, General Correspondence File, 1911–1935, RG 75, NARA-DEN. On racialized expectations regarding Indian veterans, R. L. Barsh, "American Indians in the Great War," 282; and "With the Boys in the Service," *Rapid City Daily Journal*, 23 August 1918, 2. On the V.A. in veterans' old days, see the files of Alphonse Bearghost, Joseph Chapman, and Joseph Grey Day, Veteran Service Officer's office, County Courthouse, Fort Yates, North Dakota; and interview of M. Trudell by H. Hoover, 14.

Chapter Five. Patriotic Rewards, New Freedoms

1. On self-determination, see for example Charles A. Eastman, "The Indian's Plea for Freedom," *American Indian Magazine* 6, no. 4 (Winter 1919): 162–65.

2. On the nation's debt toward its veterans, see Theda Skocpol, *Social Policy in the United States: Future Possibilities in Historical Perspective* (Princeton,

N.J.: Princeton University Press, 1995), 47–52; and Skocpol, *Protecting Soldiers and Mothers;* Amy E. Holmes, "'Such Is the Price We Pay': American Widows and the Civil War Pension System," in *Toward a Social History of the American Civil War: Exploratory Essays,* ed. Maris A. Vinovskis (Cambridge: Cambridge University Press, 1990), 171–95. On the War Risk Insurance, see Keene, *Doughboys,* 171. On Indians in the fight for the bonus, see "Leg Amputated with Penknife," *Pittsburgh Chronicle,* 29 August 1921, in "Brightlight, John," Card File Relating to Indians in World War I, 1916–1920, killed in action, wounded, died at home, box 3, entry 977B, RG 75, NARA-DC.

3. On the Sioux Jurisdictional Act and similar legislation, see Harvey D. Rosenthal, "Indian Claims and the American Conscience: A Brief History of the Indian Claims Commission," in *Irredeemable America: The Indians' Estate and Land Claims,* ed. Imre Sutton and Ralph L. Beals (Albuquerque: University of New Mexico Press, 1985), 35–70; and "Lead Up to the Indian Claims Commission Act of 1946," available at www.justice.gov/enrd/3147.htm. On treaties and enlistment on Pine Ridge, see statement by Margaret B. Mewhirter, 23 August 1942, box 39863-1942, entry 725, Pine Ridge Agency, CCF 1907–1939, RG 75, NARA-DC. On the Black Hills Council at Crow Creek, see Edward Lazarus, *Black Hills/ White Justice: The Sioux Nation Versus the United States, 1775 to the Present* (New York: HarperCollins, 1991), 136–38. For a similar interpretation of treaties as prohibiting war with whites, see, among Shawnees, Jesse Chisholm, "Interview with John Spybuck," *Indian-Pioneer Papers,* vol. 86, 342, unnumbered interview, University of Oklahoma Libraries Western History Collections, Norman, Oklahoma.

4. On Gandy and Williamson, see E. Lazarus, *Black Hills/White Justice,* 138; "Speech of Hon. Harry L. Gandy, May 28 1920," "Black Hills Claims 1918–1924, folder 2," box 256, DCF, 1906–1959, SRA, RG 75, NARA-KC; Butte Creek Local Council, 8 January 1920, and Carlos Gallineaux to Homer P. Snyder, 23 January 1920, "HR 400" and "S. 1018, 66th Congress," box 11, 66th Congress accompanying papers to specific bills and resolutions, RG 46, NARA-DC; W. Williamson to Peter Norbeck, 17 November 1924, A. G. Granger to W. Williamson, 9 November 1924, W. Williamson to Martin B. Madden, 10 December 1924, Frightened to W. Williamson, 13 February 1923, "Black Hills Claims," Indian Materials, William Williamson Papers, Archives and Special Collections, University of South Dakota, Vermillion, South Dakota; and Elmer R. Rusco, *A Fateful Time: The Background and Legislative History of the Indian Reorganization Act* (Reno: University of Nevada Press, 2000), 13.

5. "Indians of Age Are Legal Voters," *Sioux County Pioneer,* 14 May 1916; "Indians Have No Time for the Non-Partisans," *Sioux County Pioneer,* 7 April 1920. On the petition and the court decision, see *Swift v. Leach,* 45 N.D. 437, 178 N.W. 437 (1920); Sioux County Judgment Book, 1,

70–72, and Commissioner's Record Book, vol. 1, 137, Sioux County Archives, Sioux County courthouse, Fort Yates, North Dakota; in the *Sioux County Pioneer,* see "Fort Yates Wins County Seat Contest by 103 Majority," 7 November 1918; "Results of Official Canvas Sioux County: Election Returns," 21 November 1918; "Heavy Vote Polled," 28 November 1918; "County Seat Contest Has Been Filed," 12 December 1918; "County Seat Removal Election Hearing Is Held Here," 12 June 1919; see also *The Northwestern Reporter* 177 (14 May–9 July 1920) (St. Paul, Minn.: West Publishing, 1920), 4437–43. Outside of North Dakota, see *Opsahl v. Johnson* (1917) 138 Minn. 42, 163 N. W. 988; *Porter v. Hall,* 34 Ariz. 308, 271 P. 411, 412 (1928); S.D. Codified Laws Ann. 92 (1929).

6. On Bonnin, see Gertrude Bonnin, editorial comment, *American Indian Magazine* 6, no. 4 (Winter 1919): 161–62. On her activism during the 1920s and 1930s, see especially Rusco, *A Fateful Time,* 65–66, 169–70.

7. On the 1920 elections in North Dakota, see "Presidential Election Returns," *Sioux County Pioneer,* 4 November 1920. On the Legion's position on Indian citizenship, see "Indian Affairs Convention Mandates," 1948, "U.S.—G–W—Indians," Correspondence—Subject Files, American Legion Library, American Legion Headquarters, Indianapolis; "Detroit Post of American Legion Passes Resolution to Aid Indians," *The Tomahawk,* 1 January 1920, 1; "Convention Resolutions Referred to the Americanism Commission," c. 1949, "U.S.—G–W—Indians," Correspondence —Subject Files, American Legion Library, American Legion Headquarters, Indianapolis. On the Indian Rights Association, see "The Indian Rights Conference," *Southern Workman* (March 1919): 101–3; and *Report of the Board of Indian Commissioners to the Secretary of the Interior* (Washington, D.C.: GPO, 1921), 10. On the 1924 legislation, see Gary C. Stein, "The Indian Citizenship Act of 1924," *New Mexico Historical Review* 47, no. 3 (1972): 257–74.

8. On the presidential certificate, see "War Honors for Indians," *New York Times,* 29 June 1924, 14; "Indians Get Token from Pres. Pershing," *Mandan Daily Pioneer,* 5 July 1924, 2; Alfred B. Welch, *Indian Celebrations,* 73–74; Superintendent of Crow Reservation to Commissioner of Indian Affairs, 8 December 1924, and "Minutes of Ceremony in Connection with Presentation of Certificate of Appreciation," 21 February 1925, 5, file "156 War Matters, 1920–1925," box 34, Numerical Correspondence File, 1914–1927, Crow Agency, RG 75, NARA-DEN; Eugene D. Mossman to A. B. Welch, 19 June 1924, and E. D. Mossman to Commissioner of Indian Affairs, 4 August 1924, "610, Indians in the World War, 1 of 2," box 287. On Indians' endorsement of presidential candidates, see "Frosted Chairman Hoover-Curtis Campaign Committee," *Sioux County Pioneer,* 27 September 1928; "Indian Writes to Coolidge," *New York Times,* 24 July 1927, 9.

9. For the Indian plank in the Republican platform in 1928, see Donald

Bruce Johnson and Kirk H. Porter, *National Party Platforms, 1840–1972* (Urbana: University of Illinois Press, 1973), 290.

10. On Oneidas in Wisconsin, see Laurence M. Hauptman and L. Gordon McLester, *The Oneida Indians in the Age of Allotment, 1860–1920* (Norman: University of Oklahoma Press, 2006), 219. On the Iroquois declaration of war against the German Empire, see Hertzberg, *The Search for an American Indian Identity*, 175; Arthur C. Parker to Major F. S. Hutchinson, 25 June 1918, reel 9, pt. 2, series 1, Correspondence of the Society of American Indians, 1911–1923, *The Papers of the Society of American Indians*, Scholarly Resources, Wilmington, Delaware, 1987; and L. M. Hauptman, *The Iroquois Struggle for Survival: World War II to Red Power* (Syracuse, N.Y.: Syracuse University Press, 1986), 7–9. On the land controversy in New York state, see Anthony Wayne Wonderley and Hope Emily Allen, *Oneida Iroquois Folklore, Myth, and History: New York Oral Narrative from the Notes of H. E. Allen and Others* (Syracuse, N.Y.: Syracuse University Press, 2004), 204–9. For the quotations taken from the Everett Report, see New York State Indian Commission, *Report of the New York State Indian Commission, March 17, 1922*, Albany, New York, 1922, 12–13, 34, 41–42, New York State Library, Digital Collections, Native American Materials, available at www.nysl.nysed.gov/scandocs/native american.htm.

11. Report of the New York State Indian Commission, 67, 97–99.

12. Ibid., 98, 312–13.

13. L. M. Hauptman, *The Iroquois and the New Deal* (Syracuse, N.Y.: Syracuse University Press, 1981), 11.

14. Report of the New York State Indian Commission, 292–97.

15. "Europeans, not Indians, Cruel: Original Americans in Advance of 'Discoverers,' Speaker Says," *Niagara Falls Gazette*, 1 March 1932, 3; and William B. Newell, "Indian Contributions to Modern Civilization," *36th Annual Archaeological Report, 1928, Appendix to the Report of the Minister of Education* (Toronto: King's Printer, 1928), 18–26.

16. Edward S. Rogers and Donald B. Smith, eds., *Aboriginal Ontario: Historical Perspectives on the First Nations* (Toronto: Dundurn Press, 1994), 245–48.

17. "Deskaheh's Last Speech," in *Canadian Literature in English: Texts and Contexts*, vol. 1, ed. Cynthia Sugars and Laura Moss (Toronto: Pearson Longman, 2008), 518–19; and Joëlle Rostkowski, "The Redman's Appeal for Justice: Deskaheh and the League of Nations," in *Indians and Europe: An Interdisciplinary Collection of Essays*, ed. Christian F. Feest (Aachen, Germany: Rader Verlag-Herodot, 1987), 435–53.

18. Donald B. Smith, "Deskaheh," *Dictionary of Canadian Biography Online*, available at www.biographi.ca/fr/bio/deskaheh_15F.html.

19. "The American Indian's Part in the World War: Shall He Fight in Segregated Race Units or Side by Side with Other American Soldiers?" *American Indian Magazine* 5, no. 3 (July–September 1917): 146–53; circular

1378, 26 November 1917, "U.S. Department of Indian Affairs, World War I," box 2, Native Americans, Kautz Family, YMCA Archives, University of Minnesota, Minneapolis, Minnesota; Henriette J. Lunds to Mae Ricketts, 22 May 1919, "Soldier boys," box 345, Rosebud Agency, RG 75, NARA-KC; and Susan Applegate Krouse, *North American Indians in the Great War*, 32, 162.

20. "Bonus Commission Starts," *New York Times*, 26 April 1921, 14; "State Indian Expert Lauds Redman's Part in Downing Germany," *Knickerbocker Press*, 18 September 1921; "Indians Urge Fair Play in Bonus Award," *Post-Standard*, 21 June 1921, 5; "Bonus Ruling Slams Indian War Veterans," *Duluth News*, 20 June 1921, 2; "Indians to Get Soldier Bonus, Newton Rules," *Hampton Press*, 10 August 1921; Clarence A. Anderson, "Lo, The Poor Indian," *Minneapolis News*, 28 May 1921; and "Indian Assails State War Bonus," *Schenectady Gazette*, 22 June 1921, "Indian Should Get His Bonus," *Albany Journal*, June 1921, Charles D. Newton to Edward H. Gohl, 25 July 1921, file 66126, entry 125, General Services, Central Classified Correspondence, 1907–1939, RG 75, NARA-DC.

21. On voting discrimination in Indian country, see Alison R. Bernstein, *American Indians and World War II: Toward a New Era in Indian Affairs* (Norman: University of Oklahoma Press, 1991), 32; and Jeanette Wolfley, "Jim Crow, Indian Style: The Disenfranchisement of Native Americans," *American Indian Law Review* 16, no. 1 (1991): 167–202. On voting rights in Eastern Cherokee country, see George Owl to Edgar Merritt, received 17 October 1917, file 96432, entry 125, Cherokee Nation, CCF 1907–1939, RG 75, NARA-DC; John R. Finger, *Cherokee Americans: The Eastern Band of Cherokees in the Twentieth Century* (Lincoln: University of Nebraska Press, 1991), 36, 39–40, 44–52; George Allen Owl, in "Hampton Normal and Agricultural Institutes, American Indian Students, 1878–1923," ed. Jon L. Brudvig; "81st Division Reunion Scheduled September 27–29," *Ocala* [Florida] *Star-Banner*, 3 September 1963, 13; George E. Frizzell, "The Politics of Cherokee Citizenship, 1898–1930," *North Carolina Historical Review* 61, no. 2 (1984): 22; Margaret Allen, "Living in Two Worlds," *Profile, The Magazine of Lenoire-Rhyne College* 57, no. 3 (Winter 2007): 10–11; Elizabeth C. Duran, "David Owl, Eastern Cherokee Among New York Iroquois," *Journal of Cherokee Studies* 4, no. 6 (1981): 4–13; "Indians Form Veterans Post," *Niagara Falls Gazette*, 26 October 1946, 20; Daniel F. Littlefield and James W. Parins, eds., *American Indian and Alaska Native Newspapers and Periodicals* (Westport, Conn.: Greenwood Press, 1984), 385–86; and Marion Eleanor Gridley, *Indians of Today* (Chicago: Indian Council Fire, 1937), 87.

22. On veterans' struggles during the Great Depression, see Keene, *Doughboys*, 70–178, 181, 203, 262.

23. On Kenoi, see Michael Lieder and Jake Page, *Wild Justice: The People of Geronimo vs. the United States* (New York: Random House, 1997), 75; on

scouts on Pine Ridge, see files 541 to 548, entry 725, "Classified Correspondence Files, 1907–1939," Pine Ridge, NARA-DC; Jerome Greene,
*Indian War Veterans: Memories of Army Life and Campaigns in the West,
1864–1898* (New York: Savas Beatie, 2007), xxi–xxxv. On the Cheyenne,
see Little Wolf to Joseph K. Dixon, 10 December 1940, WW-3, Wanamaker Documentation.

24. Clyde Ellis, Luke E. Lassiter, and Gary H. Dunham, *Powwow* (Lincoln:
University of Nebraska Press, 2005), 19; Ben Black Bear and Ron D.
Theisz, *Songs and Dances of the Lakota* (Aberdeen, S.D.: North Plains Press,
1984 [1976]), 87; Thomas Frosted, file 98473, box 24, entry 155, CCF
1907–1939, SRA, RG 75, NARA-DC.

25. Asa Littlecrow, Acting farmer, Cannonball substation, to Superintendent
Kitch, 14 January 1920, box "73, Indian Dances 1/2."

26. Jerome Cottonwood and John Littlecrow to Charles H. Burke, 28 February 1923, and Claude Killspotted, Red Tomahawk, James All Yellow
to C. H. Burke, n.d., box; and E. D. Mossman to Guy H. Houchen, 20
October 1923, file "73, Indian Dances 1/2."

27. James McGregor to James B. Kitch, 8 February 1921; E. D. Mossman to
Farmers, 28 October 1921, C. C. Covey to Farmers, 23 December 1916;
E. D. Mossman to P. F. Frazier, 30 November 1932; E. D. Mossman to
G. H. Houchen, 20 October 1923; file "73, Indian Dances 1/2;" and
E. D. Mossman to Commissioner of Indian Affairs, 10 February 1922,
file "73, Indian Dances 2/2."

28. Forest F. Bliss to E. D. Mossman, 16 October 1922, Arthur Pratt to E. D.
Mossman, 16 October 1922; Roy Shipman to E. D. Mossman, 30 July
1925, file "73, Indian Dances 1/2."

29. On veterans' involvement in dances, see interview with Germaine Eagle
Iron Thunder, 23 July 2008, Rock Creek, South Dakota; G. H. Houchen
to E. D. Mossman, 6 July 1925, 2, file "73, Indian Dances 1/2." On
Crowskin, see "Kenel Kernels," *Sioux County Pioneer,* 10 July 1924. On
veterans in organizing committees, see for example "Arrangements for
4th July Celebration," *Corson County News,* 3 June 1921, 1. On Red Legs,
see interviews with Etta Taken Alive, 29 July 2008, Bear Soldier, South
Dakota; and Adele Little Dog, 16 July 2008, Little Eagle, South Dakota;
Olley Little Eagle, 8 August 2008, Rock Creek, South Dakota; Benedict
Red Legs, box Oversize (OS) 36, Family Information Survey 1922–1923,
SRA, RG 75, NARA-KC. "Dedication Program, Saturday, July 28, 1934,"
file "44, Standing Rock Memorial Celebration," box 152, SRA, RG 75,
NARA-KC. Lastly, Benedict Red Legs, box 380, Family Survey 1935,
SRA, RG 75, NARA-KC.

30. Joe Gray Day to J. H. Sinclair, 2 April 1923, box 28148, box 24, entry 155,
CC 1907–1939, SRA, RG 75, NARA-DC; Asa Littlecrow to Superinten-
dent Kitch, 14 January 1920, and Joseph Otterrobe et al. to Charles H.
Burke, 17 January 1927, file "73, Indian Dances 1/2."

31. On the project to push the candidacy of a veteran to the position of Indian Commissioner, see James Irving to Arthur C. Parker, 14 January 1920, pt. 1, ser. A. Correspondence of the Society of American Indians, 1911–1923, *The Papers of the Society of American Indians* (Wilmington, Del.: Scholarly Resources, 1987).

32. On Tafoya, see Joe S. Sando, *Pueblo Profiles: Cultural Identity Through Centuries of Change* (Santa Fe: Clear Light Publishers, 1998), 65–69; and *Senate Survey*, 19 (1931), 9060–61. On factionalism in Santa Clara in general and on Tafoya's role in it, see Marilyn Norcini, "The Political Process of Factionalism and Self-Governance at Santa Clara Pueblo, New Mexico," *Proceedings of the American Philosophical Society* 149, no. 4 (2005): 544–90.

33. Young Hawk, Edward, Family Information Survey, 1922–1923, box OS 36, SRA, RG 75, NARA-KC; Eugene Younghawk, "Major James McLaughlin, Inspector Interior Department, Wash. DC, Standing Rock Allotments," reel 9, microfilm edition of James McLaughlin Papers, SHSND; E. Younghawk, Family Survey 1935, box 385, SRA, RG 75, NARA-KC; Application for Unit Charter of the American Legion Auxiliary, Bullhead Post no. 82, 15 February 1926, and Post Application for Permanent Charter, Brought Post no. 82, 24 August 1932, American Legion Headquarters' Archives, Watertown, South Dakota; Eugene Younghawk et al. to Indian Affairs Committee, 14 March 1933, file 11550-1932, box 9, SRA, CCF 1906–1939, NARA-DC; E. Younghawk to E. D. Mossman, 13 February 1930, Younghawk et al. to C. J. Rhoades, 25 February 1930, file "73, Indian Dances, 2/2," box 174, DCF, 1906–1959, SRA, RG 75, NARA-KC; interviews with Olley Little Eagle, 8 August 2008, Rock Creek, South Dakota, and Linnus Grey Eagle, 30 June 2009, McLaughlin, South Dakota; James Red Fish et al. to E. D. Mossman, 24 April 1931, file "076 Forms of Government, Indians Judges etc.," box 174, DCF, 1906–1959, SRA, RG 75, NARA-KC; and E. Younghawk to Mr. Campbell, 14 June 1930, box 18, box 108, research Correspondence V–Y, Walter Stanley Campbell Collection, Native American Collections, Western History Collections, University of Oklahoma, Norman. On general councils, see Richmond L. Clow, "A New Look at Indian Suits: The Sioux Nation's Black Hills Claim as a Case for Tribal Symbolism," *Plains Anthropologist* 28, no. 102 (1983): 316.

34. John Runs the Middle to Lynn J. Frazier, 14 February 1924, Thomas Frosted to J. E. Sinclair, 18 February 1924, Frank B. Streeter "to whom it may concern" 28 February 1924, David M. Means et al. "to whom it may concern," 12 March 1924, David M. Means to Jack Williams, 14 March 1924, Charles A. Eastman to Charles H. Burke, 10 April 1924, Francis B. Bullhead to E. D. Mossman, 22 May 1924, E. D. Mossman to T. B. Roberts, 12–13 July 1924, Thomas Frosted to W. I. Glover, 18 July 1924, W. I. Glover to Charles H. Burke, 4 August 1924, E. D. Mossman

to Charles H. Burke, 23 August 1924, file 63689, box 22, entry 154, SRA, CCF 1907–1939, RG 75, NARA-DC.

35. The senatorial investigation was published in 41 volumes between 1927 and 1943. For context, see Robert A. Staley, "Congressional Hearings: Neglected Sources of Information on American Indians," *Government Information Quarterly* 25 (2008): 526–31.

36. On Steele, see Mead Steele, "Card File Relating to Indians in World War I, 1916–1920," box 15, entry 977B, CCF 1907–1939, RG 75, NARA-DC; Meade Steele's interview with Joseph K. Dixon, 19 September 1919, WW-32, 25, Wanamaker Documentation; "Report of William Madison, Secretary of the Society of American Indians as to the Conditions on Fort Peck, Blackfeet and Flathead Reservations," 1923, pt. 2, ser. 1. Correspondence of the Society of American Indians, n.d. and 1906–1946, *The Papers of the Society of American Indians*; Congress, 68th Cong., 1st sess., *Congressional Record*, 1924, LXV-9, 847; David Reed Miller, *The History of the Fort Peck Assiniboine and Sioux Tribes, 1800–2000* (Helena, Mont.: Fort Peck Community College, 2008), 262–64; Congress, House, Committee on Indian Affairs, 69th Cong. 1st sess., *Reservation Court of Indian Offenses, Hearings on HR 7826*, 13 February–20 May 1926, GPO, Washington, D.C., 1926, 21; *95th Annual Conference of the Church of Jesus Christ of Latterday Saints, April 4, 5, and 6 1925* (Salt Lake City: Church of Jesus Christ of Latterday Saints, 1925), 96; E. D. Mossman to Scott Leavitt, 14 April 1926, file "National Council of American Indians, 1927–1930," box 175, DCF, 1906–1959, SRA, RG 75, NARA-KC; "Indians to Meet at Helena Soon," *Laredo Tribune*, 5 June 1926. On opposition to HR 7826, see Gertrude Bonnin and Meade Steele, "To All Indians," 5 March 1926, file "National council of American Indians, 1927–1930," box 175, DCF, 1906–1959, SRA, RG 75, NARA-KC; and Basil Reddoor et al. Committee to "Dear Fellow Tribesmen," 12 March 1926, file "024, Congressional Committee, 1926–1923," box 148, DCF, 1906–1959, SRA, RG 75, NARA-KC. On Senate Resolution 79, see E. R. Rusco, *A Fateful Time*, 168–74. On the end of Steele's career, see Congress, Subcommittee of the Committee on Indian Affairs, 74th Cong., 1st sess. *Indian Conditions and Affairs: Hearings Before the Subcommittee on General on General Bills of the Committee of Indian Affairs, HR 7781, February 11, 1935*, GPO, Washington, D.C., 1935, 545.

37. Joseph White Plume et al. to Lynn J. Frazier, 11 March 1929; Meade Steele to Chairman, 26 March 1928; testimonies by James Tattoed (8 June 1928), Thomas Frosted (6 June 1928), Ben Has Horns (21 June 1928) and Ella Gleyum-Ke-Win (n.d.), Joseph Leaf (n.d.); "A Protest to the U.S. Senate by Representative Indians of the Standing Rock Indian Reservation," 29 July 1929, and Francis Red Tomahawk et al. to Lynn J. Frazier, 21 October 1929; Luke Speaks Walking to Straight Pine, 8 August 1929;

file "Senate 83A-F59 SRA," box 109, Committee on Interior and Insular Affairs, North Dakota, RG 46, NARA-DC; Testimony of Thomas
Frosted, Court Claims of the U.S., Docket C-531, *The Sioux Tribe of Indians v. United States of America* (1923), 296, Docket 74, RG 279; Minutes
of Standing Rock Tribal Business Council, 15 July 1929, 82, file "Minutes
of Tribal Council 1912–1916, 1928–1932," box 326, Tribal Council and
Committee 1880–1932, SRA, RG 75, NARA-KC.

38. For George Sleeps From Home's father, see Oliver Sleeps From Home,
Family Information Survey, 1922–1923, box OS 36, SRA, RG 75,
NARA-KC. On his occupational history, see Family Survey 1935, box
384, SRA, RG 75, NARA-KC. On his dancing, see Eugene Bearking to
E. D. Mossman, 5 July 1924, file "73, Indian Dances 1/2," box 174, DCF,
1906–1959, SRA, RG 75, NARA-KC. On Sleeps From Home's involve-
ment with the American Legion, see Application for Post of the Ameri-
can Legion, Martin Yellow Fat Post no. 232, 28 February 1924, American
Legion Headquarters' Archives, Watertown, South Dakota, and E. Bearking to E. D. Mossman, 6 July 1927, file "047, Fair Grounds," box 153,
DCF, 1906–1959, SRA, RG 75, NARA-KC. On his political projects, see
Senate Survey, 1929, 9, 3149–50 and 3210, and Henry Ankle to E. D.
Mossman, 29 January 1924, box 9315-1924, box 7, entry 53, SRA, CCF,
1907–1939, RG 75, NARA-DC.

Chapter Six. A Dream of Emancipation

1. Loretta Fowler, "Wind River Reservation Political Process: An Analysis
of the Symbols of Consensus," *American Ethnologist* 5, no. 4 (1978): 758;
Loretta Fowler, *Tribal Sovereignty and the Historical Imagination: Cheyenne-
Arapaho Politics* (Lincoln: University of Nebraska Press, 2002), 79; Loretta Fowler, "Political Middlemen and the Headman Tradition Among
the Twentieth-Century Gros Ventres of Fort Belknap Reservation,"
Journal of the West 23 (1984): 54–63. See also J. R. Fox, "Veterans and
Factions in Pueblo Society," *Man* 61 (October 1961): 173–76. Interview
of Jesse Rowlodge by Julia A. Jordan, T-239, 16 April 1968, 10, DCAIOH.
Interview of George Kills In Sight by J. H. Cash, MS-15, Summer 1967,
3, American Indian Research Program, South Dakota Oral History Center, Institute of American Indian Studies, University of South Dakota,
Vermillion, South Dakota.

2. J. R. Fox, "Veterans and Factions," 174, and L. Fowler, *Tribal Sovereignty*,
79.

3. Constitution and Bylaws of the Rosebud Sioux Tribe of South Dakota,
20 December 1935, available at www.narf.org/nill/Constitutions/rosebud
const/rstconst.htm; American Legion Preamble to the Constitution,
10–12 November 1919, available at www.legion.org/preamble. On Kills
In Sight's career as a veteran, see "Parmelee Indians celebrated Novem-

ber 11," *Todd County Tribune*, 19 November 1925; Archie B. Beauvais, "Descendants Seek Return of Sicangu Chief Possessions," *Lakota Country Times*, 29 January 2009.

4. Antoine DeRockbraine, Isaac Hawk, Edward Youngeagle to the President of the United States et al., n.d., file "Senate 83A-F59 SRA," box 109, Committee on Interior and Insular Affairs, ND, RG 46, NARA-DC; and Eugene Younghawk et al. to Indian Affairs Committee, 14 March 1933, and Joseph Brave Thunder and William Good Eagle to Honorable President of the Senate's Indian Committee, 11 March 1933, file 11550-1932, box 9, SRA, CCF 1906–1939, NARA-DC.

5. On Logerwell, see Harry D. Williams to Hon. John W. Collier, 1 February 1934, as well as Exhibit 1, and Willis White Mountain to John Collier, 23 October 1934, file 15834-1933, entry 54, SRA, CCF 1907–1939, RG 75, NARA-DC. On the New Deal on Standing Rock in 1935, see Vine Deloria, ed., *The Indian Reorganization Act: Congresses and Bills* (Norman: University of Oklahoma Press, 2002), 99–100. On the "Indian Self-Government" circular, see Francis Paul Prucha, *The Great Father: The United States Government and the American Indians*, 2 (Lincoln: University of Nebraska Press, 1995), 955. J. Collier to L. C. Lippert, 22 June 1934, file "065 Elections, 1933–1935," box 166, DCF, 1906–1959, SRA, RG 75, NARA-KC; "Many Attend the Celebration and Dedication at Little Eagle," *Sioux County Pioneer*, 3 August 1934; L. C. Lippert to Commissioner of Indian Affairs, 23 January 1935, file 9755-1936, box 11, entry 68, SRA, CCF 1907–1939, RG 75, NARA-DC.

6. George Sleeps From Home to J. Collier, 16 January 1935, file 9755-1936, box 11, entry 68, SRA, CCF, RG 75, NARA-DC; Minutes of Standing Rock Tribal Business Council, 29 December 1934, file 47401-1935, box 9, entry 54, SRA, CCF 1907–1939, RG 75, NARA-DC; L. C. Lippert to Commissioner of Indian Affairs, 4 November 1935, and Antoine DeRockbraine et al. to Commissioner of Indian Affairs, 3 November 1935, Standing Rock Sioux Tribe—National Archives 1935–1937, Fort Yates, North Dakota.

7. Minutes of the Commissioner of Indian Affairs, 24 [after L. C. Lippert to Commissioner of Indian Affairs, 14 January 1936], file 47401-1935, entry 54, box 9, SRA, CCF 1907–1939, RG 75, NARA-DC; George White Bull et al. to Commissioner of Indian Affairs, 5 March 1934, and Report of the Constitution and By Laws Committee to Tribal Business Council, 11 May 1936, entry 54, box 9, SRA, CCF 1907–1939, RG 75, NARA-DC; "Indian Delegation of 7 to Go to Washington, D.C.," *McLaughlin Messenger*, 22 May 1936; box 17624-1938, box 11, entry 66, SRA, CCF 1907–1939, RG 75, NARA-DC. On attempts to design "natural communities," see Memorandum on the Proposed Standing Rock Constitution, 3 June 1936, 1, file 9755A-1936, NARA-DC; and Akim D. Reinhardt, *Ruling Pine Ridge: Oglala Lakota Politics from the IRA to Wounded Knee* (Lubbock:

Texas Tech University Press, 2007), 89. On referenda, see Eugene Young-hawk et al. to Hon. Harold Ickes, 21 September 1939, box "9755-A-1936, part III," box 11, entry 68, SRA, CCF 1907–1939, RG 75, NARA-DC; and Lawrence C. Kelly, "The Indian Reorganization Act: The Dream and The Reality," *Pacific Historical Review* 44, no. 3 (1975): 301–4.

8. Roger Bromert, "The Sioux and the Indian-CCC," *South Dakota History* 8, no. 4 (1978): 355; Thomas J. Malone, "On the Warpath Again," *American Legion Monthly* 18, no. 4 (April 1935): 28–29, 61–62; Keene, *Doughboys*, 201. On Many Deeds and Yellow Earrings, see their files in box 380, Family Survey 1935, SRA, RG 75, NARA-KC. On Little Eagle, see L. G. Lippert to Commissioner of Indian Affairs, 9 April 1937, file "Little Eagle, Alex," box 200, DCF, 1906–1959, SRA, RG 75, NARA-KC. Acting Assistant to the Commissioner to L. G. Lippert, 26 February 1937, file "Little Eagle, Alex," box 200, DCF, 1906–1959, SRA, RG 75, NARA-KC; and Edward A. (Alex) Little Eagle Card, file "Little Eagle, Alex," box 200, DCF 1906–1959, SRA, RG 75, NARA-KC.

9. Minutes of Standing Rock Tribal Business Council, 28 September 1935, and Local Council to L. C. Lippert, 17 April 1935, file "064 Minutes and Correspondence 1934," box 161, DCF, 1906–1959, SRA, RG 75, NARA-KC. Eugene Young Hawk, Family Survey 1935, box 385, SRA, RG 75, NARA-KC. J. Collier to Usher L. Burdick, 10 February 1936, in response to Alphonse Bearghost et al. to Usher L. Burdick, 27 January 1936, box 564, box 26, entry 155, CCF 1907–1939, SRA, RG 75, NARA-DC.

10. On veterans as defenders of the people, Minutes of Standing Rock Tribal Business Council, 16 September 1941, file "9755-E-1936," box 9, entry 54, SRA, CCF 1907–1939, RG 75, NARA-DC; G. Sleeps From Home to Francis H. Case, 1 December 1937, box 9755-1936, box 11, entry 68, SRA, CCF 1907–1939, RG 75, NARA-DC. On petitions, see Thomas Grillot, "Frontières du politique: La pratique pétitionnaire sur une réserve indienne (1880–1980)," *Politiques Américaines* (forthcoming). On interpersonal conflicts, see Benjamin Reifel to Commissioner of Indian Affairs, 1 March 1938, file 17624-1938, box 11, entry 66, SRA, CCF 1907–1939, RG 75, NARA-DC.

11. "Emancipation Memorial," 26 June 1937, file "Sen 83A-F9, new box 36, box 30 folder 2, South Dakota Tribe, Amend Wheeler-Howard Act," box 16, Indian Affairs Investigating Subcommittee, Committee on Interior and Insular Affairs, RG 46, NARA-DC. On veterans defending private property but eventually rallying to the Indian Reorganization Act, see the testimony of Jesse Rowlodge, in Congress, House, Committee on Indian Affairs, 73rd Cong., 2nd sess., *Hearings on S. 2755 and S. 3645, part 2, April 26, 28, 30 and May 3, 4, 17, 1934*, GPO, Washington, D.C., 1934, 108. Dan Yellow Earrings et al. to L. C. Lippert, 23 October 1937, file

"Bullhead Blackhorse, Tribal Council, October 23 1937," box 169, DCF, 1906–1959, SRA, RG 75, NARA-KC.

12. Marci Barnes Gracey, "Joseph Bruner and the American Indian Federation: An Alternative View of Indian Rights," in *Alternative Oklahoma: Contrarian Views of the Sooner State*, ed. Davis D. Joyce (Norman: University of Oklahoma Press, 2007), 63–86; and, in the January 1928 edition of *The American Indian*, the Society of American Indians' journal: "The Indians Make an Enviable Record During the World War," 12; in the August 1928 edition: "Romance of a Doughboy with a Maiden in Sunny France," 10–11; and the June 1930 edition: "War Generals Pay Tributes to the Valor of Indian Soldiers," 14.

13. On Bruner, see *Senate Survey* 37, 1940, 21377. On Jemison, see *Senate Survey*, 4, 1939, 2466–67; *Senate Survey* 37, 1940, 21711–17; and Laurence M. Hauptman, *The Iroquois and the New Deal*, 35–46, 63–69; Laurence M. Hauptman, "Alice Lee Jemison: A Modern 'Mother of the Nation,'" in *Sifters: Native American Women's Lives*, ed. Theda Perdue (New York: Oxford University Press, 2001), 175–86. On veterans as anti-IRA witnesses, see *Senate Survey* 37, 1940, 20526; and Eugene Younghawk et al., petition, 9 March 1938, box 17624-1938, box 11, entry 66, SRA, CCF 1907–1939, RG 75, NARA-DC; Congress, House, 75th Cong., 3rd sess., and 78th Cong., 2nd sess., *Investigation of Un-American Propaganda Activities in the United States: Hearings Before a Special Committee on Un-American Activities on H. Res. 282*, 4, 1939, 2467 and 2475. On the American Indian Federation's and the Black Hills Treaty Council's links to reservation communities, see Richmond L. Clow, "'We Do Not Always Agree': Eugene Little, the Indian New Deal, and Changing Rosebud Leadership," *South Dakota History* 33, no. 2 (Summer 2003): 176–77; and Lawrence M. Hauptman, "The American Indian Federation and the Indian New Deal: A Reinterpretation," *Pacific Historical Review* 52 (1983): 378–402.

14. See Eugene Younghawk et al. to Elmer Thomas, 18 February 1937, file "Sen 83A-F9, new box 36, box 30 folder 2, "South Dakota Tribe, Amend Wheeler-Howard Act," box 16, Indian Affairs Investigating Subcommittee, Committee on Interior and Insular Affairs, RG 46, NARA-DC; and file "S. 2103," box 64, Papers Accompanying Specific Bills and Resolutions, RG 46, NARA-DC.

15. "To the Honorable President and Congress of the United States of America," file "Sen 83A-F9, new box 36, box 30 folder 2, South Dakota Tribe, Amend Wheeler-Howard Act," box 16, Indian Affairs Investigating Subcommittee, Committee on Interior and Insular Affairs, RG 46, NARA-DC; Memorandum of Instructions to the Delegates to Washington, D.C. From the National Indian Voters' Association, received on 11 February 1936, box 6943-1936, box 9, entry 54, SRA, CCF 1907–1939,

RG 75, NARA-DC; *Senate Survey* 37, 1940, 21586; Minutes of Standing Rock Tribal Business Council, 6 June 1938, 7, box 9755-E-1936, box 9, entry 54, SRA, CCF 1907–1939, RG 75, NARA-DC.

16. For other Lakota reservations, see *Senate Survey* 37, 1940, 21537, 21538, 21557, 21559, 21563, 21569, 21571–72, 21616–17; Earl S. Cleaver to W. O. Roberts, 14 January 1935; J. Atwood Maulding to Wallace Murray, 7 November 1940; and the attached petition in file "610 Indians in World War, American Legion," Rosebud Agency, RG 75, NARA-KC. For Iroquois, see Lawrence M. Hauptman, "Alice Jemison, Seneca Political Activist: 1901–1964," *The Indian Historian* 12, no. 2 (Summer 1979): 16–19; and Lawrence M. Hauptman, "The American Indian Federation," 393.

17. Ella Deloria, *Speaking of Indians* (Lincoln: University of Nebraska Press, 1998 [1944]), 137, 140–41, 144, 148.

18. On the BIA during the war, see K. R. Philp, "Termination: A Legacy of the Indian New Deal," *Western Historical Quarterly* 14, no. 2 (1983): 173; K. R. Philp, *John Collier's Crusade for Indian Reform, 1920–1954* (Tucson: University of Arizona Press, 1977), 202–5; Donald Lee Fixico, *Termination and Relocation: Federal Indian Policy, 1945–1960* (Albuquerque: University of New Mexico Press, 1986), 116.

19. Congress, Senate, Committee on Indian Affairs, 78th Cong., 1st sess., *Partial Report 310*, GPO, Washington, D.C., June 1943. On Francis H. Case, see Kenneth R. Philp, *Termination Revisited: American Indians on the Trail to Self-Determination, 1933–1953* (Lincoln: University of Nebraska Press, 1999), 76. On the Indian Claims Commission, see Harvey D. Rosenthal, "Indian Claims and the American Conscience: A Brief History of the Indian Claims Commission," in *Irredeemable America*, ed. Sutton and Beals, 35–70. On the Cold War as a context for termination, see Paul C. Rosier, "'They Are Ancestral Homelands': Race, Place, and Politics in Cold War Native America, 1945–1961," *Journal of American History* 92, no. 4 (2006): 1300–1326.

20. On White Mountain, see Willis (White) Mountain, Family Survey, 1935; W. White Mountain to Francis H. Case, 30 January 1947, and F. H. Case to W. White Mountain, 8 February 1947; F. H. Case to Commissioner of Indian Affairs, 28 October 1943; Arthur Juhnke to W. White Mountain, 26 January 1945; F. H. Case to W. White Mountain, 8 November 1945; W. White Mountain to F. H. Case, 30 January 1947; F. H. Case to W. White Mountain, 8 February 1947; F. H. Case to Commissioner of Indian Affairs, 3 June 1947; W. White Mountain to F. H. Case, 7 June 1947; W. White Mountain to F. H. Case, 12 January 1948; W. White Mountain to F. H. Case, 23 June 1952; D. S. Myer to F. H. Case, 18 July 1952; in Correspondence and related papers exchanged between Francis Case and individual Indians in South Dakota, Francis H. Case Papers, Dakota Wesleyan University, Mitchell, South Dakota.

21. On veterans' preference, see Minutes of Standing Rock Tribal Business

Council, 7 December 1943, file "9755-E-1936," box 9, entry 54, SRA, CCF 1907–1939, RG 75, NARA-DC. On Brownotter, see interviews with Cecilia Brownotter, 23 July 2008, Rock Creek, South Dakota, and Melvin Shoots The Enemy, 9 July 2009, Fort Yates, North Dakota. On Wakeman, see "Gordon Weston Indian Veterans Lodge," Flandreau Santee Sioux Tribe, available at http://fsst.org/GordonWestonMain.html. On the Legion post on Pine Ridge, see Fred H. Daiker to William Firethunder, 5 April 1945, file "600, Military Activities, 1942–1946," box 656, Pine Ridge Agency, General records, Main Decimal Files, RG 75, NARA-KC. On Standing Rock, see "Solen Legion Post Starts This Week," *Sioux County Pioneer*, 16 November 1945; American Legion—History Committee of the North Dakota Department of the American Legion, *The American Legion: The First Seventy-Five Years in North Dakota, 1919–1994*, American Legion, North Dakota, 1999, A-141. On posts among the Osage, see Interview of David Pitts, T270-2, 16 May 1968, 6, DIOHC; on the Iroquois, see "Indians Form Veterans Post," *Niagara Falls Gazette*, 26 October 1946, 20; on the Pueblos, see A. R. Bernstein, *American Indians and World War II*, 134. On Rowlodge, see his interview by David Jones, T-125, 28 July 1968, 12, DIOHC; and Fowler, "Political Middlemen."

22. "Our Indian Boys in the Service," *Corson County News*, 9 August 1945, 1.
23. On the BIA's planning for relocation for returning veterans, see K. R. Philp, ed., *Indian Self-Rule: First-Hand Accounts of Indian-White Relations from Roosevelt to Reagan* (Logan: Utah State University Press, 1995), 161. On the American Legion's involvement in Indian citizenship, see Resolution 60, 1943, "Convention Resolutions Referred to the Americanism Commission," c. 1949, and Indian Affairs Convention Mandates, 1948, in "U.S.—G–W—Indians," Correspondence—Subject Files, American Legion Library, American Legion Headquarters, Indianapolis. For Kelly's quote, see "Hearing at Pierre, South Dakota, July 27, 1944," 14, in box 1, Transcripts of Investigative Hearings on Indian Affairs, 1937–48, Division of Administration, RG 75, NARA-DC. On the NCAI and veterans, see Mark L. Burns to Tribal Councils and Indian Leaders, 16 October 1944, NCAI records, National Anthropological Archives, Suitland, Maryland; and Thomas W. Cowger, *The National Congress of American Indians: The Founding Years* (Lincoln: University of Nebraska Press, 1999), 37, 64–65.
24. Speech by E. Y. Berry, 18 June 1935, file "045 Addresses (Speeches) 1923, 1932–1938," box 152, DCF 1906–1959, SRA, RG 75, NARA-KC; Richard R. Chenoweth, *Francis Case, a Political Biography* (Ph.D. diss., University of Nebraska, 1977), 12; Ronald Briley, "Lynn J. Frazier and Progressive Indian Reform: A Plodder in the Ranks of a Ragged Regiment," *South Dakota History*, no. 7 (1977): 438–54; "Langer Initiation," *Sioux County Pioneer*, 26 May 1933. On Langer as a "Friend of the Indians," see

Minutes of Standing Rock Tribal Business Council, 27 October 1941, file "9755-E-1936," box 9, entry 54, SRA, CCF 1907–1939, RG 75, NARA-DC. On Mundt, Gurney, and Bulow, see Minutes of Standing Rock Tribal Business Council, 18 December 1941, file "9755-E-1936," box 9, entry 54, SRA, CCF 1907–1939, RG 75, NARA-DC. On Berry, see "Judge Berry Makes Inspiring Memorial Day Address Here," *Sioux County Pioneer*, 5 June 1924; Steven C. Schulte, "Removing the Yoke of Government: E. Y. Berry and the Origins of Indian Termination Policy," *South Dakota History* 14, no. 1 (Spring 1984): 52–56, 59.

25. Finger, *Cherokee Americans*, 84–85, 96, 107–8, 135; *Senate Survey* 37, 1940, 20683, 20686; Ogle and Thompson, *History of the Sam White Bear Post no. 251 of the American Legion*, 18; Joe Jennings Collection, 1802–1967, "Archives of Appalachia" (Eastern Tennessee State University, Johnson City), available at http://archives.etsu.edu/agents/211?agent_type=agent _person; Joe Jennings to Harry Edward Neal, 13 November 1946, and Joe Jennings to Donald Q. Palmer, 7 November 1946, file "Letters to Others, Oct. 1–Dec. 31, 1946," box 18, Series 6, General Correspondence, RG 75, National Archives, Morrow, GA; and Joe Jennings, "Eastern Cherokee Indians. Recent Progress," 1954 (Statement to FBI investigators), box 8, box 11, Series 6, and Joe Jennings, "July 31, 1946" (Statement to FBI investigators), box 11, box 54, Series 4, Jennings Collections East Tennessee State University, Johnson City, Tennessee.

26. On Sleeps From Home, see Minutes of Standing Rock Tribal Business Council, 1 February and 5 April 1943, file "9755-E-1936," box 9, entry 54, SRA, CCF 1907–1939, RG 75, NARA-DC; George Sleeps From Home to Francis H. Case, 6 January 1943, 9 June 1943, 6 December 1944, 3 February 1946, 7 October 1946, Correspondence and related papers exchanged between Francis Case and individual Indians in South Dakota, Francis H. Case Papers, Dakota Wesleyan University, Mitchell, South Dakota. On Case's bill, see K. R. Philp, *Termination*, 76. On Standing Rock veterans' trip to Washington, see Erma O. Hicks to Division Directors, 28 May 1946, box 31364-1943, box 9, entry 56, SRA, CCF 1940–1957, RG 75, NARA-DC. For Younghawk's quote, see Congress, House, Committee on Indian Affairs, 79th Cong., 2nd sess., *"Removal of Restrictions on Property of Indians who served in the Armed Forces," Hearings on S. 1093 and S. 1194, June 12, 1946*, GPO, Washington, D.C., 1946, 10; for another invocation of Lincoln in Lakota country, see Richmond L. Clow, "'We Do Not Always Agree': Eugene Little, the Indian New Deal, and Changing Rosebud Leadership," *South Dakota History* 33, no. 2 (Summer 2003): 178.

27. For Sleeps From Home's testimony, see Congress, House, Committee on Indian Affairs, 80th Cong., 1st sess., *Hearings on HR 2958, HR 2165, and HR 1113, April 8, 9, 10, 11, May 15, 1947*, GPO, Washington, D.C., 1947, 29; G. Sleeps From Home to Francis H. Case, 21 October 1946, Fran-

cis H. Case Papers. On Sleeps From Home's support for the Indian Claims Commissions, see Congress, House, Committee on Indian Affairs, 79th Cong., 2nd sess., *Hearings on HR 4997, June 1 and 12, and July 13, 1946*, GPO, Washington, D.C., 1947, 29. On claims and state jurisdiction, see Congress, House, Committee on Indian Affairs, 79th Cong., 2nd sess., *Hearings on HR 3680, HR 3681, and HR 3710, May 6 and June 13, 1946*, GPO, Washington, D.C., 1946, 42–45. For the petitions cited here, look, in the same volume, on pages 35, 45, 47 and in Congress, House, Committee on Indian Affairs, 79th Cong., 2nd sess., *Hearings on S. 1093 and S. 1094, June 12, 1946*, GPO, Washington, D.C., 1946, 10.

28. *Standing Rock Eyapaha*, April 1950, 1, file "Standing Rock Eyapaha 1950," box 150, DCF 1906–1959, SRA, RG 75, NARA-KC; Congress, 82nd Cong., 2nd sess., *Congressional Record*, 1952, vol. 98, 3619; George Sleeps From Home to Francis H. Case, 6 January 1950, Francis H. Case Papers; Congress, House, 80th Cong., 1st sess., *Report 1488, 80th Cong., 2nd Session, to accompany S. 543, Enforcement of Penal Laws of the States of North and South Dakota on the Standing Rock Indian Reservation, June 4 (legislative day, June 1), 1948*, GPO, Washington, D.C., 1948; K. R. Philp, "Dillon S. Myer and the Advent of Termination: 1950–1953," *Western Historical Quarterly* 19, no. 1 (1988): 37–59, 47–49, 73; D. L. Fixico, *Termination and Relocation*, 40, 47.

29. On veterans fighting the Oahe Dam, see Michael L. Lawson, *Dammed Indians: The Pick-Sloan Plan and the Missouri River Sioux, 1944–1980* (Norman: University of Oklahoma Press, 1994), 75; Michael L. Lawson, "The Oahe Dam and the Standing Rock Sioux," *South Dakota History* 6, no. 2 (1976): 203–28; and "HR 3544, HR 3602, HR 5608, Friday, June 24, 1955," 233, 239; unpublished hearing, Library of Congress. Cf. On Keith, see Russel Lawrence Barsh, "War and the Reconfiguring of American Indian Society," *Journal of American Studies* 35, no. 3 (December 2001): 383.

Conclusion

1. On race-based patriotism, see Higham, *Strangers in the Land*, 204–12; Ford, *Americans All!* 25; Gary Gerstle, "Liberty, Coercion, and the Making of Americans," 552–53.

2. Jonas M. Poweshiek, "An Autobiography," *Annals of Iowa* 20 (1936): 435–43; and "Indians Again on the Warpath," *Annals of Iowa* 26 (1945): 291–99; Jonas Poweshiek to Editor, 4 December 1917, file 4655, box 112, Series 1327, RG 75, NARA-DC; "Poweshiek, Jonas," box 6, MS 4802 Sol Tax-Fox Field Notes and Fox Project records 1932–1959, National Anthropological Archives, Smithsonian Institution, Washington, D.C.

3. On the Flag Song, see Black Bear and Theisz, *Songs and Dances*, 33; and William K. Powers, "Contemporary Oglala Music and Dance: Pan-Indianism Versus Pan-Tetonism," in *The Modern Sioux: Social System and*

Reservation Culture, ed. Ethel Nurge (Lincoln: University of Nebraska Press, 1970): 283. For James Emery's flag, see "Proposed Tribal Flag and Related Letter," box 1121, Records of the Oglala Sioux Tribal Government, Pine Ridge Agency, RG 75, NARA-KC. On Pine Ridge from 1965 to 1968, see Robert E. Daniels, "Cultural Identities Among the Oglala Sioux," in *The Modern Sioux*, ed. Nurge, 198–245. On Lamont, see Tom Rice, "Warrior: Rest in Peace, Buddy Lamont," available at http://tom fooleryadventures.blogspot.com/2009/05/warrior-rest-in-peace-buddy -lamont.html.

4. On American nationalism's capaciousness, see Gerstle, *American Crucible;* for a look at the practical consequences of the mix of colonialism and anti-colonialism and its role in the United States' rise to hegemony, see Anne L. Foster, *Projections of Power: The United States and Europe in Colonial Southeast Asia, 1919–1941* (Durham, N.C.: Duke University Press, 2010).

5. On the relative conservatism of, among others, African veterans of World War I and World War II, see T. H. Parsons, *The African Rank-and-File: Social Implications of Colonial Military Service in the King's African Rifles, 1902–1964* (Portsmouth, N.H.: Heinemann, 1999); Hal Brands, "Wartime Recruiting Practices, Martial Identity, and Post–World War II Demobilization in Colonial Kenya," *Journal of African History* 46 (2005): 103–25; James K. Matthews, "World War I and the Rise of African Nationalism: Nigerian Veterans as Catalysts of Change," *Journal of Modern African Studies* 20, no. 3 (1982): 493–502; Joe Lunn, *Memoirs of the Maelstrom: A Senegalese Oral History of the First World War* (Portsmouth, N.H.: Heinemann, 1999); David Killingray and Richard Fogarty, "Demobilization in British and French Africa at the End of the First World War," *Journal of Contemporary History* 50, no. 1 (2015): 100–123. On the founding principles of the "settler colonial" approach, see Lorenzo Veracini, "Introducing *Settler Colonial Studies*," *Settler Colonial Studies* 1 (2011): 1–12; Patrick Wolfe, "Settler Colonialism and the Elimination of the Native," *Journal of Genocide Research* 8, no. 4 (2006): 387–409; Patrick Wolfe, "Land, Labor, and Difference: Elementary Structures of Race," *American Historical Review* 106, no. 3 (2011): 866–905.

6. Trans-imperial comparisons have been made on specific subjects, such as recruitment policies. See for example Christian Koller, "The Recruitment of Colonial Troops in Africa and Asia and Their Deployment in Europe During the First World War," *Immigrants and Minorities* 26, nos. 1/2 (2008): 111–33. Most studies, even comparative, confine themselves to intra-empire comparisons. On indigenous peoples, see in particular Timothy C. Winegard, *Indigenous Peoples of the British Dominions and the First World War* (New York: Cambridge University Press, 2012).

7. An imperial and transnational framework has already proved a fruitful way to renew our understanding of immigration policies and race. See

in particular Paul A. Kramer, *The Blood of Government: Race, Empire, the United States, and the Philippines* (Chapel Hill: University of North Carolina Press, 2006); Ngai, *Impossible Subjects*; and Seema Sohi, "Race, Surveillance, and Indian Anticolonialism in the Transnational Western U.S.-Canadian Borderlands," *Journal of American History* 98 (Sept. 2011): 420–36. The "Indian" of the title refers to the Indian subcontinent. American Indians have been strangely absent from this conversation.

8. On the anti-colonial politics of "Red Power" in the United States, see Gyorgy Ferenc Toth, *Red Nations: The Transatlantic Relations of the American Indian Radical Sovereignty Movement in the Late Cold War* (Ph.D. diss., University of Iowa, 2012). On the complex relationship between self-determination and anti-colonialism in the indigenous movement, see Ayako Uchida, "Searching for Indigenous Alliances: International NGOs of the United States and Canada in the 1970s," *Japanese Journal of American Studies* 23 (2012): 209–30. For a view from Australia, see Bastien Bosa, "Les mots et les choses: Les Aborigènes et la décolonisation," *Genèses* 61 (2005): 70–97.

9. On graves, monuments, and commemorations in Africa, see Marc Michel, "Mémoire officielle, discours et pratique coloniale. Le 14 juillet et le 11 novembre au Sénégal entre les deux guerres," *Revue française d'histoire d'Outre-mer* 77, no. 2 (1990): 145–58; Gregory Mann, "Locating Colonial Histories: Between France and West Africa," *American Historical Review* 110, no. 2 (2005): 409–34; Michèle Barrett, "'White Graves' and Natives: The Imperial War Graves Commission in East and West Africa, 1918–1939," in *Bodies in Conflict: Corporeality, Materiality, and Transformation*, ed. Paul Cornish and Nicholas J. Saunders (London: Routledge, 2014), 80–90; on citizenship and the "federation moment" in the French African empire, see Frederick Cooper, *Citizenship Between Empire and Nation: Remaking France and French Africa, 1945–1960* (Princeton, N.J.: Princeton University Press, 2016).

Index